MENTAL DOMINANCE

BOOKS PREVIOUSLY PUBLISHED

by Dr. Haha Lung

The Ancient Art of Strangulation (1995)
Assassin! Secrets of the Cult of Assassins (1997)
The Ninja Craft (1997)
Knights of Darkness (1998)
Lost Fighting Art of Vietnam (2006)
Mind Control (2006)

Written with Christopher B. Prowant

Shadowhand: Secrets of Ninja Taisavaki (2000)
*The Black Science: Ancient and Modern Techniques of Ninja
    Mind Manipulation* (2001)

Written as "Ralf Dean Omar"

Death on Your Doorstep: 101 Weapons in the Home (1993)
Prison Killing Techniques: Blade, Bludgeon & Bomb (2001)

Written as "Dirk Skinner"

Street Ninja: Ancient Secrets for Mastering Today's Mean Streets (1995)
X-Treme Boxing: Secrets of the Savage Street Boxer (2002)
    with Christopher B. Prowant

MENTAL DOMINANCE

The Art of Ninja Mind Power

DR. HAHA LUNG

with

CHRISTOPHER B. PROWANT

CITADEL PRESS
Kensington Publishing Corp.
www.kensingtonbooks.com

CITADEL PRESS BOOKS are published by

Kensington Publishing Corp.
119 West 40th Street
New York, NY 10018

Illustrations by Dr. Haha Lung

All Kensington titles, imprints, and distributed lines are available at special quantity discounts for bulk purchases for sales promotions, premiums, fund-raising, educational, or institutional use. Special book excerpts or customized printings can also be created to fit specific needs. For details, write or phone the office of the Kensington special sales manager: Kensington Publishing Corp., 119 West 40th Street, New York, NY 10018, attn: Special Sales Department; phone 1-800-221-2647.

First printing: July 2009

10   9   8   7   6   5   4   3   2   1

Printed in the United States of America

Library of Congress Control Number: 2009923865

ISBN-13: 978-0-8065-3117-5
ISBN-10: 0-8065-3117-7

To Officer John Reed,

Shirley Marsee and Agnes Shifferly,

Eric Tucker, Eddie Harris,

and the Warriors of The Zendokan

CONTENTS

CONTENTS

MENTAL DOMINANCE

INTRODUCTION
"East or West: All's Fair in Love and War"

Most people figure Shakespeare said it. Their second guess is always the Bible. Sorry.

Francis Edward Smedley (1818–1864) gets the credit for the actual phrase "All's fair in love and war."

But go a little further back to Act I of Susannah Centliure's 1706 *Love at a Venture* and you'll find: "All policy's allowed in war and love."

Even further back, one hundred years earlier, in his 1605–16 *Don Quixote de la Mancha,* Miguel de Cervantes (1547–1616) penned:

> Love and War are the same thing, and stratagems and policy are allowable in the one as in the other.

Still further back? Back to where the objectivity of history and the passion of myth intermingle, always we find love and war—if not formally married to one another, then at least intimately linked (or "living in sin," if you prefer), with the former all too often proving the catalyst for the launching of the latter:

- Helen of Troy ring a bell? Those were a thousand *war*ships her face launched.
- Aeneas rejects Dido's love, dooming Carthage and Rome to six hundred years of bloody struggle.
- How many times did Delilah's treachery send Samson out to smite the Philistines?

1

- For the love of David* did not Prince Jonathan betray his father the King, even as Saul was locked in a life-and-death struggle with invading Philistines, a war that would ultimately prove fatal for both Saul and his son?
- Did not later King David send Uriah to war and certain death in order to take this loyal warrior's wife?
- For the sake of one night in Igrayne's arms, Uther Pendragon plunges a recently united Britain back into a dark age of war.

We do many strange things in the name of love—not the least of which are lie, cheat, steal—perhaps even kill.

It is as if these two—Love and War, seemingly so different—both have special dispensation to routinely traipse and tarry outside the realms of common decency.

Perhaps that's because love and war are both inherently *indecent*.

Not that love is somehow "indecent" simply because (if you're lucky) it involves plenty of nakedness. Rather, like war, love is indecent because it is brutal and uncompromising, an "all-or-nothing" proposition.

When we fall in love, all else ceases to matter or, at the very least, all else takes a backseat to our obtaining our objective—that object of our affection. Sure, we start out with the highest of morals, the best of intentions, but . . . how easy is it for love unfulfilled to turn to depression to desperation to "I'll do *anything* I have to to be with him/her!"

Worse yet is unrequited love—that pining heart we so carefully hand to another, only to find it posted the next day on eBay! Is it any wonder such love can all too easily become disillusioned to the point where it begins to despise the very thing that—only yesterday—it so cherished?

And so love turns to hate turns to war.

As in love, in war we have only one goal: Obtaining our objective. We may initially go to war with the most honorable of intentions—perhaps even going to war out of love. But should a campaign drag on long enough, inevitably we find our patience beginning to thin, and what it begins to thin in turn are those good intentions.

Ultimately, as in love so in war, temptation tests our honor.

---

*"I am distressed for you, my brother Jonathan; very pleasant have you been to me; your love to me was wonderful, passing the love of women." (2 Samuel 1:26) See "Gender-Benders" in China section.

An "easier," more expedient way to win our war (or win our love) is presented to us—one that goes against "everything we stand for," so we indignantly reject it . . . first time out. But as the body bags (and heart pangs) begin to pile up, as resources become strained, that initial "easier way" doesn't sound nearly as bad as it did at first.

And in the end, rather than see our land overrun by the Hun, rather than have our heart broken again, we give in to the expedient. We do what we must to win the war, the same as we do what we must to win our true love.

So you see, all really *is* fair in love and war—any strategy to carry the battle, any seduction to win the apple of our eye.

Or so we convince ourselves so we can better sleep at night—whether in a soft bed with something soft sleeping next to us (our reward for having mastered the Art of Seduction), or else sleeping in the overrun and hurriedly abandoned bed of our vanquished foe.

East or West, Orient or Occident: Seduction is strategy, strategy is seduction, their respective tactics and technique indistinguishable.

So "all's fair in love and war" means "anything goes," anything and everything is allowed—for so long as personal honor holds out—be it on the battlefield or in the bedroom.

But just because we decide "all's fair in love and war," using this convenience of conscience to justify all ruthless stratagem, questionable seduction, and downright skullduggery (means justifying end), we must never confuse "all's fair in love and war" for "life is fair."

Be it you've come looking for love or looking for war, you've come looking in the wrong place if you've come looking for a fair fight.

For, in the immortal words of Dr. John Becker:

"Fair" is where hogs compete for ribbons.

I

One Hand "Watches" the Other

In the West, we have a saying, "One hand washes the other," implying that helpfulness is the way to go.

Not to imply that our Asian brothers cannot be just as helpful to one another, or as friendly and beneficial to us here in the West, but there is a similar *sounding*—yet decidedly different!—saying in the East:

> "One hand *watches* the other!"

On first hearing this curious phrase, Westerners might think it a mis-translation, "Surely you mean "washes?""

No, "watches." One hand *watches* the other. In some ways this is closer to the Western warning, "Don't let the left hand know what the right hand is doing."*

In the East, rather than there being a singular path to enlightenment, or to accomplishing any earthly task for that matter, there are always thought to be *two paths* from which to choose: a Right-handed Path and a Left-handed Path.

In general, the "Right-handed" path is the straighter, the more common, usually the less difficult path to follow.

Conversely, the "Left-handed" path is the more unconventional, con-troversial, difficult—perhaps even dangerous!—path in life to tempt.

Perhaps this is the same "road less traveled" that Frost first wondered over and then wandered down?

---

*Matthew chapter 6, verse 3.

Choosing the Left-handed path, we all too often travel alone, shunned, perhaps scorned—perhaps even hated and hunted!—by our fellow man.

True, the trade-off and eventual payoff to treading this Left-handed path is often quicker—more *ruthlessly*—straight to the point. But always the price—the risk!—is thrice greater.

In the West, Left-handed-path poster children would include the impatient—or perhaps just imperious—Alexander the Great hacking his way through the Gordian Knot; Friedrich Nietzsche boldly declaring "God is dead!"—knowing full well he'd be celebrating the rest of his holidays alone; and Pablo Picasso, daring to draw outside the lines in order to see—and expose!—the naked universe in all her shame.

In many ways these Right-handed and Left-handed paths play at the extremes of the Asian concept of *yin-yang,* those seemingly contentious universal polar opposites that—despite their constant "conflict"—must nonetheless find balance—or at least tolerance—with one another lest this rudderless ship of the universe irretrievably list too far to starboard, spilling us all farther out into the unforgiving maelstrom of the Milky Way.

And so, for every patient and compassionate path to enlightenment we find in Asian teachers and texts, should we dare dig a little deeper, past those dusty scrolls and smiling souls, we'll discover as well a more expedient avenue—be it only a seldom-used shortcut down a narrow side street or sinister dark alley—that nonetheless gets us to the same goal in half the time—so long as we have only half the moral qualms.

Thus in the East, for those seeking knowledge, enlightenment—and yes, seduction and power!—it has never been their way to sophomorically demand that a serious seeker on the way confine his or her choices—their path in life—to merely *right* or *wrong.*

Instead, the East more magnanimously—realistically—gives us the choice between *right* . . . or *left.* And, depending on time and teacher and the temperament of both, Asian etiquette and indulgence may even allow us to mix the two—taking a pinch from here, a tincture from there, until our own personal alchemy finds balance.

And so "one hand *watches* the other," not so much as a prison guard watches his charge, watching not so much in order to condemn, but instead to complement—one hand adding to the other whatever strength might be missing so that both arrive at the destination together—if not hand in hand, then at least with grasping fingers relatively intact!

On second thought, "One hand *watches* the other" *is* closer akin to "one hand washes the other" than we first suspected.

But does that then open the door to perhaps East and West also being more similar in mind and kind than we first suspected?

Perhaps all the various Asian arts of strategy, seduction, and skullduggery we've gathered here to study *are* indeed similar to, if not the same as, our tried-and-true coy Western ploys, plots, and self-serving proposals?

Yet somehow we still insist upon seeing the "mysterious" East as just that—impenetrable, oh-so-inscrutable.

And so we buy the books. And we concentrate and meditate upon the ancient mandalas until we go blind, all in the hopes we'll finally see.

And we sit at the feet of the mystic du jour, bending both our body and mind into impossible contortions, all in the hope that an errant drop of their beneficent sweat will drip down, washing away our woes, finally bathing us in enlightenment . . .

But a true master never sweats. At least at the small stuff.

Still, down through the centuries, so many in the West have continued to look toward the mysterious East for wisdom and enlightenment. But, ironically, what is arguably the greatest story of personal quest and enlightenment to be found in Eastern lore, the tale of the Buddha (560–477 B.C.E.), begins with a grand *deception.*

Having been told by a seer that his young son Siddhartha would either grow up to be a great and wealthy king or else a wandering, penniless beggar, Siddhartha's father, an Indian king, staged an elaborate ruse by which he kept the boy from ever seeing anything negative about the world.

All of the young prince's servants were kept young and healthy. If illness or age began to overtake one of them, they were immediately replaced by younger, healthier servants.

Likewise, when Siddhartha traveled from palace to palace, he was always secluded inside an enclosed sedan chair, the curtains kept tightly drawn to prevent the prince from inadvertently seeing old, ill, crippled, or poor people along the way.

As the boy grew older, and correspondingly more curious, this deception became more elaborate, with whole "perfect" towns being set up along his travel routes, where there existed no ill, old, malformed, or poor people to trouble the boy's mind.

Eventually, this intricate illusion of earthly perfection was exposed and, upon realizing that there was suffering in the world, adult Prince Siddhartha abandoned his family and his kingdom to indeed become that foretold penniless, wandering beggar . . . the same penniless, wandering holy man who would one day find enlightenment and world acclaim as the Buddha.

While Buddhists worldwide take this 2,500-year-old tale as "gospel," others, especially Westerners, are more inclined to view it as a metaphor; a young, naïve prince caught up in an illusion from which he must eventually free himself is a timeless metaphor for all our lives.

Times change. Latitudes change. Attitudes seldom do.

Farther west, closer to our own time, comes a similar story of deception out of Russia—that land forever precariously balanced, one foot treading West, the other foot firmly mired in the East.

It seems eighteenth century Russian rogue Gregory Potemkin used a similar ploy to fool his mistress Catherine the Great, then empress of Russia.

In 1783, Catherine decided to test her boy toy Potemkin's sincerity and ingenuity by putting him in charge of building up a blighted area in her newly annexed Crimea region.

Thereafter, each time Potemkin returned to Moscow's royal court, he brought glowing reports of how he was indeed improving the area, of how the peasants were all happy and productive.

Delighted with her beau's reports, in 1787 Catherine decided to visit the area personally.

Traveling by ship down the Dnieper, as Catherine gazed at either shore she saw only brightly colored houses and farms sporting lush, bountiful gardens and healthy-looking cattle. Everywhere she looked new buildings were being built by smiling workmen, fields tended by smiling peasants.

Catherine was overjoyed and rewarded Potemkin lavishly.

Not until much later was it discovered that it had all been an elaborately staged play directed by Potemkin!

The brightly painted houses lining the shore were all false fronts, shells hiding decrepit hovels. The healthy cattle had been shipped in from far away, replacing the area's own diseased livestock. Even the well-fed and smiling peasants were professional entertainers paid by Potemkin to perform in one village along Catherine's route, before quickly changing costumes to hurry along to the next "village."

Still closer to our own time, during World War II the allies built entire fake military bases replete with wooden planes and even inflatable tanks and cannon that successfully fooled Axis spies.

Consider: If it's possible for such determined masters of deception to successfully deceive professionally trained observers by faking whole towns and military bases, how much easier would it be for a con man or cult leader to stage mini-dramas from behind a pulpit, a political podium, or even on our own front porch, that would successfully catch us up in confusion and illusion—confusion and illusion we would gladly pay—be it in cash or in flesh—to escape from?

We need not journey to the East to find such scoundrels. When it comes to rascals, rogues, and ruthless mind-manipulators, shameless seducers, charlatans, and "sure things," neither East nor West can dare claim monopoly.

There is no single land, no solitary people no matter how poor, that cannot still boast a plentitude of home-grown pirates and opportunists willing to peddle promises and prosperity phantasms to their hungry fellows.

In this respect, Asia can indeed boast of riches!

Thus, the Westerners hand would do well to *watch* what the Eastern hand does!

Watch and learn.

> *We study to grow strong. We study to stay strong. We study to discover the source of our enemy's strength . . . and to take that strength from him.*
>
> *—Joshua Only*

2

Seduction and Strategy: The Two-Headed Coin

Seduction is, of course, the act of seducing.

Both the definition—and the mission!—of seduction is to be found in its root, the verb "to seduce," from the Old French, by way of the medieval Latin word *"seducere,"* meaning "to lead astray."

Thumbing through the *American Heritage College Dictionary* (third edition) we find several definitions for "seduce":

- To attract
- To win over
- To entice or beguile into a desired state or position
- To lead away from accepted principles, or proper conduct
- To induce to engage in sex

Your goal in mastering the art of seduction may be one or all of these— that's your business.

Our business is teaching you how to do it better!

First, start by realizing that *seduction and strategy go hand in hand.* Some noted authorities on the subject argue they're even one and the same.

So, from now on, when you see the word "seduction" think "strategy."

Likewise, when reading respected treatises by Sun Tzu, Musashi, Machiavelli, and others on military and political *strategy,* ask yourself "How can I apply these tactics and techniques to improving my own arts of *seduction?"*

Here at the Black Science Institute* we're all about graduating with a dual (or is that "duel"?) major in both "Appreciation" and "Application."

It's not enough for we would-be Mind-wizards to only read and intellectually "appreciate" Sun Tzu, Musashi, and Machiavelli.

The key is learning the *application* of that *appreciation*.

In other words, we need to learn how to take the great seduction lessons in history, classic acts of seduction, and find practical—and profitable!—uses for them in our own lives. Thus, while an *abstract* appreciation is a good place to start, *concrete* application is the goal.

For example, if you already have what you consider to be adequate one-on-one "seduction skills" (somewhere between successfully picking up that half-drunk barfly and successfully selling that "pre-owned" SUV), odds are you're still literally "selling yourself short" if you fail to realize how your one-on-one skills of seduction (strategy) can be applied on a grander scale—from the barroom to the bedroom to the boardroom to the battlefield.

Don't sell yourself short, because, in the end, that's exactly what seduction and strategy are all about—*selling yourself,* getting your lover, customer, opponent, or blood enemy to buy into what you're selling.

Here's the secret: those same seduction skills you use to get into that barfly's pants are the same seduction skills that will land you the job of your dreams—the higher position and recognition in life you deserve.

The ancient Hindus understood this; that's why they wrote the *Kama Sutra.* At first glance, most Westerners see the Kama Sutra as only a titillating "sex manual" (primarily because most Western translations of the book concentrate on filling their pages with voyeuristic photos of naked couples cavorting and contorting into "yogic" postures "guaranteed to stimulate your sex life!").

What most Westerners fail to realize is this Kama Sutra book of *seduction* was/is first and foremost a book of *strategy* designed to help ambitious young Hindu men claw their way up India's strict socioeconomic ladder by marrying into a well-to-do family, if not into royalty. Thus, the overall lesson of the Kama Sutra is learning to use the principles of one-on-one seduction to achieve so much more than an orgasm. (For more on "Kama Sutra Karma," see *India* section.)

---

*"Black Science," generic definition: Any strategy, tactic, or technique used to interfere with and/or undermine a person's ability to reason and respond for themselves. (Lung, 2007)

In case your pesky moral qualms have decided to kick in about this point (What took you so long?), assuage any misgivings and/or guilt (and *temptation!*) you might have now (There'll be more later!) about seeking out this kind of "forbidden" knowledge by assuring yourself that, just because you learn a dangerous skill—like how to totally seduce and dominate another's mind!—that doesn't necessarily mean you have to become the next Lex Luthor . . . Heh-heh-heh.

Miyamoto Musashi (1584–1645), universally acknowledged as the greatest swordsman who ever lived in Japan, author of *A Book of Five Rings** taught his students that the same principles that work for defeating one man can easily be applied to defeating a thousand men:

> The way of war is the same if the situation is one against one
> or ten thousand against ten thousand. This should be exam-
> ined well, making the mind now large, now small.

Musashi not only meant his students could apply this principle in a thousand one-on-one singular sword duels (Musashi himself fought more than sixty to-the-death duels during his life), he also meant that the same strategy could be applied for maneuvering (seducing) a single opponent into position for delivering the coup de grâce, pulling the enemy this way, pushing the enemy that way—the same principle that can be applied by generals for skillfully maneuvering armies of thousands.

Musashi's philosophical basis for this principle is very familiar in the East: That by mastering the underlying principles (the essence) of a small skill, we can then apply those same principles on ever-larger playing fields.

In Japan, the process involved in learning such principles, as well as the application of that principle—is called "Dō" (pronounced "dough").

Dō means "the way" and is sometimes used as a synonym for the Japanese "michi" (path). When written dō, it refers to the "small dō, any skill, or experience which causes us to see, and/or can be applied to the "big" Dō on a universal scale. In this respect the "big Dō" is identical with the Chinese Taoist concept of "Tao." (More on "The Tao of Seduction" in Chapter 4: *China.*)

In Western metaphysics, this same principle is summed up as

---

*Musashi's *A Book of Five Rings* is second only to Sun Tzu's *Art of War* when it comes to Asian treatises on strategy.

As Above, So Below.
As Within, So Without.

"As Above, So Below" refers to the Eastern dō-Dō concept that understanding and mastering smaller skills and principles prepares us for effectively dealing with "The Big Picture," universal principles.

"As Within, So Without" keys us to the fact that the exterior of a thing (or person) can either mask or all too often reveal what's going on inside a thing or person, and vice versa. Ever heard of "body language"? What about "Freudian slips"?

So whether it's trying to talk your way into some lover's boudoir, successfully negotiate a corporate merger, or "shock-and-awe" your way across some other country's sovereign border, somewhere along the way, seduction will either be the key . . . or the crowbar!

The same principles—strategies and tactics—apply whether trying to seduce your way into someone's pants, into their pocketbook, or into their politics.

In the East, there's no better symbol for balancing both our mental and physical energies—in order to better focus and direct them—than the yin-yang symbol of Chinese Taoism. (See Figure 1.)

In the end the "art" of seduction is simply yin-yang, or push-pull.

For example, ever hear someone say, "he pushed her into another man's arms," meaning one lover has become so demanding and/or demean-

YIN-YANG

Figure 1.

ing as to chase off their lover? This phase is often heard in one-on-one relationships.

Consider how this *failure of seduction* can also be applied on a large scale, even on the *largest* of scales—global politics:

In the early 1960s, the U.S. government rejected Cuban revolutionary Fidel Castro's newly formed government because he had a couple communists in his Cabinet.

Our insistent demands that he remove these communists (as a precondition for the United States formally recognizing his regime) infuriated Castro, literally driving him into another's arms: the sympathetic embrace of the USSR.

"Let's keep it real!" you protest. "How is all this ancient history important in my life?" . . . Hello! "Cuban Missile Crisis" ring a bell? "Brink of World War III, nuclear destruction of every living thing on the planet!" sound familiar?

All life on Earth wiped out because some half-assed politicians decided to use the bully stick rather than the seduction carrot!

Might we not have wooed, wined, and dined Castro with all his faults (foul-smelling cigar and all), accepting him as he was, gradually "getting to know him better," before slowly—diplomatically—enticing him to change, in subtle ways at first.* (You know, the way your girlfriend/roommate slowly—imperceptibly—changes everything in the apartment over a period of time without you realizing it? Until one day you just happen to notice your prized autographed World Series baseball has been replaced on the mantel by her autographed photo of those irritating women from *The View* and . . . now that you mention it, I haven't seen Rover's doggie dish—or Rover—for a few days!

Better seduction than destruction . . . although seduction *is* often the first step to the eventual destruction of your enemy.

By now you should see seduction and strategy as two sides to the same coin—a two-headed coin.

And you never lose when tossing a two-headed coin . . . unless you let the other person choose first!

---

*Objects in motion tend to stay in motion.

THE ZEN OF SEDUCTION

Nothing whatever is hidden; from of old, all is clear as daylight.
—The Zenrin

February 7, 2008, began the Year of the Rat, the year 4706 on the Asian calendar. (More on using—and abusing!—the secrets of the Chinese zodiac in our section on China.)

Apropos, there is a story told in the East:

> One day Elder Rat and his young son were out scurrying about when, suddenly, a large, ravenous cat barred their path. Young Rat cowered behind his father, but Elder Rat stands his ground, locks eyes with the ferocious feline, and loudly barks, "Bow-wow! Bow-wow!" Startled, the cat immediately runs off. Smiling, Elder Rat tells young Rat, "Now you see why I always stress how important it is for you to learn a second language?"

In many ways, expanding our individual mental powers—expanding our defensive and offensive seductive arsenal!—*is* somewhat akin to learning a "second language." This is especially true when it comes to wielding the wisdom and wherewithal of ancient, and modern, Asian mind-masters. In other words, learning to think like they think.

The ancient Taoist masters of China had a saying:

"The journey of a thousand miles begins with a single step."

Thus the first step on our journey into the Eastern mysteries of mind-mastery will have us learning an *appreciation* for and then the *application* of, *both sides* of our brain.

You see, it's a myth that we human beings only use 10 percent of our brains. The truth of the matter is human beings use all their brain all the time. To be more precise, there's always a certain amount of blood coursing to every part of the brain all the time—otherwise the neglected parts of the brain would atrophy—stroke!—and die. (Of course there's no way of telling whether it's attention or distraction—ignorance or genius—swimming along in that blood flow!)

As a result, most people only use their brains 10 percent *efficiently.*

The bad news: That leaves a whopping 90 percent room for improvement. Or is that "the good news," since that adds up to a lot of human potential we can tap into?

Successfully tapping into that dormant 90 percent potential—whatever our morals or motivation—begins with our realizing that *the human brain is actually two brains in one,* a right hemisphere and a left hemisphere.

Each of these hemispheres specializes in looking at the world—processing information—in a different way. These two hemispheres often work at cross-purposes to one another. This is where all your indecision and confusion originates. (And you thought it was just because that third cup of coffee hadn't kicked in!)

The left hemisphere of your brain is a talker. It enjoys words, it enjoys doing math. It demands sequential, logical thinking. The left hemisphere concentrates on the details, often to the exclusion of all else.

The right hemisphere of your brain is more artistic. It enjoys music, it tends to see "the big picture." It is less organized but more creative than the left side. (See Figure 2, page 16.)

Simply put, the left brain is a more no-nonsense, "concrete" thinker. The right, more speculative, imaginative, and "abstract."

This is important because we can often get a clue to how a person processes information—right brain versus left brain dominant—simply by listening to the various words and phrases they use to express themselves. (See Figure 3, page 17.)

Learning to fully "listen" to a person, determining whether they are left-side (concrete thinker) or right-side (more abstract) brain dominant is one of the first tools we need to add to our seduction arsenal. (We'll teach you how to "listen" better in the section called "Making More Sense of Your Senses" in the section on Sexual Feng-Shui.)

If you are trying to concentrate on creating a piece of art (right-brain activity)—say, a painting—and are constantly being interrupted by an incessant talker (language processed by the left side of your brain), the result can only be frustration and eventual anger.

We need to learn to use the appropriate side of our brain to do the appropriate job, to become adaptable. Not as easy as it sounds.

World renowned twentieth century Japanese Zen Buddhist Master D. T. Suzuki realized that Eastern thought and Western ways of thinking likewise can be viewed in this dualistic light. Suzuki discovered and catalogued what he saw as the differences between Eastern and Western ways of looking at the world. (See Figure 4, page 18.)

LEFT BRAIN	RIGHT BRAIN
Verbal—uses words to describe things. Temporal—keeps good track of time. Abstract AND Symbolic—uses symbols and word representations easily.	Nonverbal, uses hands, draws pictures and designs in the air when talking. Nontemporal. Has no sense of time. Not good with schedules. Synthetic, sees the "whole," the big picture just by looking at the parts. Concrete thinking, relates to things as they are at the present time.
Logical and linear. Sequential (A-B-C . . .)	Intuitive, a good guesser! Makes cognitive leaps.
OBJECTIVE	SUBJECTIVE
Catchphrase: HMMM . . .	Catchphrase: AHA!
Mathematical (uses numbers to measure and count his world)	Metaphorical (uses images and metaphor and simile to describe his world)
Most left-brain-dominant people are LISTENERS.	Right-brain-dominant people tend towards being Watchers and Touchers. Listen for his use of words and phrases as an indication of his NLP orientation. (See *Sexual Feng Shui* section)

Figure 2. Left brain/right brain traits

Suzuki was merely being observant, not being judgmental, since he acknowledged strengths in both ways of thinking.

While differently oriented, neither of these ways is necessarily right or wrong. What we are dealing with here is developing the ability to think in more than one way. Strategy-wise (hence, seduction-wise), either/both modes of thinking are available to us, though people are usually dominated by one mode of thinking over the other.

Likewise groups, political entities, even countries tend to show a propensity for one or the other of these modes of thinking in their policy making.

Whatever our preference and propensity for one mode of thinking over the other, we should make an effort to appreciate (and actually *apply* when appropriate) the complementary mode of thinking.

Different situations demand differing responses, varying and hopefully

"ABSTRACT INPUT"

ABSTRACT INPUT	CONCRETE INPUT
"Imagine this . . . "	"Nine tomorrow morning."
"Picture this . . . "	"Twenty dollars."
"Suppose that . . . "	"My office."
"Think about . . . "	"No."
"Consider . . . "	"Hell, no!"
"Pretend for just a minute that . . . "	"White. Black. (i.e. solid colors)
"Believe what I'm about to tell you . . . "	Specific times (specify AM or PM).
"This is really going to take you back . . . "	Exact places.
"Remember when . . . "	Proper names (not "my secretary,"
"Here's an offer you've only dreamed about . . . "	"a friend," "someone").
"Wish upon a star and sometimes your wish comes true . . . "	Specific job descriptions follow introductions: "This is Ed Walsh. He is in charge of
"Behold! The answer to your prayers . . . "	the project. You will answer to him, and you will follow his instructions to the letter."

Figure 3.

creative ways of processing of information. This rule applies whether we are trying to win seductive points in the bedroom or take strategic positions on the battlefield.

As on the battlefield, so in the bedroom, seduction is strategy, strategy is seduction. We must never allow ourselves to become locked into one mode of thought only. Such people are called "hardheads," and are boring and predictable.

Wise generals will tell you there's no greater blessing (on the battlefield at least) than a *predictable* enemy.

Lovers will tell you there's nothing more *boring* than a predictable lover.

For example, in some situations deductive reasoning (Eastern mind) might need to solve a problem but, in other cases, the Western penchant for induc-

D. T. SUZUKI'S
EASTERN MIND VS. WESTERN MIND

EASTERN MIND	WESTERN MIND
SUBJECTIVE	OBJECTIVE
DEDUCTIVE	INDUCTIVE
NON-DISCRIMINATIVE	DISCRIMINATIVE
NON-SYSTEMATIC	SCIENTIFIC
NON-DISCURSIVE (i.e., "focused")	GENERALIZING`
SOCIALLY GROUP-MINDED	SELF-ASSERTIVE
INTUTIVE (rather than affective)	INTELLECTUAL
INTEGRATIVE	DIFFERENTIAL
TOTALIZING	ANALYTICAL
DOGMATIC	CONCEPTUAL
SPIRITUALLY INDIVIDUALISTIC	SCHEMATIC
SYNTHETIC (Note: This word is not used in the Western sense to mean "phony" or "artificial"; rather it derives from the word "SYNTHESIS" meaning to combine diverse elements, parts and substances to create a unified whole.)	IMPERSONAL
	LEGALISTIC
	POWER-WIELDING
(cf. Schol & Carr, 1970)	DISPOSED TO IMPOSE ITS WILL UPON OTHERS

Figure 4.

tive reasoning will more efficiently and effectively get the job done. Likewise, while it is most effective to be "socially group-minded" (Eastern mind-set)— pooling resources and working with others in order to accomplish mutually beneficial goals—at other times going it alone, being independent and self-assertive (Western mind) might accomplish the goal in half the time.

Remember *"as above, so below"* and vice versa. Hence, whether attempting to seduce a single individual or convince an entire nation, we need to understand which of these modes of thinking and perceiving and processing information we ourselves favor and which mode of perceiving and processing our potential "lover" is likely to embrace.

Thus we should not see either Eastern or Western modes of thinking as being "better" or somehow "superior" to the other. Both have their inherent strengths and weaknesses depending on how they are applied to differing challenges.

As in all things yin-yang, *balance* is the way to go. Balance and a willingness to adapt to the ever-changing needs and possibly shifting perimeters of a problem.

Nineteenth-century Prussian strategist Field Marshal Helmuth von Moltke gets the credit for first penning that "No battle plan survives first contact with the enemy."*

Whether it's changing up those tired old pickup lines that no longer seem to be impressing those fine fillies at the bar, or deciding to lay in ambush rather than meet a numerically superior enemy force head-on, a willingness to *adapt* and the ability to "think on our feet" (make decisions on the spot as new intelligence arrives) are the key to both strategy on the battlefield and seduction in the bedroom.

> *Unless it grows out of yourself no knowledge is really yours, it is only borrowed plumage.*
> —D. T. Suzuki

THE WILLOW BRANCH WAY

This book, both our map and compass to Asian arts of strategy and seduction, begins somewhere on the lower Ganges and culminates somewhere in the Japanese archipelago—but only after having ventured by way of Tibet, China, Korea, Vietnam, and a dozen other Asian locales.

And while these various Eastern cultures may appear vastly different, exotic,

---

*Actually, since the time of Hannibal, *any* general worth his salt knows this as the first and foremost of all battle adages. Or as Hannibal the Conqueror put it: "Truth #17: What I know today, my enemy knows tomorrow. What my enemy knows tomorrow is what I teach him today!" See *The 99 Truths: Hannibal's Black Art of War* by Dr. Haha Lung. Publication pending.

perhaps even forebidding and impenetrable, and while it's true each of these lands does indeed possess a uniqueness about them, once we set first foot on their land we soon discover they have *more similarities than differences* with their neighbors and with us, like most places in the world, like most people in the world.

Some of these Asian philosophical stopovers will seem more inviting, others more inscrutable. As long as we can swallow our fear and open our eyes, we will soon see that they are certain similarities of thought—*wisdom* they willingly share with any truth seeker, so long as that seeker comes harvesting similarities, not nitpicking differences.

Throughout our journey to the East we will time and again return our focus to these shared similarities of method and mind. Schools of thought, tactics, and techniques, some mind-expanding and uplifting, others insidious and self-serving, all tried-and-true, having effectively stood the test of time under a variety of banners—behind a myriad of masks!—in various parts of the Far East.

And, in the end, we'll discover that the Far East is not so "far" away after all . . . we need only look *within!* (The word "Asia" originally meant "within" and "interior.")

These shared principles of thought—mind-sets—that resonate throughout Asia are best summed up in two Japanese concepts: *ketchimyakyu* and *Masakatsu.*

Ketchimyakyu means "the Blood Pulse" and initially referred to the passing of wisdom from a master to disciple. But, on a broader scale, ketchimyakyu also refers to the way in which special and sometimes sacred knowledge passes down through the generations.

Thus we follow the trial and transmission of treaties and treasures of sacred, high-minded wisdom from India to other parts of Asia.

But we also catch a fleeting—shadowy—glimpse of the dissemination of darker, perhaps more practical—definitely more ruthless!—scrolls, scholars, and schools of strategy and seduction from one Eastern land to the next, one nefarious cadre to another, concepts flowing from place to place, mind to mind, heart to heart across the length and breadth of Asia. Thus we should not be surprised to find covert Hiraccarah of India, relentless Moshuh Nanren of China, mysterious Cao Dai "Black Crows" of Vietnam, ninja and samurai warriors and even Yakuza gangsters of Japan all employing variations of the same tactics and techniques of manipulation and mind control.

Neither should we in the West be shy in likewise doing so.

Nature gifts us with knowledge free for the taking, knowing full well those lacking in knowledge will surely be the first taken!

Sometimes these methods of mind-manipulation and mental-manhandling were outright stolen, other times traitorously bartered for, still other times literally tortured out of an enemy!

Thus we credit intrepid Bodhidharma-Tamo for braving the harsh northlands of India, for crossing the treacherous peaks of Tibet (picking up a trick or two along the way) before descending on China—there to teach a handful of monks at Shaolin . . . thereby enriching the lives of millions of seekers in a hundred generations to come.

Truly, knowledge can never be hidden under a bushel . . . especially not when you have every insatiable scholar, keen-edged samurai, and always nosy ninja in Asia trying to spy out your "hidden" secrets!

Better to "hide" your secrets in the open, where an indolent thief will pass them by, thinking them of no value. ("Otherwise they'd keep them locked away, right?")

Herein lies the biggest of ironies: That we imagine Eastern masters have "hidden" knowledge, ancient wisdoms they go out of their way to keep from prying Western eyes.

Nothing could be further from the truth.

From the tranquil beatitudes of India's Buddha and the tantalizing bedroom seductions of the Kama Sutra, to the ruthless battlefield strategies of Japan's samurai and ninja, the "secrets" of the East are as plain as the nose on your face. Ah! But like that nose on your face, to "see" the secrets of Asian strategy and seduction requires first looking in the mirror!

Thus no matter where our journey to the East takes us, we must make note of the *similar* themes and concepts taught and employed by all the seemingly different schools and scholars—*leit-motif of legerity.* This is the prime prerequisite to the mastery of first your own mind, before then venturing into the minds of others.

Our other prerequisites—and goals—along the way:

- Seeking to understand—and master!—Circumstance and flux through mastery of—or at least attention to—"The Three Knows":

    Know yourself.
    Know your enemy.
    Know your environment.

- Seeking to balance our mental and physical energies through understanding of Yin & Yang.

- Mastering our own emotions, while learning to influence the emotional state of others by way of "the 5 Movers" (See China section).
- Learning to read your lovers—and your enemies—like a book . . . before writing their final chapter, be it epilogue or epitaph!

Masakatsu! At the Black Science Institute, when rendered into English, Masakatsu! should always be spelled with an exclamation point!—to emphasize the spirit of determination inherent in the word. By any means necessary. Whatever it takes, whatever is most appropriate to the situation.

To accomplish their goals, samurai, ninja, and yakuza, all focused on this concept, applying it to both forceful as well as more accommodating methods, what in Japan is referred to as "Silk & Steel," in other words, yin & yang (Jp. *in-yo).*

Dogged determination, Nietzsche's "will to power," not taking "no" for an answer. To win our true love or win in battle. To win condemnation or praise, winner or the thinner for the experience. (Who was it that said: Experience is what you get when you don't get what you wanted.)

So Masakatsu! Masakatsu! achieved through *correct practice.*

Practice seduces chance.

The age-old saying that "practice makes perfect" requires a proviso: Practice makes perfect *only* if we practice correctly to begin with, with correct form, with correct attitude of learning.

And, when practicing, we must always apply the age-old Chinese kung-fu adage known as The Willow Branch Rule:

"He who plays with the sword will succumb to he who works with the willow branch."

3

India: The Guru Effect

> It is those who go to the extremes—the Gandhis, the
> Krishnamurtis—who seduce us.
> —Greene, 2001:358

India, "the Mother of all civilizations," was gifted (others say "cursed") by a curious mixture of its indigenous matriarchal culture and the patriarchal Indo-Aryans who invaded the subcontinent around 1500 BC, creating a unique religious tradition, taking the best from both cultures. Out of this mix came the Upanishads, the primary socioreligious "bible" of Hindu India, which recognizes two distinct types of wisdom:

- *Para vidya,* "Higher wisdom" concerned with "spiritual" matters (i.e., how to get right with the gods)
- *Apara vidya,* "lower wisdom" that concentrates on more mundane, practical matters like how to get ahead in life (up to and including taking your adversary's head!)

Thus, when we find ourselves figuratively or literally sitting at the feet of an Indian guru, we should ask ourselves what he is putting in our ear: *para vidya* or *apara vidya*? The world has need for both, and our collection of strategy and seduction methods also has room for both . . . actually *rooms* for both: the war room and the bedroom!

However, whether dealing with an Indian con man wearing a diaper, or a dapper con man in some singles bar in Indianapolis, there's a rude, crude—tried and true—adage snickered by trailer-trash gigolos and ghetto pimps from coast to coast: "If you can't get no ear . . . you can't get no rear!"

So listen and learn. Today, much of India's religious renown comes from the concept of the guru—the enlightened teacher who passes his wisdom and sometimes even extrasensory powers along to his students. Often this wisdom and these "powers" *(siddhas)* require years of hard practice by the student. Other times such "energy" comes in the form of an instant "blessing" from the guru, like an electrical spark jumping between two Tesla coils.

In his 2001 *The Art of Seduction,* Robert Greene explains this "Guru Effect":

> People do not want to hear that your power comes from years of effort or discipline. They prefer to think that it comes from your personality, your character, something you were born with. They also hope the proximity to the guru or Charismatic will make some of the power rub off on them. . . . People are naturally drawn to those who emit happiness, maybe they can catch it from you. (Greene, 2001:109–110)

All such gurus possess a certain amount of charisma, either *charisma that is a natural outgrowth* of their spiritual practices, or else *charisma deliberately crafted and cultivated* with the intent of defrauding—and perhaps deflowering!—unwary would-be disciples. (More on this in the section Darkside Dharma.)

For those unscrupulous gurus lacking natural charisma, either charisma inborn, or charisma as a *siddha* developed through years of practice, there are still other time-tested Indian arts of strategy and seduction that can be wielded for worldly gain and/or nighttime entertainment.

KARMA AND DHARMA

In the ancient Hindu holy book *Bhagavad-Gita* ("The Song of God") India's greatest warrior, Arjuna, finds himself literally standing in the middle of an Indian civil war. Seeing his brothers and cousins, uncles and teachers, ready to spill their blood on opposite sides, Arjuna is so overcome with grief that he throws down his bow and declares, "I will not fight!"

Arjuna's chariot driver (who just happens to be the god Krishna in disguise) spends the rest of the Bhagavad-Gita explaining to Arjuna that it is both Arjuna's karma (fate) and dharma (duty) that has brought him to this pivotal point in life. It doesn't matter whether Arjuna actively participates (dharma) in the coming battle or not, this battle is still going to take place (karma).

So with Arjuna, so with us all, our environment contributes to us just as we contribute to it, both by our actions and by our inaction. Recall that environment is one of "The Three Knows."*

But environment is never all-determining. Your environment should refine you, not define you.

According to Indian philosophy, our lives are a combination of both karma and dharma:

Karma is the *fate* we have written for ourselves through our past actions.

Dharma is the *duty and obligations* that arises from our karma.**

Arjuna's past actions, his karma (i.e., living the life of the warrior), brought him to that particular point in his life. His dharma (duty) were the *attachments* he had collected along the way, duties and obligations he was honor-bound to see through: Family duties, duties to his comrades and country.

Beware! Wily mind-manipulators, strategists, and seducers can play on our unguarded sense of duty and honor to push or pull us in one direction or another. One way to guard yourself against such manipulation—when someone gets in your face trying to "obligate" you into doing something by claiming "You owe me!"—is to remember this adage: "obligation" is what people foist on you. "Duty" is the debt you owe yourself!

What woman hasn't, at one time or another, felt pressured by some jerk boyfriend to "put out"? Such unscrupulous manipulators try to "obligate" the woman by making her feel "guilty" about "leading him on," "teasing him," or else implying that sex at the end of the evening is the "cost" of the movie and meal he so graciously provided.

Hence the woman feels the same "obligation" Arjuna did. As on the battlefield, so in the bedroom.

This is one of the simplest (and shadiest!) of all seduction techniques: making a potential lover feel obligated (dharma). Or else convincing them it's fate (karma) you've come together.

Of course, the better we've mastered "The Three Knows"—self, adversary, environment—the better chance we'll have of making the right choice—

---

*Know yourself, know your adversary, know your environment.

**Dharma written with a small-case "d" is used to refer to the Hindu concept of "dharma," whereas Dharma with upper-case "D" is used to mean the teachings of the Buddha.

whether to drop our panties in surrender . . . or else drop our adversary (or obnoxious boyfriend!) with a right hook and a strategic exit, stage left.

Thus, it might behoove and benefit us to take some time—before that big date, before that big battle—to examine what Indian masters of strategy and seduction had to say about why people think the way they do ("The Seven Secrets of Power"); what faults in reasoning we all share ("The City of Nine Gates"); and, most importantly, what vulnerabilities we all also possess ("The Eighteen Links") that we must first learn to guard in ourselves, before then being able to use them to rock someone else's world ("Kama Sutra Karma").

SEVEN SECRETS OF POWER

In both East and West, the number seven holds an honored place laden with superstition.

The West has the classical Seven Deadly Vices, seeds of weaknesses and temptation inherent in man that be must balanced against the Seven Universal Virtues. (See Figure 5, opposite.)

All human beings have the capacity of slipping (or being pushed!) from one of these vices and virtues to the next. Ideally we would have a balance (yin-yang) between vice and virtue (the definition of both subject to change depending on time and place). As a result of this moral fluidity, wily seducers are forever tempting us (tipping us!) one way or another, in favor of one vice or virtue.

Vice often comes before virtue, and not just in the dictionary.

According to Indian yoga gurus, we all have a mysterious, untapped energy within us known as kundalini (symbolized in Hinduism as a serpent asleep at the base of our spine).

Once awakened (through yoga, meditation, and other disciplines) kundalini spirals its way up our spine toward the crown of our head. Along this path, kundalini's passing activates seven "power centers" called chakras (Skt. Wheels). Each of these chakras controls various aspects of our physical and mental life—from basic survival needs to our desires (for sex, power, etc.) to our achieving ultimate enlightenment. (See Figure 6, page 28.)

Kundalini energy, similar in many ways to the Chinese Taoist concept of chi, follows a natural, smooth-flowing course through the body *unless interfered with by our personal hang-ups.* According to Bo Lozoff in his book *We're All Doing Time,* kundalini flows from one chakra to another naturally, except

VICE VS. VIRTUE

THE SEVEN "DEADLY" SINS	THE SEVEN "UNIVERSAL" VIRTUES	
PRIDE	FAITH	
WRATH	HOPE	("Supernatural virtues")
ENVY	CHARITY	
LUST		
GLUTTONY	JUSTICE	
AVARICE (GREED)	FORTITUDE	("Natural" or "cardinal" virtues)
SLOTH	TEMPERANCE	
	PRUDENCE	

Figure 5.

when our fears and desires push us to unnaturally manipulate the power flow, not allowing the whole system to work as it should. (Lozoff, 1985:78)

As ascending kundalini stimulates each chakra, unique energies are released, granting the guru (and us) enhanced physical and mental "powers" *(siddhas)*.

Over the centuries, gurus of kundalini and tantra have experimented with numerous ways to awaken (jump-start!) these power centers: extreme contortionists' yoga postures, masochistically laying on beds of nails; burying themselves in earth up to the level of a specific chakra; as well as mental manipulations such as drugs, meditation, and hypnosis. Oh yeah, and sex!

Extensive lists have also been compiled of chakra "correspondence"— factors and formulas designed to stimulate particular chakras, inducing particular moods and influencing thought patterns, both in your own mind and in the mind of an adversary or potential love interest. (See Figure 7, page 29.)

It's a two-way street: Our attitudes and actions help stimulate specific chakras. In turn, how we see the world depends on which chakra we're "looking through," which chakra is most active in us at any given time. During the course of any day, even from minute to minute, our mood can change as kundalini dances from one chakra to the other.

THE CHAKRAS/WHEELS OF POWER

CHAKRA SANSKRIT NAME	METAPHORIC	LOCATION	PETALS	KEY WORD	SYMBOL	
Muladhara	"Root base"	Perineum	4	Survival	Black stone	EXOTERIC
Svadhisthana	"Favored resort"	Lower Abdomen	6	Tribe	Phallus/ Serpent	EXOTERIC
Manipura	"Shining City"	Solar Plexus	10	Power	Jewel	BALANCE
Anahata	"Silent Sound"	Heart	12	Balance	Scales	BALANCE
Vishuddha	"Purifier"	Throat	16	Direction	Voice/ Arrow	BALANCE
Ajna	"Commander"	Brow	2	Mind	White stone	ESOTERIC
Sahasrara	"Thousand petaled"	Top of head	1,000	Spirit	Halo/ crown	ESOTERIC

Figure 6.

In general, upper chakras are associated with higher levels of thought and action, while lower-level chakras (though necessary for the survival of self and species) are associated with more basic (and baser) thought and action.

Much of our language reflects this natural aversion away from the lower end of this emotional spectrum, as when we're feeling *"down* in the dumps." Conversely, when things are going our way, we feel *"up*beat," and "on top" because "things are looking *up."*

When we feel positive and compassionate about the world, we're dealing from our fourth "heart" chakra. Conversely, when we're worrying about where our next meal is coming from, or fretting about personal safety, we're stuck at our lowest "root" chakra.

Remember the last time *this* happened: You're engaged in a spirited conversation about philosophy and self-realization, your energy focused and flowing through your sixth chakra. But then a devastatingly beautiful blonde struts by in painted-on jeans and, suddenly, all your thoughts go south as your focus drops from your higher sixth chakra to your lower second chakra—the chakra controlling your libido.

Gurus often used mantra (sounds) and yantra (meditation images, see

CHAKRA CORRESPONDENCE

Chakra	ONE	TWO	THREE	FOUR	FIVE	SIX	SEVEN
SANSKRIT	Muladhara	Svadisthana	Manipura	Anahata	Vishuddha	Ajna	Sahasrara
LOCATION	perineum	lower abdomen	solar plexus	heart	throat	forehead	top of the head
ELEMENT	earth	water	(fire (little fire)	air	ether, sound	light (big fire)	thought
PSYCHOLOGICAL FUNCTION	survival	emotion and sexuality	will and power	love and balance	creativity, communication	imagination	understanding
EMOTION	stillness, passivity	desire	joy and anger	compassion	enthusiasm	emotions in dreams	bliss
BODY PART	skeleton, lower intestine, legs	genitals and kidneys	stomach and muscles	cardio-vascular, arms	mouth, throat and ears	eyes	central nervous system, brain
MALFUNCTION	obesity	impotence	diabetes, ulcers	asthma, high blood pressure	thyroid, cold & flu	headache blindness, and bad dreams	depression, withdrawal
INFLUENCED BY VOWEL SOUND	Long O	OO	AH	Long A	Long E	MMM, NNN	ING
INFLUENCED BY "SEED SOUND"	LAM	VAM	RAM	SAM and	HAM	OM	SILENCE
INFLUEENCED BY VERB PHRASE	"I have"	"I feel"	"I can"	"I live"	"I speak"	"I see"	"I know"

Figure 7.

Figure 15) to help stimulate specific chakras. It's not surprising then that merely watching that blonde strut her stuff or only just hearing the sound of her voice can "activate" the chakra that controls procreation, or at least recreation!

By now you've begun to realize how easily you can use your knowledge of chakra energies to manipulate your lover's (or your adversary's) mind-set and mood.

For example, say we catch our adversary thinking "higher" positive thoughts, we can throw him off by bombarding him with unexpected *lower* chakra images, instantly bringing him back down to negative thoughts of tribe, survival, and sex.

If a lover is depressed by the (mis)deeds of the day, we deliberately raise her *("lift* her spirits") by planting positive images and words, bringing her up to the heart-level chakra. What's the chance we'll get "lucky" tonight? Raise her spirits, raise her skirt!

Conversely, if the person we're trying to seduce is "thinking" overlong about whether or not to give us a chance, we introduce an element designed to "lower" them to the perineum chakra that controls their (nonthinking) sex urges.

Can you see now how determining the chakra level at which our adversary is operating gives us invaluable insight into his character?

A common cult chakra manipulation strategy when dealing with a religious-minded seeker who is trying to channel their energy through their higher sixth and seventh wisdom and enlightenment chakras is to take them to their lower third chakra, distracting and tempting them with images of power and "forbidden" secrets.

Shakespeare's *Othello* provides us a perfect example of "evil" chakra manipulation: Othello truly loves Desdemona (fourth chakra = love and compassion), but the scheming Iago literally takes Othello *down* a notch, down to the next level (third chakra = ego power and emotions), transforming Othello's positive love into negative jealousy. The kundalini energy Othello puts out is the same, only the chakra it is being *filtered* through has changed—with disastrous results!

While this "chakra power centers" concept might at first sound far-fetched to Westerners, modern scientific studies have found intriguing correspondence between ancient Sanskrit descriptions of chakras and modern medicine's discovery of the human *endocrine* system, the seven glands that pump their mood-altering chemicals directly into the bloodstream. (See Figure 8.)

The part of the endocrine system most people have at least heard of is the adrenals, our "flight or fight" gland. "Mother lifts automobile off her trapped child" sound familiar?

If you're a smoker, what you're really addicted to is an adrenal-based secretion called epinephrine, triggered by the intake of nicotine. That's why just a few drags off a cigarette affects you so quickly, because this epinephrine chemical is flooding directly into your bloodstream. That's also why it's so hard to quit smoking, because what you're actually addicted to is a "natural" chemical in your body.

Likewise, other endocrine glands pump similar mood-altering chemicals directly into your body. This explains why one minute you're "high-minded", the next horny!

GLANDS AND CHAKRA

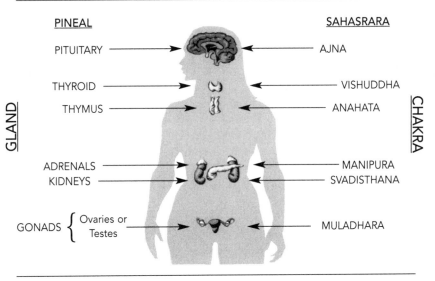

PINEAL

SAHASRARA

PITUITARY ⟶ AJNA

THYROID ⟶ VISHUDDHA

THYMUS ⟶ ANAHATA

GLAND

CHAKRA

ADRENALS ⟶ MANIPURA

KIDNEYS ⟶ SVADISTHANA

GONADS { Ovaries or Testes ⟶ MULADHARA

Figure 8.

DARKSIDE DHARMA

So you and I are the problem, and not the world, because the world
is the projection of ourselves and to understand the world we must
understand ourselves.

—J. Krishnamurti, *The First and Last Freedom,* 1954:95

We in the West are most comfortable thinking of India as the land of spiritual teachers: Buddha, J. Krishnamurti, Gandhi. After all, India gave us such "high-minded" words as: yoga, guru, swami, ashram, and mantra. But India also gave us thug and mugger!*

At first discovery of kundalini led to the development of the Indian healing arts, which in turn influenced the development of Chinese acupuncture and Japanese shiatsu. Only later, again perhaps inevitably, from those same

---

*The Indian killer cult of Kali gave us the words thug and mugger; the former shortened from *thuggee,* while the latter is an English corruption of the Hindu *magar,* British slang for Thuggee since these killers struck with the speed and ferocity of a "crocodile." (Lung, 1995)

roots came *Dim Mak*—the dreaded martial-arts "death touch" capable of killing an adversary instantly, without leaving a mark, simply by interrupting a person's kundalini chi flow (Omar, 1989; Lung, 1997a; Lung, 2002, "The Only-Eyed Snake"). Evidently, one man's healing touch is another's coup de grâce!

Perhaps it was inevitable that control of one's own body and mind proved too much of a temptation for some unscrupulous gurus, and so they were soon using their newfound powers to seduce their disciples. Not surprising then that India's noble sons include benevolent spiritual mentors, mendicants, marvelous magicians, master strategists, and martial artists . . . as well as crazed cult leaders and satyric seducers.

Thus, for every peaceful lamb, Mother India has also birthed her share of black sheep: from ruthless Rajas and scheming Hiraccarah spies, to the fourth-century B.C.E. "Machiavelli of India," Kautilya. (Lung and Prowant, 2001:136).

Kings, Kautilya, and Kipling

India's secular history is one long chronicle of constant intrigue, perpetual political and unrelenting religious strife.

Around 1500 B.C.E. lighter-skinned patriarchal (code word for "more warlike") Aryans,* nowadays called "Proto-Indo-Europeans."

By their own account, writings collected in the Upanishads and the Mahabharata (which includes Arjuna's Bhagavad-Gita), these Aryans were well-versed in both warfare and wiliness, strategy and seduction, and so quickly overpowered and then overshadowed the less savvy (i.e., less ruthless!) indigenous folk. Soon after, these conquerors imposed a strict caste system, predictably with Aryans—"nobles"—at the front of the pack, conquered peoples bringing up the rear. Thus India was ruled more or less successfully by the descendants of these Aryan invaders for the next twelve centuries—not counting constant court intrigues, the occasional coup d'etat, and a bloody civil war every now and then (like the one depicted in the Bhagavad-Gita).

---

*These invaders referred to themselves as "The Sons of Aryas," hence the now discredited (thanks to Hitler) term "Aryan" which, in ancient Sanskrit (their original language) meant "noble" and still refers to higher-ranking members of Hindu society. While we're on the subject, Hitler also stole his swastika from Aryan India (where the word and the symbol meant "good fortune").

Then in 326 B.C.E., Alexander the Great invaded into the Punjab (the northwest region of India) where he began not-so-subtly teaching the rulers of India a new thing or two about Western strategy—and seduction. Alexander succeeded—as he always had—in hacking himself off a fair-sized piece of the Punjab, opening trade routes between India and the West.

Alexander's life deserves scrutiny by any would-be student of Black Science strategy and seduction. While we are most familiar with Alexander's military conquests, via his brilliant use of battlefield strategy, the young Greek was just as adept at advantageous negotiation, using more subtle seductions. Alexander could wield charm, a vital component of seduction, to get what he wanted through diplomatic means, successfully wooing both the awed and the ambitious in the lands he'd invaded to come to his side.

Like every successful conqueror who survives long enough to become an effective ruler, Alexander made more allies than he did enemies. Allies cost more in the long run than adversaries . . . but you sleep better at night!

Following Alexander's death in 323 B.C.E., the empire he'd built was divided up among his contentious lieutenants. In other words, Alexander's empire began falling apart as a bunch of big dogs fought for major bites off the haunches of the still-warm carcass, even as a pack of lesser curs paced anxiously, licking their hungry chops in the shadows, ever alert for scraps.

Confusion and chaos feed opportunity, at least for those hungry enough to sink their teeth in and hold on for dear life.

Taking advantage of the opportunity to fill the sudden power vacuum left in India by Alexander's passing, a noble named Chandragupta Maurya seized control of the Ganges Valley state of Magadha. Over the next twenty-four years Chandragupta went on to conquer most of India. His son and grandson would complete the mission by conquering the remainder of the Indian subcontinent. The Maurya Dynasty established by Chandragupta would endure until 185 B.C.E.

In 305 B.C.E., Chandragupta proved his wile and worth by beating back Alexander's lieutenant and would-be successor, Seleucus, who was then in control of most of Asia Minor. Chandragupta nullified the threat of Seleucus through a combination of brilliant battlefield strategy on the one sword-filled fist and diplomatic "seduction" on the other, open, olive-branch-holding hand. In the end, Seleucus was convinced to give up his claims in India (the easternmost portion of his empire) in exchange for Chandragupta's promise to provide him five hundred war elephants, which both rulers knew would give Seleucus an edge over his more immediately threatening enemies in the west. Nothing dulls an angry sword blade like calm diplomacy . . . and the occasional well-placed bribe!

By all accounts Chandragupta was both a brilliant general (strategist) and wise administrator (seducer), ruling his empire from his eighteen-square-mile capital at Patna. He has been favorably compared with both King David (for strategy) and King Solomon (for his sly and seductive wisdom). Taking a page from the book of conquest penned by that great Indian Sikh warlord Khan Noonian Singh that "Conquest is easy, control is not!," heeding the advice of his chief advisor Kautilya, Chandragupta realized that to successfully supervise his vast empire would require three things: Law, Order, and Intelligence:

Law: Chandragupta set up a series of courts, starting with a lesser court in each village presided over by the village headman, up through regional courts, ultimately to the Imperial Court of final appeal, which also acted as a legislative branch, making laws.

Order: Provided by a strong, professional army (loyal only to Chandragupta, of course). Units of this army also acted as local national guard, policing specific regions. At its height, Chandragupta's army was massive, composed of 700,000 men, 9,000 elephants, and 10,000 chariots!

Intelligence: His success in winning his empire was proof Chandragupta possessed the first type of intelligence: innate intelligence, the kind you're born with. What he now needed to further safeguard his empire (and his own person!) was the gathered kind of intelligence. And so Chandragupta empowered a secret police force to keep an eye on enemies, internal and external, real and imagined; a secret police force, again answerable only to the emperor himself. According to one Greek observer of Chandragupta's reign, spies working for the emperor's secret police were so numerous they constituted a separate class of Indian society! Here then would be the origin of India's (in)famous Hiraccarah spy network of later years. (See "Craft of the Hiraccarah" in *Mind Control* by Dr. Haha Lung, Citadel, 2006).

With great power comes great responsibility, right? But with great power also comes great paranoia. Some other ass is always trying to see how well it fits your throne.

Following their Emperor's example, conspiracy became the number-one sport and pastime in Chandragupta's India. So great was the threat of espionage and treachery that Chandragupta lived most of his senior years in seclusion, attended only by a special cadre of women courtesans who doubled as bodyguards and who saw to his every need—from safety to sex.

Some researchers have suggested this highly trained cadre of women body-guards may have formed the roots of the all-female (all-lovely and all-lethal!) Black Lotus secret society that's still whispered of throughout Asia. (More on the origins and organization of this exotic—and elusive—sorority of femmes fatales in the following section on China.)

So far as Black Science overall is concerned, Chandragupta's rule also produced one of the most seductive strategists of all time, the sorely under-appreciated Kautilya, Chandragupta's chief minister and, at times, de facto ruler of the perennially absent Chandragupta's empire.

Author of the *Arthasastra* ("Treatise on Material Gain"), Kautilya has been dubbed "the Machiavelli of India" although, since the former lived nearly 1800 years earlier, perhaps the latter should be known as "The Kautilya of Italy."

Kautilya's philosophy maintained that the greatest evil in the world is confusion and anarchy. Somebody—a firm hand—needs to be in charge, preferably the best qualified man for the job. Better a bad king (which at least holds out the possibility of establishing order) than no king at all. According to Kautilya, a singular, focused authority is necessary if a state is going to accomplish its duty (dharma) of providing a stable, productive environment for its people. Like Machiavelli, Kautilya had no problem with rulers doing whatever they had to (Masakatsu!) to achieve this practical goal. Ends justified means in Kautilya's world. Any strategy and seduction, up to and including bald-faced deception and unscrupulous statecraft, was justified to attain a "noble" end.

Postscript: Following Chandragupta's death in 297 B.C.E., his son continued to ruthlessly expand his empire throughout the rest of India. However, Chandragupta's grandson Ashoka (273–232 B.C.E.), perhaps the most praised of India's rulers, had neither the stomach nor stones for bloody conquest as had his father and grandfather (either that, or he was just a nice guy). Ashoka was so horrified by war that after just his first military campaign he converted to Buddhism and thereafter made love not war, preferring diplomacy and seduction to duplicity and destruction. After this, the Maurya Dynasty faded and the empire crumbled, giving rise to numerous petty rulers (rajas) down through the centuries.

By the 1520s the Mogul empire had been established just in time to meet, but not defeat, the invading Portuguese, Dutch, French, and finally the British.

Thanks to India's volatile "tradition" of vacillating and violent politics down through its history, it's not surprising that every ambitious militarist and merchant, every suspicious raja, and every ruthless religious leader felt it necessary, if only for self-defense, to field their own spies and, when need be, assassins.

However, most of the British in India, high on newfound colonial wealth and power, remained blissfully ignorant of the Hiraccarah, the ages-old system of sophisticated skullduggery operating right under those British stiff upper lips. This was the Indian version of the grapevine: information shared, stolen, and then sold back and forth within a mercenary network of spies.

Not all Europeans were so naïve. While in India working for the East India Company, notorious freebooter and libertine Sir Richard Francis Burton (1821–1890) was initiated into both the craft of the Hiraccarah and into tantric "sex magic."

Another controversial Westerner, the occult author H. P. Blavatsky (1831–1891), also learned Hiraccarah mind-manipulation techniques of strategy, spying, and seduction that she later used in her extensive and often perilous travels throughout Asia (such as disguise techniques she successfully used when dressing as a man to penetrate the "forbidden" Tibetan capital of Lhasa). Like Burton, she is rumored to have foreplayed and fiddled around with tantric sex rituals. In 1875, Blavatsky founded the Theosophical Society. Occult oriented, this international brotherhood borrows freely from Indian fakir and Freemason alike and has done much to educate the West to Eastern mysticism, including tantra.

Mystic poet William Blake (1757–1827) was also inspired by Asian religious and mystical imagery in general and by tantric imagery in particular. Reportedly Blake used tantric techniques to achieve spiritual visions (altered states of awareness), which he then transposed into both his poetry and his artwork. (Schuchurd, 2008)

Still another noted Western author and part-time spy, Rudyard Kipling (1865–1936), understood the potential of Hiraccarah tactics. Born in India, Kipling acted as a journalist/spy in India from 1882 to 1889, during which time he became both a Freemason and a Hiraccarah adept.

Kipling journeyed widely throughout northern India, mostly spying on Russian intentions. But Kipling was also obsessed with Masonic legends of a fabled lost city hidden somewhere between India and Afghanistan. Reportedly founded by Alexander the Great, this Shangri-la was said to be the repository of the forbidden knowledge of the *Roshaniya,* the "Illuminated

Ones," mystical adepts from whose lineage so many subsequent secret societies, including the Freemasons, lay claim.

Art imitates life. Some of Kipling's actual adventures, thinly veiled, subsequently appeared in his novel *The Man Who Would Be King* (1891)—the tale of two ex-British soldiers who, after an arduous search, finally succeed in discovering just such a hidden city somewhere in the Kashmir. The heroes of Kipling's story are both Freemasons, adept at strategy and seduction, a fact that not only saves their lives but also ultimately proves to be the key to their gaining riches and power. The 1975 movie starred Sean Connery.

British successes spying in northern India and Afghanistan, along with the difficult—bloody!—lessons they learned suppressing the secretive strangler cult of Thuggee, helped the British military hone their own skills of strategy and espionage, leading to their forming special "commando" units adept at thuggee infiltration and assassination techniques, as well as specialized intelligence operatives (Lung, 1995).

Life imitates art. Homegrown Indian strategists and seducers, as well as acute and ambitious adventurers from the West, borrowed freely from age-old Indian *para vidya* ("enlightenment") texts, finding more mundane *(apara vidya)* uses for this ancient wisdom. They turned techniques originally meant for the spiritual enlightenment of self into strategies for the physical—and financial—advancement of self, as well as for the seduction of others.

For example, we've already seen how easily the Indian science of chakras, the seven "Wheels of Power," originally intended for the enlightenment of self, can give us invaluable insight into others (insight you *will* be tempted to use to further your own ends and feather your own nest!).

Relax, "temptation" is just another way of saying "choice." (And the more "choice" the cuts of meat, the greater the temptation!)

Likewise, the time-honored practice of kundalini (which when used correctly concentrates on stimulating the flow of healthful energies in the body) was soon corrupted into techniques designed to interfere with and even stop the flow of positive energies, giving birth to the Chinese art of Dim Mak, the "Death Touch." Dim Mak is adapted from the Sanskrit *marman,* "death spots," and *varma Adi,* "striking vital spots." (See "Ninja Death Touch: The Fact and the Fiction" by Ralf Dean Omar, *Black Belt* magazine, September, 1989. Also, Lung, 1997a.).

Another innocent and helpful para vidya system that easily lends itself to Black Science mind control (mis)use is Ayurveda, an ancient system of mind and body medicine at least five thousand years old.

At first glance, Ayurveda somewhat resembles the discarded Western psychology theory of "somatotypes." (See Lung and Prowant, 2001:65.)

Ayurveda maintains there are three basic principles *(doshas)* that control us: *Vata, Pitta,* and *Kapha.* These doshas correspond to everything from our body type and size to our mental attitude—emotional strengths and weaknesses.

Most people are a combination of two types of dosha, with one dosha predominating. Identifying which doshas dominate our adversaries or our potential lover helps us better plot out our approach strategy and/or seduction technique. (See Figure 9, opposite.)

Buddhist Black Science

> *All that we are is the result of what we have thought, it is founded*
> *on our thoughts, it is made up of our thoughts.*
> **—the Buddha**

No other Eastern school of philosophy has had as much influence on Western thought as has Buddhism.

Who doesn't remember "Snatch the pebble from my hand, Grasshopper," from the seventies *Kung Fu* TV series? *Kung Fu* spotlighted the Shaolin Order* of monks, a fusion of indigenous Chinese Taoism and the Buddhism brought to China from India around 520 C.E.

A thousand years earlier, Gautama Siddhartha (560–477 B.C.E.), a prince of northern India, gave up his throne to go in search of enlightenment, which he found after forty years of study and struggle, earning him the title "Buddha" ("one who is awake"). For the past 2,500 years Buddhism has collected invaluable insight into the nature of human beings. In the wrong hands, even this well-intentioned knowledge can all too easily be used to manipulate others. The Buddha left behind a simple outline for finding enlightenment in this world, his "Four Aryan Truths":

- *The nature of life is suffering.*
- *Suffering is caused by desire.*
- *Desire can be overcome.*
- *Desire is overcome by following "The Eightfold Path":* Having Right Views,

---

*We discuss the Shaolin Order and its offshoots at length in the China section.

AYURVEDA STRATEGY AND SEDUCTION

THE PERSON	VATA	PITA	KAPHA
THEIR BUILD	Thin	Medium	Solidly built
THEIR METABOLISM	Fast	Methodical	Slow
THEIR ORIENTATION	Loves excitement and change	Likes challenges, an innate drive.	Likes status quo (but needs stimulus of new sights, sounds, and people)
THEIR NATURE	Cheerful, enthusiastic.	Enterprising, energetic.	Tranquil, relaxed.
TEMPTATION TO USE	Tempt with novelty.	Always looking for "the edge," a new angle.	Needs stimulus, attracted by new sights, sounds, people and opportunity.
THEIR ENERGY LEVEL	Given to bursts of energy (impulsive).	Sharp intellect, articulate speech.	Slow and steady. Mulls things over before acting.
THEIR COPING STRATEGY	Experiences excess anxiety.	Becomes angry and irritable under stress.	Slow to anger.
HEALTH TENDENCY	Unexplained aches and pains.	Workaholic "burnout."	Prone to weight gain.
PERFORMANCE FLAWS TO EXPLOIT	Short attention span. Can't keep a routine. Light sleeper. Learns fast, forgets just as fast and quickly.	Sarcastic and critical. Too demanding. Lives by his watch. Workaholic. Never skips a meal. Never "wastes" time.	Seeks emotional comfort from overeating. Needs more sleep and wakes slower than others. Empathetic to a fault.

Figure 9.

Right Desires, Right Speech, Right Conduct, Right Livelihood, Right Endeavors, Right Mindfulness, and Right Meditation.

What makes Buddhism unique among life philosophies is that one Buddhist can't tell another Buddhist how to apply these eight principles.

At its most basic Buddhism delves into the depths of the human mind to uncover the roots of a person's desires—our often toxic attachments to the world—so it's not surprising such insightful and intimate knowledge of human character—traits, tensions, and temptations—holds the potential for misuse and abuse. The ancient *Dhammapada* (423 sayings attributed to the Buddha himself) gives us insight into ourselves and others . . . insights an unscrupulous person might all too easily use to influence an unguarded mind. For example:

> "There is no fire like lust, no spark like hatred, no snare like folly, and no torrent like greed." (Saying #251)

Lust, hatred, folly, greed . . . four insights into a lover's personality, four nails to drive into an adversary's coffin! But Buddhism teaches us to first guard ourselves by coming to grips with our own faults (before attempting to exploit the faults of others!):

> "Whatever one hater can do to another hater, whatever one adversary can do to another adversary, still your untrained mind can do you even greater harm." (#42)

And

> "The fault of others is easy to see, but our own faults are often difficult to admit. This is why a man can so easily separate his own faults from his neighbor's faults, like separating wheat from chaff. All the while he hides his own faults the way a dishonest dicer hides his snake-eyes." (#252)

And ultimately:

> "Fools are their own worst adversary. With little understanding they plant evil deeds which all too soon bear them bitter fruits." (#66)

Worthwhile advice to help us to weed our own garden while planting seeds of influence in our adversary's garden.

The Cult Seduction Method

Confusion is my method. The moment I see you accumulating something, creating a philosophy or theology, I immediately jump on it and destroy it.
—Bhagwan Shree Rajneesh

One can't help but suspect prejudice when naysayers point out the "mysterious power" that "strange" and "inscrutable" Asian philosophies have to entice and entrap the unwary Western mind, as when critics point with alarm to the inroads Asian "cults" have made into the West. These cults include the South Korea-based "Moonies" and the ubiquitous East Indian "Hare Krishna" movement. But nowhere has such criticism of Asian cult methods of sly seduction, mind control, and manipulation been more alleged (and later proven!) than with the India-based cult of the Bhagwan Shree Rajneesh.

Rajneesh was born in India on December 11, 1931, and had his first transcendental religious experience—called *Samadhi*—at age seven. By 1974, he had formed the organization that would later become his "cult," humbly calling it "The Rajneesh Foundation."

In 1981, Rajneesh moved this growing cult from India to the small town of Antelope, Oregon. Rajneesh followers then began pouring into Antelope at an alarming rate, in short order overrunning the small town. More than seven thousand Rajneeshees visited Antelope in 1982 alone and, by December 1982, Rajneesh followers had commandeered the local elections, winning the Antelope mayor's office and a majority of seats on the city council and promptly renaming the city Rajneeshpuram. Allegations soon surfaced that Rajneesh followers had used intimidation, voter fraud, and even a failed attempt to poison the town's popular salad bar with botulism in order to prevent longtime Antelope residents from voting!

By 1984, Rajneesh claimed 250,000 followers worldwide, 20,000 of those in the United States.

Eventually, a court of appeals nullified what they determined was a hijacked, jerry-rigged election and gave Antelope back to its original citizens. A moot point since, by then, the Rajneesh "Empire" had already begun to fray around the edges. First the media, and finally the authorities, began to question what an Indian holy man (one who had supposedly taken a vow of poverty) needed with *a fleet* of limousines? More ominous still, why was a

41

religious group supposedly dedicated to nonviolence seen toting around *automatic weapons?* In 1985, Rajneesh's main lieutenant was convicted of several felonies and eventually Rajneesh himself was deported and died not long after in his native India.

But this guru's powers of seduction and persuasion outlived him. At Rajneesh's cremation, one of his *several* wives committed suicide by throwing herself onto his funeral pyre, an ancient (outlawed by the British) Hindu custom known as "suttee."

A Cult of Two. It has been argued that Westerners just don't "get" gurus like Rajneesh, or other Eastern "cults" for that matter, specifically that Westerners don't understand the Indian religious tradition governing the guru/disciple relationship which recommends that, in order to reach ultimate enlightenment, a student is expected to "surrender" himself (or herself) to a recognized guru/master who is seen not only as that student's superior in all spiritual matters, but who is also the earthly embodiment of the Divine, acting in the god's, or goddess' stead. Often this requires that the student give up all their worldly wealth, making a gift of their earthly possessions to their new master who, in theory, then passes this wealth along to the truly needy . . . at least this was the explanation given for Rajneesh's fleet of limousines.

"What's all this cult crap got to do with my getting paid, or laid, or both?" you ask.

The strategy Rajneesh (and other cult leaders) used to draw in, overawe, and finally overhaul tens of thousands of followers are the same one-on-one ploys of seduction you can use to pick up that babe, schmooze up your boss, or get elected to high office.

Rajneesh had tens of thousands of followers in the end, but he had to start out by convincing (seducing) them one by one, in effect creating a "cult of two." Those two then followed the Bhagwan's now-proven strategy by seducing two of their own for the master. Thus two becomes four become eight, sixteen, thirty-six, and on and on, exponentially.

But even if you're not interested in using your Black Science to become a "prophet for profit,"* you can still use the Bhagwan's methods to seduce that barfly, creating your own "cult of two." Here's how:

---

*But if you are, see *Holy Profit, Holy Cow! How to Be a Prophet for Profit,* by Dr. Haha Lung. 2008. Publication pending.

Tailor Your Message. Like any successful cult leader, or any good speaker for that matter, Rajneesh crafted his talk(s) to fit his immediate audience: tactics, techniques, and trigger words specifically spoken with the needs (and vulnerabilities) of the targeted individual in mind.

Always talk *to* your audience. Mirror their education and cultural level. When talking to a woman, remember that women like to talk about different things than men do: Men and women start out talking about things they both care about. In order of importance these are: Family life (including home and children); good health; work (their "crummy" job); professional growth (hoping for that raise and promotion, their dumb-ass boss); and personal growth (self-actualization, hopes, and dreams).

But this is where men and women part company. The next four things men like to talk about, again in order of priority are: recreation; travel; women (especially younger women!); and sports/politics (which men seem somehow unable to separate in their minds!).

Women list their talk priorities as: clothes and shopping; recreation (not necessarily the same type of "recreation" men like!); travel (men and women differ on where to travel); and last—and perhaps least—women talk about men. Sorry, guys.

Listen to her (or him), try to use the same "level" words as they do. Don't use "big words" (you'll intimidate a "simpler" person). Don't "act dumb" or get caught "dumbing down your speech" (this will insult their intelligence).

Remember being told to "always be yourself?" Forget that! Practice being your audience. Tell them what they want to hear and tell it to them in language (including body language) they'll understand.

The Play's the Thing. Any cult leader (or any strategist/seducer for that matter) has to be a constant and consummate showman—in other words, he has to keep his followers enthralled, from the root "thrall," meaning "slave." Synonyms include servitude, slavery, and bondage. (Yeah, I thought you'd like that last one, you kinky dog!)

You gotta think like a cult leader: The more contradiction and confusion in the parishioners' minds, the more coins in the collection plate.

The more "intrigued" and curious your date is, the better the chances they'll stick around for "Act II."

In his *The Golden Guru: The Strange Journey of Bhagwan Shree Rajneesh* (1987), author James Gordon points out the fact that ancient mind-master gurus used "The 3 C's," contradiction, confusion, and continual change, to break down their disciples' preconceptions and resistance. Modern Western hypnotherapists use these same 3 C's, to induce a hypnotic trance. Not surprising Rajneesh was no stranger to hypnosis:

> In discourses and darshans [one-on-one talks] Rajneesh also used hypnotic techniques to bypass his disciples' conscious defenses, to win their assent to his words, and to enhance their "transference" to him. He created confusion and elaborate paradoxes and contradictions, which baffled their rational minds and habitual ways they looked at themselves and the world. He used his voice, varying the volume and pace of speech, punctuating, modifying his words with his hands and eyes, even with his stillness. As his disciples listened and watched their minds slowed. They followed the winding, discursive thread of his stories the way the eye follows the motions of a tiny falling feather. In trance they were more receptive and suggestible. (Gordon, 1987:235)

Did you catch all that?

- Vary your tone and pace of speech.
- Emphasize and draw attention to your *word images* through the use of your hands, your eyes, and your overall body language.
- Catch their attention. Get them to focus in on you, then focus in even more on your ever smaller gestures.
- Now then pull them in even "closer" with your words—normal volume at first, then softer (more intimate), causing them to focus even more on your words alone. (Watch for them to lean more towards you, in order to hear clearly what you're saying.)

Setting the Stage A good cult leader, like a good Broadway director, or a wily general on the battlefield—like any accomplished seducer of any sort— first sets the stage: manipulating the scenery, foreground, and background against which his actors, soldiers, or lovers will dance to and fro to his choreography and coaxing.

At his cult HQ in India, and later at his compound in Antelope, Oregon, Rajneesh masterfully manipulated setting and surroundings to maximize its effect on both the already faithful and on future followers. Flashy dramatic entrances and exits were arranged for Rajneesh, ending with him enthroned atop a raised platform, high *above* the faithful (so that they figuratively and literally had to look up to the master).

The Rajneesh compound overall was planned out to create an idyllic setting, far from the troubles (reality) of the outside world. Inside this seemingly perfect world, the pipe dreams of the cult leader weren't just so much smoke but actually seemed to make sense. In such a secluded, temperature-controlled environment, the disciple begins to believe in the message of "peace" (and absolute obedience) taught by his guru. Within the Rajneesh community, distinctions of age, class, nationality, race, and even specific religions soon became blurred in the mind of the disciple. Any past misdeeds and indiscretions were "pardoned" by the Master. Any future anxieties they might have brought with them vanished as the future ceased to exist.

Children were allowed to play and "experiment" without parental censure. Teenagers were treated like adults. Adults themselves were relieved of any responsibilities and worries of "the outside world." Here they could indulge their fantasies and explore their fears safely, the community acting as mother, Rajneesh acting as the all-knowing, all-powerful Father.

As much as possible you must control the setting of your encounters—this holds true whether in a pickup bar or on a battlefield. Know your surroundings.

Arrange *deliberate* "chance" meetings to your advantage. When you "accidentally" run into that fine filly you've been stalking (in a nice way) at a movie theater where she (or he) is going in to watch the latest "chick flick," it's the perfect time to "discover" the two of you have something in common. It's called "bonding."

When arranging such accidental meetings, always try to get your love interest alone—the last thing you want to do is have to try and pry her away from her cockblocking posse of nosy ("overly protective") girlfriends.

Control the setting to make your "target" as comfortable as possible, with as few distractions as possible. All their attention should be focused on you as you pretend to focus all your attention on them.

Out with the Old . . . By breaking down all of a disciple's traditional reference points (age, race, nationality), Rajneesh in effect destroyed that disciple's identity, in preparation for providing the disciple with a new cult identity.

. . . In with the New After the "breakdown," the systematic dismantling of the disciple's old identity, now comes the "build-up" giving them the *new* identity you've created for them. The same meditation techniques and "therapy groups" that "helped" new disciples "let go" of their old "attachments" also helped the disciple adopt their new cult identity.

If this "break 'em down" to "build 'em up" cult indoctrination sequence sounds familiar, then you've probably read about "brainwashing" in *Theatre of Hell: Dr. Lung's Complete Guide to Torture* (Loompanics, 2003).

Safe in the loving arms of the idyllic cult community, secure under the omniscient gaze of the master, the new disciple is ready to follow any order. Constant dictates from the master and from his always watchful lieutenants provide all the guidance the new disciple needs to embrace the cult's world-view.

Every one of us has prejudices and preconceptions. That fine young thing you're trying to reel in might have been screwed over in the past (a prejudice) and now thinks that all men are jerks (a preconception). You have to use every tactic, technique, and trick at your disposal (basically everything you learn in this book!) to break her out of that old way of thinking:

- Convince her she's not wrong—all men are jerks . . . except for you.
- Convince her she's not a "loser" or "stupid" for going out with jerks in the past.
- Use fresh lines of approach (fresh pickup lines and body language) to convince her you're different—you're something "new."

I'm sure you realize that the cult tactics used by Bhagwan Shree Rajneesh are in no way exclusive to cults of East Indian extraction, or even to Far Eastern cults in general. No, these methods of mind control and manipulation are universal and have been used throughout history, in every clime and time, by unscrupulous cults, cadre, and con men with varying degrees of success—the particular degree of success directly proportionate to the ruthlessness of the particular cult leader, confidence man, or would-be Casanova.

Most important to our immediate study of strategy and seduction is for you to realize that *toxic relationships are like a cult,* with one partner dominating the other by playing the role of "cult leader," while the other person in the relationship takes on the submissive "disciple" role. That's why, sadly, all the "tricks of the trade" used by cult leaders can easily be adopted and adapted for one-on-one seductions—for creating your own "cult of two."

PEEKING UNDER THE RED ROBE

They don't know the day is the dark's face and the dark the day's.

—Prabhu Allama, Lingayatas poet

In eleventh century India there was a unique sect of yogi gurus known as "Lingayatas." In India the linga (phallus) is/was the universally recognized symbol for Shiva, one of the three "faces" of the main Hindu god, Brahma.*

This curious Lingayatas sect was founded back in the tenth century by the guru Deavara Dasimayya. Deavara was a severe ascetic, into doing the whole fast-till-you-drop, sleep-on-a-bed-of-nails type of thing. That is, until, in a vision, Shiva told Deavara to stop fasting, to put away the pincushion, and, from that day forth, worship only the sacred phallus. Thus, to this day, following Deavara's example, Lingayatas practice bhakti (devotional) rituals to Lord Shiva, mixing tantra and other forms of yoga in with their adoration of the divine creative urge (symbolized by the erect penis). Ultimately, Lingayatas wanted to do away with useless ritual animal sacrifice in favor of sacrificing the bestial human self. (Ramanujan, 1973:147)

Lingayatas, a.k.a. "Vacanas," taught the common people through their poetry (a convenient device, since most peasants were illiterate). These poems were specially crafted, incorporating their mystic knowledge of mantras and hidden subliminal verb influences. (See Figure 13.)

Some Vacanas developed "Siddhas" and formed the Order of the Red Robes.

These Siddha *Pabhu* (literally, "power masters") taught simple yet effective techniques for achieving mystical union with Lord Shiva (a.k.a. "Ramanatha," "Lord of the Meeting Rivers," ad infinitum): asceticism, meditations, and, listening to specially crafted mantras and poems designed to stimulate kundalini flow and open the chakras. In these poems we find not only "spiritual" insight but also practical insight into the varieties, vanities, and vulnerabilities of human nature.

For example, twelfth-century Power Master Mahadaviyakka, a woman, left us this poetic insight into human weaknesses:

> Lust's body: site of rage, ambush of greed, house of passion,
> fence of pride, mask of envy.

Notice how closely her catalog of human lusts stacks up against "the Five Movers" (a.k.a. "Warning F.L.A.G.S.") that we discuss at more length in the section on China. (See Figure 10, page 48.)

---

*Brahma—the one God—has three "faces" he shows the world, three different aspects of himself: Brahma the Creator, Vishnu the Preserver, and Shiva the Destroyer.

MAHADAVEYAKKA'S "LUST'S BODY"	SYMBOL	THE FIVE MOVERS (a.k.a. "THE 5 WARNING F.L.A.G.S")
Envy	Mask	Fear
Passion	House of Prostitution	Lust
Rage	Site (Funeral Pyre)	Anger
Greed	Ambushing (Robbery)	Greed
Pride	Fence	Sympathy

Figure 10.

Nine Hounds at the Nine Gates

Siddha Padhu Allama warned us of the vulnerability of "the Nine Gates":

Closed and shut the bolts, of the nine gates and locked them
up, killed nine thousand men till he was left alone.

As every Black Science student knows, "the Nine Gates" is the oft-used metaphor in the East symbolizing the nine "openings" in the body through which "temptation" can enter: eyes, ears, mouth, nostrils, urethra (sex organ), and anus (Lung and Prowant, 2001, 2002.).

Siddha Pabhu Basavanna (1106–1167) used similar symbolism when he warned us to beware "the Nine Hounds" of the uncontrolled mind and body:

Nine hounds unleashed on a hare, the body lusts . . . will my
heart reach you, O Lord of the meeting rivers, before the
sensuous bitches touch and overtake?

Does it seem strange to hear a "holy man" speak of "lust" and "sensuous bitches"? Basavanna was no ordinary holy man. Unlike most of his more secretive brethren, Basavanna often took center stage as a political activist and reformer. Basavanna was also often accused of being a political conspirator by his *many* enemies. Part Machiavelli, part Rasputin, as his fame as a Power Master grew, Basavanna became court advisor (and eventually brother-in-law) to Bijjala, king of the Mangalavada region of India.

Since Basavanna also practiced tantra, disregarding time-honored Hindu customs of sex and caste restrictions, rejecting the complex and often lucrative religious rituals of his day, his enemies attacked him with gossip and accusations that scandalized and threatened to undermine the kingdom until finally Basavanna was forced to leave Mangalavada in order to prevent a civil war. But as he exited the kingdom, poet Basavanna left behind a final verse, a succinct observation and condemnation of human nature:

What shall I call such fools, who do not know themselves?

In the Buddha's *Dhammapada* we likewise find several verses comparing our body and mind to a city as well as all admonishing us to guard it jealously:

- "Restrain your eye. Restrain your ear. Restrain your nose. Restrain your tongue. Restrain your body. Restrain your speech. Restrain your mind. Restraint in all these is the key." (sayings #360–361)
- "A well-guarded fortress, defenses inside and out, that is how a man is to guard himself." (#315)
- "With sincerity as your watchman, guard your thoughts well. Raise yourself above evil the way the noble elephant pulls himself from the suck of the muck." (#327)
- "Hold yourself dear by guarding yourself dearly. The wise man keeps watch himself at least one of the three watches of the night." (#157)
- "Guard well your thoughts though they be difficult to perceive, crafty, and running about here and there. Thoughts well guarded bring joy." (#36)

Seducing the Five Virgins

There are many schools of yoga, some of which concentrate on physical practices (Hatha Yoga), others on observation of traditional rituals (Raja Yoga), while still others concentrate on selfless acts and devotional duties (Bhakti Yoga). As already mentioned, Kundalini Yoga specializes in techniques designed to stimulate and direct Kundalini. More exotic still, further off the beaten path is Tantric Yoga.

Over the years, in large part due to prurient interest in wildly exaggerated Western reports, Tantric Yoga (with both Hindu and Buddhist branches) has gotten a bad reputation for encouraging disciples to indulge in sensual pleasures, and especially for teaching a form of meditation that prolongs and heightens sexual pleasure—techniques for delaying orgasm for hours in order to experience an orgasm lasting for hours!

This is hard for some Westerners to swallow.

Recall our already mentioning that in the East in general and in yoga practice in particular there are two paths: the Right-handed path and the Left-handed path.

A quick review: Yogis following the Right-handed path abstain from worldly pleasures (meat, alcohol, drugs, and sex). By abstaining it is believed that the flame of desire will die out for lack of fuel. Once this flame of passion dies out, the yogi becomes "enlightened".

Conversely, the Left-handed path allows—indeed, encourages—practitioners to indulge their passions. The argument is that, since God is "every, always, and perfect," there is not more of God (enlightenment) "here" and less of God "over there." Thus a seeker is just as likely to "find God" in a whorehouse as in a temple. Meat, alcohol, and all manners of "sex, drugs, and rock-n-roll" are permitted to a practitioner of the Left-Hand path. By indulging their passions they burn up (and "burn out") all the fuel of passion until, all on its own, the flame of passion sputters and dies—and the yogi attains enlightenment.

Needless to say, many Westerners are interested in practicing this Left-handed tantra . . . *as often as possible!* But whichever yoga path we decide to study, all such study begins with our understanding the "Six Senses," and then the "Five Virgins."

The Six Senses. There are, of course, the universally accepted five senses of smell, taste, sight, touch, and hearing, to which yogis further add a sixth "feeling" (a.k.a. "heart"). (See Figure 11, opposite.)

Mastery of these Six Senses unlocks "powers" (Skt. *siddhas)* that allow yogis to free themselves from the physical and mental restrictions that hold the rest of us down.

Keep in mind that, from a Black Science perspective, both our adversaries and our potential lovers are all susceptible to these six senses. Thus we have two reasons for mastering our six senses:

- First, in order to better regulate our own lives, in order to better protect ourselves from the potential danger and disaster of allowing our senses to run wild, their ruling us and not the other way around.
- Second, to more easily influence (seduce) others.

On a purely physical level, the reward for learning to control our five "animal" senses is that it takes us to a new level of individual awareness of ourselves, of others, and of our surroundings—the Three knows again.

THE SIX SENSES

ELEMENT	EARTH	WATER	FIRE	AIR	SKY	SPACE
	SMELL	TASTE	SIGHT	TOUCH	HEARING	FEELING (HEART)
OUTER SENSE						
INNER SENSES	CITTA	BUDDHI	AHANKARA	MANAS	JNANA	BHAVA
SAKTI TYPE (Divine power)	KRIYA (action)	JNANA (knowing)	ICCHA (will)	AD (creating)	PARA (power)	CIT (intelligence)

Figure 11.

In turn, practicing this "advanced" level of awareness makes it appear to others that we possess some sort of ESP when, in fact, all we are doing is not allowing ourselves to be distracted by the itchin', twitchin', and bitchin' of our five senses, freeing us up to pay closer attention to the world around us.

The Five Virgins. As we master each of our five physical senses, we are rewarded by a gift of one of the "Five Virgins," so-called because these five powers are considered "pure" gifts from a divine source. In Hinduism this divine source is called *Sakti,* the feminine side of Shiva, the Destroyer.

They are *Kriya, Jnana, Iccha, Adi,* and *Para.* (See Figure 12, page 52.)

Mastery of Kriya—the sense of smell—gives us the power to act instantly, to turn our thoughts into action, testifying to the power of smell to instantly change our mind, to transform our thought into action.

Having lost touch with our bestial roots, humans don't like to be reminded how often they are literally led around by the nose. Keep in mind that women have a more highly attuned sense of smell than men. (More on training your sense of smell and other senses, in the section called "Senses Training," in our China chapter.)

Mastery of Jnana gives us the power to create and destroy with just a word. Science teaches that all physical objects are simply collections of vibrations oscillating at various wavelengths, the vibrations of one thing influencing another, like ripples colliding and connecting in a pond.

THE FIVE VIRGINS

KRIYA	The power of action	The power to instantly change thought into action; energy (thought) into action. $E=MC^2$
JNANA	a.k.a. Mantra, the power of the word	The power to instantly create effect with just a spoken word; to control self and others through vibrations (words).
ICCHA	The power of wish and Will	The power to simply desire an object and/or outcome and thus bring it into reality.
ADI	The power of primal creativity	The power to innovate and create completely new ideas. The power to create "something" from "nothing."
PARA	Transcendent Power	The power to create effect(s) that seem outside the laws of physics; to create "magical" effects; to transcend physical and mental restrictions of thought and action.

Figure 12.

We all experienced how spoken words (endearments, racial slurs, etc.) can instantly affect us emotionally: making us laugh when we feel depressed, at other times inciting us to violence in an instant with a single insult.

In the East, mantras (spoken power phrases, often a single syllable) are used to affect body and mind, not only of self, but of others as well.

Each of the Five Virgins has a specific, unique sound (vibration) associated with it, as do chakras (refer back to Figure 6, page 28). These mantras are used by yogis to influence (confuse and control) the five senses:

For example, Kriya is associated with the element Earth and controls the body's skeletal system, legs, and large intestine. Kriya acts as natural Prozac, helping regulate our mental equilibrium. Mastering Kriya gives us the power to instantly transform thought into action. To activate this power, chant the seed mantra "LAM" and "O-LAM," since a long "O" sound is the major vowel vibration a person dominated by the element Earth responds to best. You can also use English words that contain this syllable sound.

Once we discover that our adversary or potential lover is predisposed/ dominated by the element Earth, we can seed our speech and writings we aim at them with words that emphasize the sound of long "O."

Writing words implanted with specific vowel vibrations works just as well as actually speaking such words because when we read words and phrases our brain "pronounces" the words silently.

Ancient poets, East and West, understood this principle. That's why reading romantic poetry (Shakespeare's sonnets, for example) can calm us and lull us into a more receptive mood. Some music (tone and lyrics) can also "subliminally" affect us. Likewise, the poetry of William Blake and mystical writings such as the Bible's Book of Revelation are believed to help induce altered states of consciousness when read aloud.

So whether we hear these words (subliminal sounds) or see (visualize) them in our mind, our brain still "hears" and internalizes them. Thus you can easily influence your adversary or prospective lover by peppering your spiel with this particular "verb influence," a phrase "I have" catches and holds the person's attention.

So how do you learn to discern what a particular person's verb influence is? You listen. That phrase most oft repeated by the person (I have, I speak, I feel, I live, I can) links them with a particular element. The person may not always repeat their actual verb influence, for example verbalizing "I have" over and over. Sometimes they use synonyms and similar phrases that mean the same thing. "I speak" becomes "I'm always telling people" . . . or "You know what I mean," "You hear me," and so on.

Mastery of Jnana helps us learn to listen and "hear" better, giving us the advantage over our adversary by allowing him to give himself away.

Learning to listen to a potential lover's verbal (and body) language is chapter one, verse one in the seducer's bible! (See Figure 13, page 54.)

Mastery of Iccha hones our desires, giving us the power to conjure a desired object or event into reality. If you can see it in your "mind's eye," if you can "visualize" it, you can make it happen. If you can "see" it, you can be it. You have to hold it in your mind before you can hold it in your hand. This rule applies whether you're imagining what it will feel like to win a major battle or what she (or he) will feel like when you succeed in getting them alone.

Iccha is controlled by the element Fire, which in turn controls our sense of sight, since we are often led by our sight when it comes to the things we desire. This includes our "mind's eye."

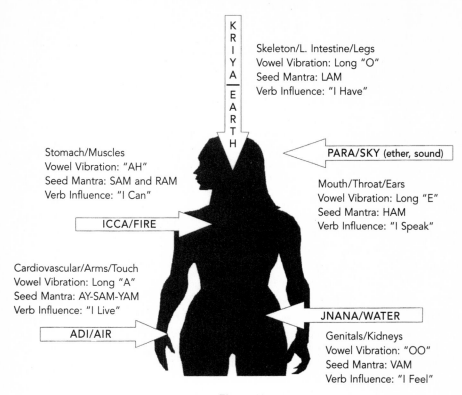

Figure 13.

Human beings are visually oriented creatures. Our seeing leads to our desiring (Fire) and our troubles begin. Don't we fall in love "at first sight"?

The exercise of "will" lets us break free of desires. Exercising our willpower makes our willpower stronger. We can then use our newfound willpower to bring us our heart's desire—anything we can *wish* for we can now *will* into existence. This is why the verb influence for Iccha declares "I can!"

On the downside; those dominated by Iccha or Fire are easily led astray by the "Three A's":

- Anger (evidenced by muscle tension)
- Appetites (symbolized by the stomach)
- Arrogance ("I can!")

Discovering that an adversary or potential lover is ruled by Fire makes it easy to lay seductive snares for them based on their predisposition toward anger, appetites (lusts and desires), and their arrogance (overconfidence).

Mastery of Adi unleashes the power of creativity within us all, power to innovate and invent, to see a problem from all angles before then creating appropriate and unique solutions to that problem.

Adi is governed by the element "Air." This is Plato's realm of pure ideas, from which all our hopes and dreams and desires are drawn, to become manifest in the physical world through our focus and intent. Once those ideas manifest, we can then physically touch the objects and participate in the events we helped bring to fruition. Thus Adi is also associated with our sense of touch.

We focus *Adi* by meditation on the mantra "Ay-Sam-Yam."

The verb influence for Adi is the positive assertion "I live!" a simple celebration of life. *Positive* Adi individuals are balanced and loving and are prone to find true love in their lives. Conversely, for a *negative* person dominated by this kind of mind-body attitude, "I live" implies selfishness. These negative *Adi*-dominated people are out of yin-yang balance and are hate-filled, drawing negative, destructive, and self-defeating influences to them.

To bring down an adversary who has a cynical outlook, you have only to agree with his cynical outlook, reinforcing his cynicism, fanning the flames of his dissatisfaction like a strong wind until it literally sucks the air (Adi) out of his body! A person predisposed/dominated by the element Air will have trouble with their heart and lungs.

To court an obviously Adi-dominated lover can lead to true love—so long as you are processing Adi-energy positively.

Mastery of Para focuses our innate inner energies outward, giving us the power to affect the people and places around us.

Para is dominated by Sky (sometimes written as ether or sound). Hearing is the key to mastering Para. Para/Sky controls the mouth, throat, and ears—our organs of communication. That's why Para's verb influence is "I speak."

In our previous books on Black Science we devoted more than a chapter or two to the power of the spoken word, using words against our adversaries while, at the same time, learning to guard ourselves and our loved ones from becoming victims of "word slavery." (See Lung and Prowant. 2001; Lung and Prowant, 2002; Lung, 2006.)

Learning to recognize and control the words that control us is one of the most important courses taught at the Black Science Institute. If you learn nothing else from your study of the Black Science, learn to *really listen* and thus to *really hear* what other people are saying . . . or what they're *not* saying.

The Eighteen Weaknesses

Lingayata Vacana Deavara is said to have developed a martial art that allowed his body to absorb any poisons his enemies used. Could this be the origin of the dreaded Chinese Dim Mak "Death Touch"? (See Omar 1989; Lung 1997; Lung and Tucker 2007.)

Deavara was also a master of "flexible martial-arts weapons" and once wove an enormously long "magical" turban cloth. When a thief tried to steal this turban, a sharp wheel whirled out of it, slashing the thief. We bring up Deavara's martial-arts mastery of flexible weapons because in his most well-known poem he uses the metaphor "eighteen links of a chain" to represent what he saw as the eighteen human weaknesses:

> You have forged this chain of eighteen links and chained us humans: You have ruined us, O Ramanatha, and made us dogs forever on a leash.

You'll no doubt notice that these "eighteen links" include not only Mahadeviyakka's "Body Lusts" (refer again to Figure 10, page 48), but also the "Five Movers" (Warning F.L.A.G.S.), as well as the "Nine Gates." (See Figure 14, opposite.)

During the course of any day, or over a lifetime, our mind moves back and forth from one of these links to another, to another. These Eighteen Links are not just everyday wants and worries; rather they are major traits and predispositions, one of which predominates in each of us because of our karma (past actions) and our dharma (filial and social duty).

Though dominated by one of these eighteen links, at any given time our mind can embrace—or be overcome by—another of the Eighteen Links. For example, you're driving along, racking your brain on problems from the past, present, or future, when you're suddenly cut off by some lead-footed jerk who adds insult to injury by flipping you a one-finger salute. In an instant your mind shifts gears, first to self-regard, then to anger and then to wounded pride, as you begin to indulge your lust for revenge!

But, as with all things in life, just because we have an "inclination" or even a predisposition toward one of these eighteen weaknesses doesn't necessarily mean we have to act on that weakness, allowing ourselves to be controlled by said weakness.

THE EIGHTEEN LINKS

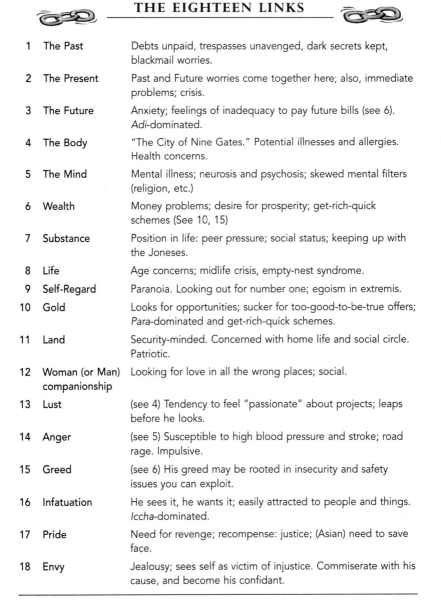

1	The Past	Debts unpaid, trespasses unavenged, dark secrets kept, blackmail worries.
2	The Present	Past and Future worries come together here; also, immediate problems; crisis.
3	The Future	Anxiety; feelings of inadequacy to pay future bills (see 6). *Adi*-dominated.
4	The Body	"The City of Nine Gates." Potential illnesses and allergies. Health concerns.
5	The Mind	Mental illness; neurosis and psychosis; skewed mental filters (religion, etc.)
6	Wealth	Money problems; desire for prosperity; get-rich-quick schemes (See 10, 15)
7	Substance	Position in life: peer pressure; social status; keeping up with the Joneses.
8	Life	Age concerns; midlife crisis, empty-nest syndrome.
9	Self-Regard	Paranoia. Looking out for number one; egoism in extremis.
10	Gold	Looks for opportunities; sucker for too-good-to-be-true offers; *Para*-dominated and get-rich-quick schemes.
11	Land	Security-minded. Concerned with home life and social circle. Patriotic.
12	Woman (or Man) companionship	Looking for love in all the wrong places; social.
13	Lust	(see 4) Tendency to feel "passionate" about projects; leaps before he looks.
14	Anger	(see 5) Susceptible to high blood pressure and stroke; road rage. Impulsive.
15	Greed	(see 6) His greed may be rooted in insecurity and safety issues you can exploit.
16	Infatuation	He sees it, he wants it; easily attracted to people and things. *Iccha*-dominated.
17	Pride	Need for revenge; recompense: justice; (Asian) need to save face.
18	Envy	Jealousy; sees self as victim of injustice. Commiserate with his cause, and become his confidant.

Figure 14.

When attempting to seduce someone, whether for business or for pleasure, recognize that your prospective "target" is influenced by one (or more) of these eighteen links. This will give you the best strategy to best approach that target.

So whether our motivation is to guard ourselves against outside manipulation, or instead to ourselves influence (manipulate) current adversaries and future lovers, we will benefit from a deeper examination of each of the Eighteen Links:

The Past (1) makes us dwell on debts we have yet to pay (literal as well as figurative debts), and "trespasses" against us we have yet to avenge (read "The Cask of Amontillado" by Edgar Allan Poe [1809–1849]).

Those "trapped" in the past are often staunch conservatives, traditionalists, and religious fundamentalists. They dream of a time gone by, one where they imagine themselves having a bigger, more potent part to play than that afforded by their present life.

We can deliberately bring the past back to haunt our adversaries by digging up all the "dark secrets" they try to keep buried. These include birth secrets, body flaws, failure secrets, sex secrets, crime secrets, illness secrets, and death secrets. (See "Blackmail/Dirty Laundry List" in Lung and Prowant, 2006.)

When going into any relationship, you have to be on guard for any "baggage" your new lover brings with them from their past. As with blood enemies, so with potential lovers, the more you know about their past, the more cozy your future together!

Often we can catch a potential love interest's attention by waxing nostalgic, by reminding them of pleasurable past experiences. Describing past pleasures they've experienced (thanks to a little investigative research beforehand) will help establish a common bond and help lull them into a receptive mood.

For example, say you have your eye on seducing that new girl (or boy) in the office. First find out something—everything!—you can about them beforehand.

Say you've just found out the person is from Vermont . . . get them talking about how beautiful it is there in autumn, walking among the trees—with someone you love. Or, perhaps they've just came back from a vacation in Florida. Get them talking about how nice it was. Then, as they describe the warm sun, soothing water, repeat the positive adjectives they use, reinforcing how "warm" it was, how "soothing," how "relaxing" . . .

This deliberate reinforcing and refocusing of their "nostalgia" is an old

hypnotism trick designed to make a subject more receptive. Relaxing +
Reinforcing + Refocusing = More Receptive.

Conversely, anxieties can be heightened and angers inflamed by repeating "hurt" words a person uses when describing (ranting!) about an injustice
they've suffered. "He screwed me over!" the person declares. You nod, agreeing, repeating, "screwed you over."

The Present (2) has plenty of worries to keep us busy, from bothersome
duties and obligations, to unforeseen crises that demand our immediate
attention, drain our already rationed energies, and throw us off our already
demanding schedule. To make matters worse, both the past and the future
live in the present, so we can't seem to prevent our indiscreet and incon-
venient past from rearing its ugly head, nor that terrifying hydra of future
commitments and responsibilities from growing yet another hungry head.

One of the main keys to a successful seduction is to make your "target"
focus on the "here and now." If she's dwelling on all the guys who screwed
her over in the past, you'll probably never get around to becoming one of
those guys! Likewise, if she's worried about what she'll "feel like in the
morning," there's a good chance you got no chance of feeling any part of her
tonight!

She's looking for "Mr. Right," you need to be "Mr. Right-Now" and
you can only accomplish this by keeping her in the Right Now.

The Future (3) never arrives, but that doesn't keep us from projecting
yesterday's mess-ups and today's anxieties onto tomorrow and the next day,
and the next, ad infinitum.

Who among us doesn't have doubts or feelings of inadequacy when our
mind races headlong into the future? Will I be able to pay my bills on time?
Will I get that promotion? Will she say yes?

Worries about the future are even more distracting and debilitating than
dwelling on the past. The past is at least "fixed" . . . fantasies and worries
about the future can be endless—limited only by our out-of-control anxieties
and the expiration date on our Valium prescription!

The Body (4) is susceptible to ailments and allergies of all kinds, all of
which we should be more than willing to help our adversary acquire!

An adversary who is overly body conscious (i.e., dominated by the body)
is likely to be a hypochondriac—a neurosis we should go out of our way to
reinforce.

And let's not forget our body is that poorly guarded "City of Nine
Gates," those nine potential openings in our mental (and physical) defenses

through which an adversary can ninja into our mind and have his way with us.

The body wants what the body wants. Her lips say "no" but the rest of her body (language) is screaming "Let's go!" (See "Chinese Face Reading 101" in our China chapter)

The Mind (5) is all we've got to work with—unfortunately. The human animal is plagued by more mental illness, neurosis, psychosis, and more philias, phobias, and fetishes than you can shake a bottle of Prozac at. The brain, that oh-so-complicated, twisting and turning labyrinth. And somewhere, lost, either stumbling blindly or else hurtling helter skelter down those synaptic hallways, bouncing off the padded walls of paranoia, is our "mind," that sum of all we are that, in its delusions of grandeur, imagines itself somehow greater than its parts put together: three pounds of confusion, contorted by childhood trauma, drama, and mama, by societal stricture, schizophrenic scripture, and a dozen other mental and moral filters—some of which parents and pastors were kind enough to beat into us, the rest of which we seem to go out of our way to collect faster than a lifer collects tattoos!

When it comes to seduction, the rule is: the mind wants what the body wants. And the body wants what the body wants! In a fight between "the big head" and "the little head," the little head doesn't fight fair and always kicks for the crotch!

Wealth (6) Money problems tax us all. We mortgage our morality to keep up with the Joneses, only to watch the Joneses slide into foreclosure! We awfulize day-to-day money problems, trying and dying to make a living till the day we finally drop dead.

A lot of guys make the mistake of throwing their money around, thinking this will impress the girls. Oh they'll help you spend it all right. But you're missing one very important fact: Ever wonder why you always see those devastatingly beautiful women married to fat, ugly, myopic nerds? Women have an innate "nester" urge (yeah, yeah, I'm an insensitive male chauvinist pig, I know!), so they sleep with the cool and sexy guys . . . but they marry "providers". Is the woman you're trying to seduce looking for a "player" or a "payer"?

On the battlefield of life, strategy-wise, let's hope your adversary is obsessed with wealth since this is the perfect opening for you to hit him with your latest no money down!, interest-free!, get-rich-quick! scheme. In other words, "win the battle, get the booty." As on the battlefield, so in the bedroom.

Substance (7) refers to your position in life, where you see yourself stand-

INDIA: THE GURU EFFECT

ing in the "great pecking order." A true "man of substance" never frets over such things since he is confident of his place in the grand skein of life.

Other, not-so-confident people obsess over their social status. These sort of people are susceptible to peer pressure (yeah, just like in high school!). They have to "keep up with the Joneses" (See 6, above).

If this sounds like your adversary, show him how you can help him get one up on his neighbor or be the envy of all his coworkers and he'll be eating out of your hand. Or, seed his mind with thoughts of how he's not keeping up with the Joneses, tempting him to get in over his head in debt.

For women looking to settle down, wealth and substance are one and the same. For ambitious gigolos thinking to marry for money, there's that old saying, "if you marry for money, you'll end up earning every dime!"

Life (8) Age concerns haunt many, and not just the elderly and the vain.

Noted psychologist Erik Erikson (1902–1994) mapped out several stages of human development, each stage possessing a psychological brass ring we need to grab hold of if we are to maintain good mental health and a feeling of self-worth (see Lung and Prowant, 2006).

For example, teenagers strive to establish a unique identity. At this age they want to look older, and act older (by drinking, smoking, having sex, all that good stuff adults do!). That's why this is the perfect time for gangs, cults, and online predators to draw kids into their web.

Once we reach our twenties, we're expected to move out on our own, get a job or a college education, start a family, all "milestones" on the road to "maturity" and "independence." Not surprisingly, we often feel like failures if we don't live up to these societal "cookie-cutter" expectations.

According to Erikson, by middle age women begin experiencing "empty nest syndrome" (a feeling of uselessness after all her children have grown up and moved out), while middle-age men go through a "midlife crisis" (during which fast cars and fast younger girls may catch their attention).

Seniors suffer through age difficulties as well, not the least of which is what Erikson calls the "Integrity vs. Despair" stage, when a senior begins to look back on his life, taking an accounting of what he's accomplished. Or what he failed to accomplish.

Confidence men know that this vulnerable period is the perfect time to target wealthy seniors.

Factoring in age is important for both strategy and seduction. The young tend to be vain and impetuous. Thus a young adversary (with something to prove) will impatiently fall to your strategy, while a young love interest will often think they (1) deserve attention and (2) are "too cool to fool." Both are easy marks who never see reality coming until it hits 'em in the ass (uh, figuratively speaking, of course!).

As for more "mature" women (those "empty nesters" and those just coming off a midlife divorce), making them feel "useful" is the first step to making them feel other things.

As for middle-aged men, get into their good graces with either a "peach" or a "teach":

- Young girls (a "peach") can easily catch the eye of older men. Give him one as a "gift" (with plenty of strings attached). Spies call this a "honey pot" trap.
- Younger men wishing to influence (seduce) older men can easily do so by asking the older man to "teach" them something. This "student-teacher," "master-disciple" relationship allows the younger hustler (or his handler) to infiltrate the targeted older man's sphere of influence.

Self-Regard (9) There's nothing wrong with looking out for number one. Except when we lose sight of the fact we share this world with another six billion human beings—some of whom just might prove useful to us!

Always show your target what's in it for them, why it's in their best interest to follow your lead. Dangle the carrot of gain (the promise of making their life better), or else shake the stick at them (the promise of making their life a living hell should they go against you). Yin and Yang. Push-pull.

An adversary (rival general, for example) can easily be led astray if you first "run" from him, avoiding battle until he begins to think you're afraid to face him, and he begins to think how "great" a general he is; in other words, inflate his ego.

Likewise, go out of your way to "puff up" your prospective paramour's ego. Compliment them appropriately—be sincere, compliment them personally, don't overpraise their clothing and jewelry, since these are superficial. Instead concentrate on their laugh, intelligence, smile, and skills (dancing, for example).

Gold (10) doesn't just mean the heavy, shiny $1,000-an-ounce stuff that dreams are gilded of. It means always being on the lookout for that "golden opportunity," a chance to get ahead. This isn't necessarily a bad thing in and of itself, only when it becomes an obsession, when there is a total disregard for the welfare of others.

The "Gold" type personality is a sucker for a "too good to be true" offer, easily seduced by "get rich quick!" schemes. In this way he is similar to those dominated by too much *Self-Regard* (9).

However, whereas someone dominated by self-regard might be smart enough to see how allying himself with others of like mind might benefit them, the *gold*-dominated personality is blinded by his "gold fever," refusing to even consider an alliance of convenience. In other words, he's too paranoid and too shortsighted to see how such an alliance might benefit him in the end. This kind of person is easy to seduce, since their only loyalty is to getting ahead.

Gold personalities make good spies, but when employing such a spy, make sure you are always the one holding the pursestrings or else he'll sell you out to a higher bidder. Read Sun Tzu's *Ping-Fa,* chapter 13.

Likewise, beware the "gold digger" when looking for love. Women (and men) looking for a "sugar daddy" (or "phat girl" as the case may be) will say anything, do anything to (1) get in your good graces (2) get in your pocketbook and/or panties—yeah, they *are* just like a politician!

Land (11) Owning land (i.e., material goods and property of all sorts) allows us to see ourselves—and to be seen by others—as being "prosperous" and "wealthy," as having economic and social stability.

Beware: the more things you have, the more things have you. And the more the chance a wily adversary will find ways to use those possessions against you. Again, Edgar Allan Poe's "The Cask of Amontillado."

Gold (10) and Land (11) are very similar, the main distinction being that psychologically, *Land* includes such abstract things as family, clan, and even country identification. Die-hard patriots fall into this category (see 15, below).

Woman (12) The desire for companionship is strong in all of us: from friends and familiars to spouses and "significant others," from social get-togethers to intimate pairings—male and female, and every combination in between.

Remember the rule about never going grocery shopping while hungry? The same rule applies when "shopping" for a lover. Don't bite off more than you can chew.

Lust (13) This isn't only physical lust, it's also the tendency to feel truly "passionate" about some person or some thing, art, a religious or political cause. "Rebels" are dominated by this *Lust* category. (Unlucky #13 if there ever was one!)

Find what the person you are trying to seduce is passionate about. It's called "shared interests" and "something in common," and is the basis for establishing a long-term relationship but also necessary for simply starting a conversation.

Shared interests often grow out of shared experience (real or manufactured by you). For example, some creep (who you paid) is harassing some pretty young thing you're trying to get close to. You step in and, with a few stern words or that well-choreographed aikido wristlock, you "chase off" the creep to become her "hero"—you and her now share "an experience" in common. Sometimes this is as simple as sharing some not quality time suffering together in that long line down at the DMV.

On the more benign side, "accidentally" meeting a woman in the grocery store gives you a chance to "bump carts" and commiserate about the high price of vegetables, before she checks out your zucchini and invites you to thump her melons!

Anger (14) People dominated by anger are susceptible to high blood pressure, stroke, and fits of "road rage." Sun Tzu, Musashi, and Cao Cao all speak often and at length on what a godsend it is to have an adversary who is easily provoked to anger (See 15, 17).

She's mad at her husband, boyfriend, her ex—she's willing to "use" you to teach him a lesson. "Use" away!

Greed (15) As used here is different from the obsession with (physical) gold and wealth. This greed is rooted in insecurity and safety issues, surrounding and insulating yourself with "walls" constructed of physical possessions and psychological coping mechanisms. These insulating layers represent security from want and worry, and sometimes from responsibility.

The best example of this type of person is Adolf Hitler. The future dictator lived many years of his early life with his mother during a time when their financial life was precarious and their future uncertain. Later he would spend a dismal period as a starving artist in Vienna before the outbreak of World War I. After the war, he continued to agonize over his future as he wandered about a postwar Germany on the brink of civil war. But finally, as he began to accumulate political position and power, he began figuratively, and in some cases literally, to build walls to insulate himself against the poverty and powerlessness he so feared from his childhood.

Fast-forward a few years: if we look at Nazi Germany at the height of Hitler's reign, we find a succession of concentric "security" circles, leading ever inward toward the innermost circle that Hitler occupied—safe at last from abuse, poverty, and hunger, the security he never experienced in his youth.

To approach such an adversary, one who builds "greedy" walls around himself but who can never seem to get enough (or feel safe enough), we either offer to help him build those walls—thicker and higher until they become his prison!—or else we begin slowly chipping away at his safety and security insulation. As with Hitler, so with our own adversary: As his insulating security walls begin to crumble one by one and the outside world of reality draws ever closer toward the center where he anxiously cowers, so too his confidence and ultimately his sanity will begin to crumble (see 6 and 10).

Coming off a sour relationship, that woman you're eyeing may be looking for some "insulation," determined not to let her heart be broken again. Become her "walls" in order to break down her walls.

Instead of trying to boneheadedly break through her defenses, become those defenses. Become the friendly, understanding, and comforting arms that enfold her, sympathizing and empathizing your way into her confidence and ultimately into her bedroom.

Infatuation (16) He sees it, he wants it. So if it's something you want him to have in his life, show it to him. Just make sure it has plenty of flashing lights attached since this type of personality is visually oriented. Being visually oriented, he is easily distracted. He has a short attention span, he falls in love quickly (with people, places, and things) and just as quickly loses interest. (See "Mastery of Iccha," above)

We are forever trying to distract our adversary, luring his mind away from the important things he should be paying attention to, on to the more trivial. Thus our strategy is: Attract to distract.

Human beings have three types of orientation: *Visual* ("watchers"), *auditory* ("listeners"), and *tactile* ("touchers"). This will be described fully, along with strategies for dealing with each of these orientations, in our section on Sexual Feng-shui. See also *Black Science* (Lung and Prowant, 2001), and *Mind Manipulation* (Lung and Prowant, 2002).

Pride (17) In the Far East, this is called saving face, or regaining face after a failure or an insult. To Asians, "face" is synonymous with "honor." This type of pride longs for recompense and revenge. More often than not, these people convince themselves that the vengeance they're seeking is rooted in "justice," but that's often just the excuse used to put the bullets in the gun. In America, the street vernacular for redressing one's wounded pride is "getting your manhood back."

Convince your adversary he's been "punk'd out," made to look the fool, and he'll already be headed out the door, rage in one hand, revenge in the other (see 14).

To get her pants down, first build up her pride.

Envy (18) Envy is a mix of hate and greed and jealousy. This type hates everybody and everything—God, fate, and the universe included—because others get ahead while his genius remains unrecognized. He sees himself as a victim of injustice, passed over for promotion and unappreciated. Sun Tzu points to this personality type as a prime candidate for recruitment as a spy.

Commiserate with his cause. The world doesn't recognize his genius, his uniqueness, so as soon as *you* do, you'll become his bestest new buddy. Soon he will become hungry, even dependent on your praise. You can then direct his envy (hate) against another of your adversaries. Two birds, one stone.

KAMA SUTRA KARMA

The "yoga of love" encourages self-exploration and the search for a balance between the masculine (Shiva) and the feminine (Shakti) side within us all. Tantrism is not exclusive to sexual activity, but can be explored through meditation. Before you say, "That's getting too deep for me," open your mind to new experiences. By thinking you're too cool for some spirituality you could be giving up the best sex you'll ever have.

—Leslie Daniels, *Tantric Sex: Something Worth Exploring* **(2007)**

Vatsyayana's Aphorisms on Love (commonly called the Kama Sutra) contains about 1,250 verses arranged into four overlapping areas of concern: Methods of Sexual Congress, Methods of Seduction, Marriage, and a concluding section on the duties and dirties expected of courtesans.

Little is known about Vatsyayana except that his given name was either Mallinaga or Mrillans and that Vatsyayana was his family name. Even the years he lived are sketchy, usually placed somewhere between the first and sixth centuries C.E.

He alludes in his writing to having written the Kama Sutra while "wholly engaged in the contemplation of the Deity" while a religious student at Benares (a popular Hindu training center). Prior to penning his Kama Sutra, he claims to have studied all available ancient texts on Tantra, most notably *The 64 Means of Babhravya.*

Vatsyayana believed that "the arts of love" should be studied by both men and women. His own work being top of the list:

> Men should study the Kama Sutra and the arts and sciences subordinate thereto, in addition to the study of the arts and sciences contained in dharma and artha. Even young maids should study this Kama Sutra along with arts and sciences before marriage, and after they could continue to do so with the consent of their husbands . . . It is a work that should be studied by all both old and young; the former will find in it real truths, gathered by experience, and already tested by themselves, while the latter will derive the great advantage of learning things, which some perhaps may otherwise never learn at all, or which they may only learn when it is too late to profit by the learning . . . It can also be fairly commended to the student of social science and of humanity, and above all to the student of those early ideas, which seem to prove that the human nature of today is much the same as the human nature of long ago. (*The Kamasutra of Vatsyayana,* Lustre Press translation/New Delhi, India 1993)

But, up front, Vatsyayana tells us to keep it in our pants:

> This book is not to be used merely as an instrument for satisfying our desires. A person acquainted with the true principle of this science . . . is sure to obtain mastery over his senses. That is, an intelligent and knowing person who attends to his *dharma* (duty), *artha* (wealth and worldly matters), and *kama* (pleasure and satisfaction through mastery of the senses), without becoming slave to his passions, that one will obtain success in everything he undertakes. (Ibid.)

To help us accomplish this lofty goal Vatsyayana begins by outlining all the subsequent arts that should be studied in connection with the art of making love. It's a long list, one that basically mentions every possible skill designed to give us the edge in winning and then sinning with some fine piece of eye candy. To mention just a few skills that might come in handy with that candy:

- Learning to appreciate music and play musical instruments.
- Learning to dance.

- Learning how to entertain properly.
- Personal considerations like grooming, makeup, and wardrobe.

In addition to these, one should learn the arts of gambling and should know about sports of all sorts. While you're at it, hedge your bets, learning magic both sleight-of-hand and mystical conjuring.

More sinister (perhaps more useful?), Vatsyayana advises we master a virtual "black bag" of espionage skills that include "knowledge of the art of war," secret writing and deciphering of codes, using disguises (both on yourself and on others), and "obtaining possession of the property of others by means of mantra and incantations"!

In other words, all's fair in love and war and, anything that could be used to obtain your objective should be used.

Always remember that, while it appears at first glance to be merely a book of sexual positions (thanks to all those glossy Western editions of the Kama Sutra liberally peppering their pages with what amounts to medieval Hindu porn!), the Kama Sutra is first and foremost a book of strategy—detailing how aspiring and ambitious upper-crust Indians (men and women) can obtain a "profitable" marriage further up the social tree and maintain that lofty perch by keeping self and partners satisfied with a daily slap-and-tickle:

> Even the bare knowledge of them gives attractiveness to a woman, though the practice of them may be only possible or otherwise according to the circumstances of each case. A man who is versed in these arts, who is loquacious and acquainted with the arts of gallantry, gains very soon the hearts of women, even though he is only acquainted with them for a short time . . . Having thus acquired learning, a man, with the wealth that he may have gained by gift, deposit or inheritance from his ancestors, should become a householder, and pass the life of a citizen.

In many ways Vatsyayana was ahead of his time. He emphasized the need for foreplay:

> [Lovers] should carry on an amusing conversation on various subjects, and may also talk suggestively of things which would be considered as coarse, and not to be mentioned in society.

But he also teaches Afterplay that should be carried on "at the end of sexual congress." (Yeah, it's called "cuddling!")

Chapter 13 of his Kama Sutra even instructs us on the use of "toys" (i.e., extensions and dildos).

Indeed, the Kama Sutra is a virtual catalog of delight (or depravity, depending on your outlook). Instead of the "twelve days of Christmas," Vatsyayana's list reads more like the "365 days of sex-mas." Although he would have probably approved of some "Lords a' leaping" (depending on exactly whom they were "a' leaping"!), "Maids a' milking" (depending perhaps on exactly what they were "milking"!), and the occasional addition of both a "partridge" and a "pear tree," if it in any way helped to spice up your sex life:

- The seven types of congress (i.e., sexual intercourse)
- Nine kinds of unions according to the dimensions of the sexual organs involved (evidently, one size does not fit all!)
- Nine kinds of union according to force of passion and desire
- The three kinds of men and women according to timing
- Nine kinds of sexual intercourse
- Four kinds of love
- Four kinds of embrace
- Seven kinds of kissing
- Eight kinds of pressing with the nails (marking)
- Eight kinds of crying out during lovemaking
- Eight kinds of biting during lovemaking
- Eight things done by a eunuch (see "Gender-Benders" in China chapter)
- Five things a man can learn from body language
- Twenty-two reasons a woman might reject you
- Twenty-four types of men who are generally successful with women
- Thirty-eight types of women who are easily gained over
- Twelve types of women not to be enjoyed
- Seven kinds of friends
- Three weaknesses of a harem guard
- Nine causes of the destruction of a woman's chastity
- Five kinds of women not to seduce (i.e., apprehensive, timid, not to be trusted, well-guarded, and those possessing a possessive father-in-law and/or mother-in-law)

- Five results of a perfect union
- Sixteen things a potential mate should possess
- Twenty-one causes and faults for not marrying a girl
- Four things to make a girl worthy
- Four things to build a girl's confidence
- Three types of women a wife should avoid (nutshell: You're known by the company you keep!)
- Five causes of divorce and remarrying
- The nine ploys of a polygamist
- Nineteen types of men whores target for money
- Twenty-one good qualities of a man
- Ten qualities all women share
- Ten types of men courtesans should avoid
- Nine causes for a courtesan to resort to men
- Four attachments to a woman
- Twenty-six means of getting money
- Eight signs of waning love
- Twenty-eight ways to get rid of your lover (Only twenty-eight? Paul Simon had "fifty ways to leave your lover.")

Vatsyayana finishes up by giving us practical advice on aphrodisiacs and on what material dildos should be made of and, more importantly, what kinds of vegetables (and other common household objects) can double as dildos in a emergency—"a tube made of wood apple," "tubular stalk of bottle gourd," and "a reed made soft with oil and extracts of plants" (but, one would hope not too soft!).

The Four Types of Love

The Kama Sutra tells us that love comes from four sources: from habit, from imagination, from belief, and from our (often faulty!) perception of external objects:

- *Love from habit:* By constantly performing an act we can come to love performing that act—this rings true from stamp collecting to love-making. Likewise, we often fall in love with friends we've known for some time, never having realized before that what we've been look-ing for in all the wrong places has been right under our noses all along.

- *Love from imagination:* They say "the fantasy is always better than the reality"; we guess that should depend on how good your imagination is. The whole power of creation depends on imagination, likewise the fulfillment of both love and lust. First we *imagine* the possibilities. It's never really "love at first sight." We always first fall in love in our imagination.
- *Love from belief:* First love believes in us, then we believe in love. In a more mundane vein, we have to *believe* we can successfully pluck the apple of our eye before we can screw up enough courage to even reach for it.
- *Love from perception of external objects:* First impressions lie through their teeth. You can't trust your senses, your perceptions . . . and knowing this proven fact will not prevent you from tumbling head over spiked heels in love (or at least slip-sliding into lust!) the next time your perceptions (seeing, hearing, smelling, touching) latch onto something (or someone) finer than April wine!

The Ten Degrees of Love

Vatsyayana then outlines for us the "Ten Degrees of Love" which, upon reflection, almost read like the ten steps of an unrequited or failed love experience:

- Love of the eye. (We see it, we want it. That's why it's called "eye candy.")
- Attachment of the mind. (We can't stop thinking about it!)
- Constant reflection. (We really can't stop thinking about it!)
- Destruction of sleep. (We toss, we turn, because they won't toss us a turn!)
- Emaciation of the body. (We can't eat.)
- Turning away from the objects of enjoyment. (Nothing else fills the void.)
- Removal of shame. (We begin making fools of ourselves, becoming lap-dogs just to get some lap!)
- Madness. (Yes, you have lost your MF'n mind!)
- Fainting. (You doth swoon.)
- Death. (If *Romeo and Juliet*— the "greatest love story ever told" so easily turned into a tragedy, what chance do a couple suckers like you and I got of coming out of this thing alive!)

Yeah, ol' Vatsyayana sure makes love sound like something to look forward to!

The Nine Types of Union

Evidently, in Vatsyayana's corner of the world, size does matter, but only for practical "someone-could-lose-an-eye-if-you're-not-careful-with-that-thing!" reasons:

> [IV] Man is divided into three classes, viz. the hare man, the bull man, and the horse man, according to the size of *lingam*. Woman, also according to the depth of her *yoni,* is either a female deer, a mare, or a female elephant. There are thus three equal unions between persons of corresponding dimensions, and there are six unequal unions, when the dimensions do not correspond, or nine in all.

He goes on to clarify that there are "nine kinds of union according to dimensions" and "nine kinds of union according to the force of passion or carnal desire." This mitigated by "three kinds of men and women, viz. The short-timed, the moderate-timed, and the long-timed, and of these as in previous statements, there are nine kinds of union."

> There being thus nine kinds of union with regard to dimensions, force of passion, and time. Respectively, by making combinations with them, innumerable kinds of union would be produced. Therefore in each particular kind of sexual union, men should use such means as they think suitable for the occasion.

The Sixty-four Ways

Part V of the Kama Sutra, dealing with sexual intercourse, is called *Chatushshashti* ("sixty-four") and teaches eight subjects: embracing, kissing; scratching with the nails or fingers; biting; lying down; making sounds during lovemaking; playing the part of the man by the woman; and the *Aurparishtaka* "mouth congress". (Note: Aurparishtaka mouth congress is polished off at length in the chapter on "Gender-Benders," in our China chapter.)

Each of these eight subjects being of eight kinds, multiplies to sixty-four methods. But these eight are further broken down, ad infinitum it seems, into numerous subspecialties. For example, at least seven different types of "kissing" are taught in the Kama Sutra and "embrace" alone is further divided into the "touching" embrace, "piercing" embrace, "rubbing" embrace, and "pressing" embrace, and even further broken down into colorful categories such as "the twining of the creeper" embrace, the "milk and water" embrace, ad nauseum.

Still, Vatsyayana assures us it will all pay off for us, you guessed it, in the end:

> A man, employing the sixty-four means taught by Babhravya, obtains his object, and enjoys women of the first quality. A man devoid of other knowledge, but well-acquainted with the sixty-four means, becomes a leader in any society of men and women. He is looked upon with love by his own wife, by the wives of others, and by courtesans.

Mars versus Venus

One thing we realize from reading the Kama Sutra is that, the more things change, the more they stay the same, especially when it comes to sex:

> If a male be *long-timed,* the female loves him the more, but if he is *short-timed,* she is dissatisfied with him.

Vatsyayana, quite the psychologist ahead of his time, taught concepts such as "body language," pointing out the fact that we are often unaware of how our most intimate thoughts (subconscious) might be reflected in our mannerisms and actions:

> Women should be judged by their conduct, by the outward expression of their thoughts, and by the movements of their bodies.

Vatsyayana seems to have recognized women as equal partners (or at least equal players) in the love game; weighing in on such debates as "Do women have orgasm?":

> Auddalika says, "Female do not emit as males do. The males simply remove their desire, while the females, from their consciousness of desire, feel a certain kind of pleasure, which gives them satisfaction, but it is impossible for them to tell you what kind of pleasure they feel. The fact from which this becomes evident is that males, when engaged in coition, cease

of themselves after emission, and are satisfied, but it is not so with females . . . It may be said that if the ways of working in men and women are different, why should there not be a difference even in the pleasure they feel, and which is the result of those ways . . . On this again some may say that when different persons are engaged in doing the same work, we find that they accomplish the same end or purpose; while, on the contrary, in the case of men and women we find that each of them accomplishes his or her own end separately.

True, but it helps if we have a piece of their "end" to help us accomplish our end!

So in the end, each person is responsible for their own orgasm. But it might be in your best interest to help your partner get off, huh?

He who is acquainted with the true principles of this science of love pays regard to *Dharma, Artha, Kama,* and to his own experiences, as well as to the teachings of others, and does not act simply on the dictates of his own desire. . . . Whatever things may be done by one of the lovers to the other, the same should be returned by the other.

Like many, Vatsyayana compares lovemaking to making war:

Sexual intercourse can be compare to a quarrel, on account of the contrarieties of love and its tendency to dispute.

In fact, in India people were actually sometimes *killed* during lovemaking. The Kama Sutra (apropos chapter 13) mentions women, including a noted queen, killed and another girl *blinded* during some especially adventuresome lovemaking. (I've always heard that you could put an eye out with that thing!)

One who is well acquainted with the science of love, and *knowing his own strength,* as also the tenderness, impetuosity, and strength of the young woman, should act accordingly. The various modes of enjoyment are not for all times or for all persons, but they should only be used at the proper time, and in the proper countries and places.

As in strategy, so in seduction, knowing the mind of your adversary is job one:

> When a man is trying to gain over a woman, he should exam-
> ine the state of her mind, and then act.

Likewise:

> A woman should always know the state of mind, of the feel-
> ings, and of the disposition of her lover towards her, from
> the changes of his temper, his manner, and the color of his
> face. A wife that reveals the secrets of her husband is despised
> by him. . . . She should, moreover, make herself acquainted
> with the weak points of her husband's character, but always
> keep them secret.

Of course there's a lot of practical hands-on instructions in the *Kama
Sutra* to be found. From "one-on-one" sexual encounters:

> When a woman forcibly holds the *lingam* in her *yoni* after it is
> in, it is called the "mare's position." This is learnt by practice
> only.

and

> When a woman stands on her hands and feet like a
> quadruped, and her lover mounts her like a bull, it is called
> the "congress of a cow." At this time, everything that is ordi-
> narily done on the bosom should be done on the back. In
> the same way can be carried on the congress of a dog, the
> congress of a goat, the congress of a deer, the forcible mount-
> ing of an ass, the congress of a cat, the jump of a tiger, the
> pressing of an elephant, the rubbing of a boa, and the mount-
> ing of a horse. And in all these cases the characteristics of
> these different animals should be manifested by acting like
> them.

to "the more, the merrier":

> When a man enjoys many women altogether, it is called the
> "congress of a herd of cows" . . . In Gramaneri, many young
> men enjoy a woman, who may be married to one of them,
> either one after the other, or at the same time.

Vatsyayana clearly tells us what to look for:

Signs of the enjoyment and satisfaction of the woman

- Her body relaxes.
- She closes her eyes.
- She puts aside all bashfulness.
- She shows increased willingness to unite the two orgasms as closely together as possible.

And what to "Look out!" for:

Signs she is not enjoying herself and/or is unsatisfied

- She shakes her hands.
- She does not let you get up after love-making.
- She feels dejected.
- She kicks you.
- She continues pleasuring herself after you're finished. (Dah. Can you say, "Pass the batteries?")

Of course, back then they had some curious (and, by today's standards, downright illegal!) ideas about how women could be wooed. For example, when all else fails to win the hand of the one you love, you could turn to date rape:

> The man should on occasion of festivals, get the daughter of the nurse to give the girl some intoxicating substance and then cause her to be brought to some secure place before she recovers from her intoxication. . . . The man should, with the connivance of the daughter of the nurse, carry off the girl from her house while she is asleep, and then having enjoyed her before she recovers from sleep, should bring fire from the house of a Brahman, and proceed as before.

Word to the Wise (or at least to your attorney): Before following this Kama Sutra advice, please consult your local, state, federal laws concerning conspiracy, kidnapping, the possession and use of roofies, and, or yeah, rape!

Of course, this could backfire. Careful you don't "turn her" into a lesbian:

> Women being a tender nature, want tender beginnings, and when they are forcibly approached by men with whom they

are but slightly acquainted, they sometimes suddenly become haters of sexual connection, and sometimes even haters of the male sex.

Date rape aside, Vatsyayana's "technique for winning over a woman is fourfold:

- *Step one:* pre-flight intelligence-gathering. First, ascertain whether or not the woman is "available," especially figure out what her present mind-set is concerning courting overall, and, if possible, being courted by *you* in particular. This means getting inside her head. You have to know where she coming from before you can take her where you want to go. To repeat: "When a man is trying to gain over a woman, he should examine the state of her mind."

According to Vatsyayana, the best way to get inside a woman's head is by getting close to those closest to her. Vatsyayana was thus no stranger to the "six degrees of separation," as in using the (often unrealized) connections between people to help you get closer to your intended target. These include family, the mother or brother for instance, as well as friends of the family, merchants and establishments the target frequents, maids, wet-nurses, or servants of your intended target, and other agents, what Vatsyayana calls "an exceedingly clever go-between."* You could use "secret agents":

These friends should bring to the notice of the girl's parents the faults, both present and future, of all other men that may wish to marry her, and should at the same time extol, even to exaggeration, all the excellences, ancestral and paternal, of their friend, so as to endear him to them, and particularly to those that may be liked by the girl's mother. One of the friends should also disguise himself as an astrologer, and declare the good fortune and wealth of his friend by showing the existence of all the lucky omens and signs, the good influence of planets, the auspicious entrance of the sun into a sign of the Zodiac, propitious stars and fortunate marks on his body. Others should rouse the jealousy of the girl's mother from some other quarter, even a better girl than hers.

---

*Now would be a good time to (re) read chapter XIII of Sun Tzu's *Art of War* on the different types of, and uses for, secret agents.

- *Step two:* the introduction. Actually getting yourself introduced to the girl can also best be accomplished by means of a third party (preferably one already in your favor, if not your actual employ).

  There is no time limit on the other three steps. You can take as much time (the more the better) gathering information about your intended target. In fact learning more about her (or him) should be carried on throughout your relationship. Likewise, maneuvering yourself for a "proper" introduction can also require time to first win over one of her friends. And, even after you meet her, dropping hints that you'd really like to get with her also isn't stuck to any particular time table.

  But when you first meet a person, you have about sixty seconds— that's right, only sixty seconds!—To make them like you. First impressions can make or break. Sure, there's always a chance you'll get a second chance to clean up all the mistakes you make during your first impression . . . but can you really afford to take that chance?

- *Step three:* hinting. Having been introduced to her, you now begin making subtle hints of your desire for her. These hints can be by way of "side-talking," talking to a third party while in earshot of her—or else knowing that the information will be passed along to her, wherein you casually mention the "perfect" kind of woman you're looking for, making sure to match all your "expectations" to what you already know about her:

  > A conversation having two meanings should also be carried on with a child or some other person, apparently having regard to a third person, but really having reference to the woman he loves, and in this way his love should be made manifest under the pretext of referring to others rather than to herself.

Don't neglect your body language. "He should express his love to her by manner and signs other than by words."

- *Step four:* the conversation. First impressions can either be a *lasting* impressions or else your *last* impression, before she blows you off— and not in the way you'd like.

This is where all the "tricks of the trade" come into play: Listening to her, mimicking (matching and mirroring) both her patterns of speech and her body language, putting yourself more in synch with her, causing her to relax more. (More on "matching and mirroring" in the section on "Sexual Feng Shui.")

> He who knows how to make himself beloved by women, as well as to increase their honor and create confidence in them, this man becomes an object of their love.

Man Manipulation 101

Part IV of the Kama Sutra deals with coy and crafty courtesans.

Many researchers suspect that within the lore, legends, and actual loves of these accomplished courtesans of ancient India can be found the roots of the Black Lotus secret society of Asian femme fatales. In fact, Part IV of the Kama Sutra sounds a lot like a training manual for Black Lotus novices— Man Manipulation 101, if you will:

> By having intercourse with men courtesans obtain sexual pleasure, as well as their own maintenance . . . She should form friendships with such persons as would enable her to separate men from other women and attach themselves to herself, to repair her own misfortunes, to acquire wealth, and to protect her from being bullied or set upon by persons with whom she may have dealings of some kind or another.
>
> These persons are: the guards of the town, or the police; the officers of the courts of justice; astrologers; powerful men, or men with interest; learned men; teachers of the sixty-four arts; Pithamardas or jesters; flower sellers; perfumers; vendors of spirits; washermen; barbers; beggars; and such other persons as may be found necessary for particular object to be acquired.

It then goes on to list "nineteen types of men a courtesan takes up with simply to get their money." Not surprising, this list runs from the young and naïve, to wizened men who have influence with the king and his ministers.

> The extent of the love of women is not known, even to those who are the objects of their affection, on account of its subtlety, and on account of the avarice and natural intelligence of womankind . . . Women are hardly ever known in their true light.

Thus, if men and women act according to each other's liking, their love for each other will not be lessened even in one hundred years. (IX)

Seventeen Ways to Get Lucky

Desire which springs from nature, and which is increased by art, and from which all danger is taken away by wisdom, becomes firm and secure. A clever man, depending on his own ability, and observing carefully the ideas and thoughts of women, and removing the causes of their turning away from men, is generally successful with them.
—The Kama Sutra of Vatsyayana

As previously mentioned, the Kama Sutra is arguably the most (in)famous treatise ever written on the art of love or, to be more precise, on the art of *seduction* since, at its core, the Kama Sutra is a book of *strategy,* originally meant to instruct ambitious Indian courtiers how to marry further up the sociopolitical food chain.

Less well known, but no less informative is the Hindu Art of Love, which advises us: "Boldness is the rule, for everything is to be gained, and nothing lost."

Compiled and edited into English by Edward Windsor, this opus lists the seventeen types of women most "easily won over to congress" (led into the bedroom):

- A woman who looks sideways at you
- A woman who hates her husband
- A woman who has not had any children
- A woman who is very fond of society
- A woman who is apparently (outwardly) very affectionate toward her husband
- The wife of an actor
- A widow
- A woman fond of enjoyments
- A vain woman
- A woman whose husband is inferior to her in rank or ability
- A woman who is proud of her skill in the arts
- A woman who is slighted by her husband without cause
- A woman whose husband is devoted to traveling

- The wife of a jeweler
- A jealous woman
- A covetous woman.

Focus 101

If the Kama Sutra teaches us nothing else, it tells us that before trying to influence the minds of others, we first must rein in our own restless and undisciplined mind.

In the East, the uncontrolled mind of man is symbolized by the scampering, easily distracted monkey. Rather than being "deaf, dumb, and blind," the three "hear no evil, see no evil, speak no evil" monkeys of the Far East are actually a Buddhist depiction of the proper way to meditate: by closing off the senses and eliminating distractions, thus calming and focusing the mind.

To increase your own powers of focus, sit in a comfortable position and breathe in slowly, deeply, and deliberately several times. When breathing in slowly, imagine yourself smelling a flower, deeply inhaling the sweet, pleasant aroma. (When smelling something pleasant, we naturally inhale deeper.) Hold this deep breath for a couple of seconds, before allowing it to slowly leave your body. This is called "flower breathing." (More on this meditation technique in our China chapter.)

Now practice concentrating on the yantra meditation image below. (Figure 15).

YANTRA

Figure 15.

After concentrating on this yantra for thirty seconds, close your eyes and try to hold the afterimage of the yantra in your mind's eye as long as possible. Once the afterimage fades, open your eyes and repeat the process. Soon you will be able to retain the afterimage for longer and longer periods of time. Don't forget your slow, deep, and deliberate breath while "visualizing" the yantra.

The calming effect of this concentration/meditation exercise alone makes it worthwhile, but the ultimate goal and benefit will be your reaching the point where, without having to look at the yantra, you can visualize this calming image—or anything else you choose to visualize—simply by closing your eyes and concentrating.

To enhance this experience, use scented candles. Specialty candles can be found designed to aid relaxation and stimulate seduction.

Vatsyayana's parting advice:

> *This book, which is intended for the good of the people, and to teach them the ways of guarding their own wives, should not be made use of merely for gaining over the wives of others. [Don't go over to the dark side, Luke!]*

4

Tibet: Snow Lion, Fire Dragon

When iron birds fly, and horses run on wheels, when the Tibetan
people are scattered like ants across the world, then the Dharma*
will come to the land of the Red men.

—Ancient Tibetan prophecy

For untold centuries the inhospitable Himalayas kept hidden the secrets of
Tibet, jealously safeguarding a mysterious magic-based shamanistic religion
known as Bon, the origins of which stretch back to before recorded time.
Eventually, Buddhism from India penetrated into Tibet, mixing with Bon to
create mystical Lamaism.

For centuries explorers and would-be occult students from the West
risked life and limb—and in many instances their sanity!—trying to penetrate first the precipices and then the mysterious porticos of this isolated
land. The most (in)famous of these adventurers (or "adventuress," in this
case) was our old friend Helena Blavatsky, who disguised herself as a man in
order to penetrate into the hidden heart of Tibet. She would later incorporate what she learned into her Theosophical Society.

Some of these intrepid souls ventured to Tibet in search of wisdom.
Some came looking for mystical power. Still others made the hazardous
journey in search of the secret of immortality believed housed in the fabled

---

*Teaching of Buddha.

City of Seers, that utopia known as Shangri-la, sometimes called Shamballah.*

Ironically, while so many Westerners were packing their bags for Tibet, Tibet was already heading west.

After Tibet was overrun by Chinese Communists in 1949, millions of Tibetans followed their spiritual leader, the Dalai Lama, to the West. Tibet's loss is the world's gain as many of the Lamaists' heretofore secret meditation and mind-control methods were finally revealed to eager Western eyes. These include not only techniques of meditation and mind-control previously only taught to Tibetan Lamaist monks, but also physical-mental techniques designed to synchronize body and mind, for example martial arts (similar to Chinese kung-fu) like those practiced by the *sDop sDop* warrior-monks of Tibet.

One such modern school combining Tibetan mystery and martial arts, teaching both physical and mental mastery, is Boabom. The principal Boabom School in the United States is in Boston.** Ostensibly an art of self-defense, as with most traditional Asian schools of martial art, the dedicated student who comes to Boabom for the "fighting" quite often stays for the "enlightenment."

According to Boabom Master Asanaro in *The Secret Art of Boabom: Awaken Inner Power through Defense-Meditation from Ancient Tibet:*

> The roots of Boabom are lost in time. Its origin is in ancient Tibet, several thousand years before the birth of the Buddha, before the Vedas*** were written, and before the Chinese Emperor even thought to exist. (Asanaro, 2006:7)

As in all serious disciplines, be they martial or mystical or both, adaptability is the key in Boabom:

> Our Art can flourish in any place, large or small, comfortable or rough, with great resources or with great lack, yet always on the condition that wherever its seed may fall, it shall be

---

*Yes, just like Three Dog Night singing "On the road to Shamballah," and Bob Seger trying to "get outta here and go to Katmandu"—which is actually the capital of Nepal, Tibet's next-door neighbor. And didn't John Lennon promise us "Theres a little yellow idol to the north of Katmandu . . ."?

**E-mail: Boabom@boabom.org.

***Original Hindu holy books.

the right soil, meaning that it shall be valued, and paid the attention and care that it requires. (Ibid., 47)

Down through the centuries Tibetan mystics developed many methods of mind mastery for self and mind manipulation of others. None of these methods can be judged as either inherently benign or malevolent—to the Western mind, good or evil—rather, they are what they are: *insights into human nature.* How we choose to use those insights—as curing pill or to induce an ill—is what paints them brightly or else taints them darkly—and our souls as well.

Thus from the Tibetans we glean the Six Dusts, the Seven Fears, and the Eight Minds.

SEM YUNG: THE SIX DUSTS

You deserve this teaching. Yours is the right soil, the proper field.
The crops that we shall cultivate and harvest will depend on your
determination, strength, and persistence over time.
—Asanaro (2006:4)

A mirror is used in both Buddhism and Japanese Shinto to represent our pure "original mind," a mind unstained by worldly desires.

Unlike Western religions, which teach that man is "born into sin" with two strikes already against him, Buddhism maintains that the original nature of man is perfect, likening our mind to a beautiful mirror, crafted to perfectly reflect the perfect will of the Universe.

Unfortunately, "dusts" obscure our otherwise perfect mind-mirror, preventing us from seeing our *true* self reflected. Where do these "dusts" come from?

Six kinds of worldly dust prevent us from seeing correctly: Form, Sound, Scent, Taste, Touch, and Dharmas (i.e., external opinions and views). These dusts are similar to the perceptual mind "filters" we've already discussed—fears and prejudices that prevent us from processing information accurately.

Esoteric Tibetan tantricism calls the Six Dusts *Sem yung,* "mental factors."

Sem yung are thus the *Rtsa nyon,* six "root afflictions" that stand in the way of our seeing clearly (enlightenment): Desire, Anger, Pride, Ignorance, Doubt, and Afflicted views (egotism and attachment). The goal then, via meditation and other Buddhist practices, is to gradually polish away these worldly dusts in order to accurately reflect reality as it really is, rather than as we'd really like it to be.

However, with all due respect to the Buddha, first comes survival, *then* comes enlightenment. While the Buddha would undoubtedly frown at our "misusing" his insights and observations for personal gain, from a Black Science perspective, the more "dust" we can blow into our adversary's eyes, the better for us.

> Human beings are unpredictable, contradictory, most of them do not value, only treasure, do not learn, only imitate. (Asanaro, 2006:290)

THE SEVEN FEARS (AND THEIR SOLUTIONS!)

The "Six Dusts" often manifest as what Tibetans call "The Seven Fears."

Fear is perhaps our most powerful emotion, the first of the "Warning F.L.A.G.S." that control our world: Fear, Lust, Anger, Greed, Sympathy.

Not content to merely identify fear as a major player, Tibetan Masters were able to further break down fear into seven specific areas. Identifying these seven areas is the first step in finding solutions for them. (See Figure 16.)

Being able to recognize that our foe, or future lover, is influenced by one (or more) of these fears, we take the first step to getting inside their head and into their bed by simply offering to be the "solution" to that fear.

THE EIGHT MINDS

The mind, as well as its physical manifestation the body, is infinite.
—Asanaro (2000:66)

Tibetan Lamaism teaches that the six *Rtsa Nyon* (root afflictions) manifest through a collection of "minds" that we mistakenly think of as our one, single mind.

These eight minds, called *Nam She Tsoq Gye,* are: eye consciousness, ear consciousness, nose consciousness, tongue consciousness, overall body consciousness, mental consciousness, afflicted consciousness, and ground consciousness. (See Figure 17, page 88.)

Eye Consciousness We think "we" see things and we identify with the things we think we see. Light impacts on the eye, sending signals to the brain/mind,

FEARS (Actual and Metaphysical)	SOLUTIONS
Afraid of being afraid	"Castle" (Shelter) A safe port in the storm
Cold (fear of being alone)	"Garment" (clothing and comfort)
Poverty (fear of being inadequate)	"Wealth" (remind them of what they have to offer)
Hunger (fear of being left out)	"Food" (include them in the feast, help them profit)
Thirst (fear of missing out)	"Drink" (invite them to the party)
Melancholy (sadness, feeling of uselessness)	"A Friend" (be their friend . . . filial or false)
Fear of straying (from the correct path)	"Focus" (Help them to keep their eyes on the prize . . . the prize *you* want to win!)

Figure 16.

which then deciphers said signals through our distorted mind filters. Therefore "we" don't really see the true object with the unfailing organ of the eye, but rather a reconstruction with our all-too-fallible mind.

We see a piece of "eye candy" and that "seeing" causes us all manner of false identification. The mere sight causes our thought to "go south," to our base (lust and reproduction) chakra.

Ear Consciousness Same as with the eye: "We" only think we hear because we identify with the organ of sound.

We think "we" are hearing what others are saying, thus we are easily swayed by their words, which we identify with either positively or negatively—"purr words" or "slur words." Even sounds that aren't even words— sighs, whistles, groans, music—can all influence us, often without our consciously being aware of it.

Nose Consciousness Same as with the eye and the ear. Reacting to sex pheromones and the like, our sense of smell can instantly affect our mood and—literally—lead us around by the nose.

TIBETAN EIGHT-MINDS

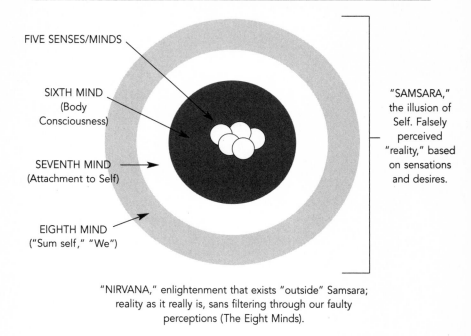

FIVE SENSES/MINDS

SIXTH MIND
(Body
Consciousness)

SEVENTH MIND
(Attachment to Self)

EIGHTH MIND
("Sum self," "We")

"SAMSARA,"
the illusion of
Self. Falsely
perceived
"reality," based
on sensations
and desires.

"NIRVANA," enlightenment that exists "outside" Samsara;
reality as it really is, sans filtering through our faulty
perceptions (The Eight Minds).

Figure 17.

Tongue Consciousness Same as the eye and ear and nose. We'll discuss how to learn to control these *false* sense identifications in our next China section and in our section on Sexual Feng Shui.

Overall Body Consciousness FYI: These first five "minds" are called *Bang She* (and, no, they weren't named for your ex-girlfriend!).

Neither our sense of touch, taste, nor "our" other senses combined are really "us." They are simply impulses of sensation information sent to the brain for storage. We receive sensations ("impressions") in through these five sense "minds" and falsely believe *"I am seeing," "I am hearing,"* when it is merely the sense organ "mind" experiencing the sensation event.

The remaining four "minds" are mental processes (like a library) where we record and recall the sensations we experience through "our" senses.

Mental Consciousness Tibetan masters disagree with Descartes (1596–1650) "Cogito, ergo sum" ("I think, therefore I am"), countering "You only think you are thinking because you falsely think you actually have a 'you' to do the thinking with!"

In actuality, say these Himalayan masters, what we think of as "I" and "me" are only the restless monkey of the mind(s) playing with itself (as monkeys are wont to do).

Afflicted Consciousness Afflicted consciousness (attachment to self) means thinking there is a real "I" apart from the sensations we experience and identify with, a real "I" that lives, dies, and "feels" a whole lot of pain in between because of our attachment and desire.

Ground Consciousness Ground consciousness binds these previous seven consciousness together to give us the illusion there really is an "us" apart from the sensations we feel.

This is where "the whole becomes greater than the sum of its parts." In effect, these seven separate minds come together and now falsely believe they are a single mind, a single being—an "I," a "me"—rather than simply a collection of parts.

In other words, our mind is an ever-changing stream of thoughts and feelings and *not* a solid, separate "self." But so long as we identify with these various senses and thoughts, we remain susceptible to outside influence . . . but so do all our foes and future flames!

Since our adversary also identifies with *his* "eight minds" sensations, we can easily distract him by dazzling his five physical senses while masterfully manipulating his three mental consciousnesses, in effect filling up his already confused mind with sights and sounds and sensations guaranteed to seduce his senses even more.

TUMO: FIRE DRAGON MASSAGE

Tibetan monks can sit half-naked in freezing snow and, through force of will alone, melt all the snow around them up to a six-foot radius. Sure, sounds far-fetched. However, recent Western laboratory experiments monitoring meditating Tibetan monks have discovered that these monks brains give off curious radiation signatures, almost as if their brains are creating (or at the very least channeling) increased energy levels.

Get the point? What's this got to do with "getting lucky"?

To a great extent sex (and sexual attraction) is simply *heat*. Excitement raises skin temperature. A warm touch excites us even more. One fire feeding another.

And I know you've at least seen the hundreds of books written on "sensual message"?

Rub your hands together—vigorously for a full minute. Feel the heat?

Do this next time before shaking hands with that prospective love interest (or business associate for that matter). Warm hands always make a nice first impression.

When attempting to woo a honey out onto the dance floor—or back to your place for a different kind of dance—first warm your hands and then touch the inside of her arm at the bottom of her bicep before slowly allowing your hand to slide down to the inside of her elbow.

This is "the sweet spot." Nerves joining the upper arm to the lower arm also run up to where lymph nodes responsible for our immunity and overall health are located at the juncture of your arm and chest.

In the same way acupuncture and acupressure stimulates chi, so too simply massaging "the sweet spot" (especially after warming your hand) sends soothing impulses up the arm, stimulating the lymph nodes and engendering an overall feeling of euphoria and relaxation.

Our lymph system doesn't have a "pump" (like the heart) and so depends on such things as exercise and massage to help "squirt" its health-promoting juices out into the body.

This is another reason "sensual massage" is so relaxing and stimulating (!) simultaneously.

If you're trying to spice up your love life, don't waste your money on all those sensual massage books and DVDs (unless you plan on doing some "self-massaging," you lonely bastard!).

Just as there is no such thing as bad oral sex so far as a man is concerned, so far as a woman is concerned there's no such thing as a bad massage.

Warm your hands first, okay?

By the way, men also respond to "the sweet spot" . . . *some* men. (See "Gender-Bender" section.)

5

China: The Tao of Seduction

INTRODUCTION: "STRATEGY IS SEDUCTION, SEDUCTION IS STRATEGY."

Few lands have been as blessed (or is that "cursed"?) as has China when it comes to having birthed both philosophers and generals—the two often being one and the same.

Likewise, whether delving into the strategies of Sun Tzu, or diving into the willing and thrilling arms and charms of an accomplished Black Lotus concubine, either way, you all too soon discover that, in China, strategy is seduction, seduction is strategy, twin edges of the same jeweled dagger, a dazzling but deadly dirk wielded as adroitly by a *wu shu* war-master on the battlefield as by a secret society–trained femme fatale in the bedroom!

From the Emperor on down to the cagy general, the wise monk, the coy concubine, the sexy spy trying to—literally—squeeze your secrets from you, all know well (after a "mere" five thousand years of continual practice!) that a good blade cuts both ways—*strategy is seduction, seduction is strategy.*

HORNY EMPERORS: THEN AND MAO

The Chinese Imperial Court has always been a hotbed of seduction, strategy, and skullduggery. This holds true from the first Emperor of China, Ying Zhing, down to the most recent "Emperor" of China, Mao Zedong.

The fifth century B.C.E. was China's "Warring States" period (453–221 B.C.E.) a time of "silk and steel"—steel blades and subtle-as-silk plots of seduction and sedition.

It was during this turbulent period in Chinese history that Fu Chai, king of the state of Wu, defeated and captured his main rival, Kou Chien, King of the state of Yueh. After humiliating Kou Chien (by forcing him to shovel manure in the royal stables), Fu Chai finally released his rival back into his own kingdom under the condition that Kou Chien continue to pay yearly tribute in the form of gold and gifts. Despite agreeing to the terms of his release, Kou Chien never forgot his humiliation at the hands of Fu Chai.*

Biding his time, Kou Chien plotted his revenge, surreptitiously rebuilding his forces toward the day he could once again test his "steel" against the steel of Fu Chai. But, until that time came, Kou Chien wisely sought to undermine Fu Chai with a clever "silk" strategy.

Staying true to their treaty, Kou Chai was never late with his annual payment of tribute to Fu Chai. Most often the payment would be in the form of gold and jewels, but other times in fine horses, rare animals, and other exotic gifts. Then came the year when, as part of his payment, Kou Chien sent Fu Chai a beautiful young courtesan named Hsi Shih.

Fu Chai took one look at Hsi Shih and fell madly in love . . . just as Kou Chien had planned. You see, Kou Chien had spent a small fortune, first scouring his kingdom to find the most flawless of maidens, then sparing no expense having Hsi Shih instructed in all the arts of seduction: how to dress, how to speak properly—yet suggestively, how to move gracefully—yet provocatively. In other words, Hsi Shih was trained to be the perfect distraction.

Having instantly fallen head-over-heels in love with Hsi Shi, Fu Chai could not stand to be parted from her for any length of time. First he began allowing her to attend councils of state (unheard of for a woman!) and soon she was advising him on important state matters, even to the exclusion of better qualified ministers (none of whom dared the King's wrath by speaking against his new love).

When Hsi Shih expressed her dislike and discomfort with Fu Chai's old palace in the old capital, the enamoured King immediately set about building her a lavish new palace all her own, away from the old royal capital. Soon, overseeing the intricate demands of the construction was taking up

---

*"Slay, but never humiliate a man." (Okinawan Shotokan Karate Master Gichin Funakoshi).

all the King's time, especially with Hsi Shih changing her mind (and his!) constantly. Soon the extravagant cost began to strain, and finally bankrupt, the royal treasury.

Fu Chien was still obsessing over new additions to Hsi Shih's palace, agonizing over where he would get the money to finally satisfy her dream, when frantic word reached him that his kingdom had been overrun by an army Kou Chien had built up in secret!

In desperation and despair—perhaps realizing at the end how he had been wrapped up in a silken trap, Fu Chai committed suicide.

Success breeds imitation. This same scenario was played out again in eighth-century C.E. China when Emperor Ming Huang fell in love with his son's new concubine, Yang Kuie-fei. He too build his new love the grand-est—most expensive!—of palaces, ultimately bankrupting and destroying his kingdom in the process.

Yes, the Chinese learned early on that where steel fails, silk succeeds, a lesson learned—and practiced—by the very first Emperor himself.

In 221 B.C.E. Ying Zheng (a.k.a. Zhao Zheng), King of the state of Qin, became the first Emperor of a united China after forty years of putting the "steel" to neighboring kingdoms: Han, Zhao, Yan, Wei, and Chu. Ironically, Ying Zheng's rise to power began with a well-planned ploy of "silk" seduction.

This plot began long before his birth: When, in 260 B.C.E., young and lonely Prince Yiren of Qin, being held hostage in Zhao, fell in love with Zhaoji, the beautiful concubine owned by an ambitious merchant named Lü Buwei.

In 258, Zhaoji gave birth to Yiren's son and heir, Ying Zheng.

Eventually Yiren, Zhaoji, and little Ying Zheng are ransomed back to Qin. To express his gratitude for helping him find his true love, Yiren appoints Lü Buwei his chief advisor and takes Lü with him to Qin.

In 246, Yiren dies* and Lü Buwei becomes "regent" to the now thir-teen-year-old King Ying. For many years thereafter, Lü Buwei, "a lowly mer-chant," is the eminence grise behind the Imperial throne of China up until his death in 235.

Having seen how lonely (hence vulnerable) Yiren was during his captivity, Lü Buwei had deliberately steered his well-trained concubine in Zhaoji Yiren's direction. Some sources even believe that Zhaoji may have *already* been pregnant with Ying Zheng before ever gracing Yiren's bed—pregnant with Lü Buwei's

---

*Some sources maintain Yiren died "of *suspiciously* good health!"

child! If so, silken-tongued Lü Buwei—a lowly merchant adept in salesmanship (another synonym for seduction!) succeeded not only in ruling the country of Qin for several years from behind the scenes but ultimately succeeded in making his son—a man of common blood—the first Emperor of China.

Call it "strategy," call it "salesmanship," but seduction by any other name still *sells* as sweet!

The lesson here is that the thing or person we are so often blindly attracted to (in this case, a beautiful concubine) is not always necessarily the seducer, but rather merely a tool in the hands of the true seducer, hidden behind a nearly black curtain.

> *In war it is best to attack minds not cities. Psychological warfare is better than fighting with weapons.*
> —Mao Tse-tung

Madame Mao We need not confine ourselves to "ancient" testimonials to the Chinese arts of seduction. There are just as viable modern-day examples, some involving the twentieth-century "Emperor" of China, Mao Zedong.

Much has been made—and justifiably so—of the strategy and cunning of Mao Zedong. One of the great military minds of the twentieth century, Mao made no bones about where he came by his strategy, often openly praising masters who came before him, such as Sun Tzu.

But one often overlooked component of Mao's success comes from the fact that he had good advisors; he had back-up, in the modern vernacular, a good "posse." In Mao's "posse" were not one, but two master strategists—master seducers!—one female, the other male.

There's that oft-repeated quip, "Behind every great man there a woman . . . bitching, bitching, bitching!" Well, in Mao's case, that's not far from the truth. Except that, in this case, the woman behind the man Mao was always scheming, scheming, scheming!

One of Mao's major assets was his wife, the controversial Jing Qing, later called Madame Mao, who had first met him in 1937, wen she was an actress in Shanghai. It was during this time, many believe, she was recruited into the Black Lotus, the female triad secret society. (More on this mysterious cadre in a minute.)

Jing was nothing like the awestruck and impressionable peasant girls with whom Mao was used to being surrounded. She was savvy and sophisticated, coy and occasionally controversial, a little too "flamboyant" for many of the staunch, stuck-in-the-mud Communist party leaders. But Mao was instantly taken with her. In short order, she became Hillary to his Bill.

Many of the other Communist Party members resented the influence Jing immediately exercised over Mao (especially after Mao left his first wife for her) but, with her influence growing every day, they feared to openly speak out against her. (Yeah, just like Hillary!)

Jing, as "Madame Mao," would, eventually become one of the most powerful women of the twentieth century and reign as the most powerful woman in China for decades. But unlike Fu Chai and Emperor Ming Huang, Mao seemed more to benefit from the added ruthlessness of "Madame Mao." His "kingdom" prospered.

Mao's other great asset was his friend and silken-tongued second-in-command Zhou Enlai, who has been called "the consummate chameleon." (Greene, 2001:93)

In 1936 it was Zhou Enlai who convinced Mao the Communist that it was in their best interest to form a temporary alliance with their old friend—now bitter enemy—Chiang Kai-shek, leader of the hated Nationalists. Zhou convinced Mao that, rather than execute the recently captured Nationalist leader, they needed to free him and create a united front with him against the invading Japanese—who were too powerful for either Mao's Communists or Chiang's Nationalists to defeat on their own. Never was there a clearer case of the even then old adage: "The enemy of my enemy is my friend."

To convince rivals Mao and Chiang of this necessity, Zhou first accused them of not seeing "the big picture," of not being able to see the forest for the trees. Zhou then went on to use the analogy of two woodsmen wanting to cut down a great tree: To cut down a great tree woodsmen could individually chop away at the tree, each with their small axes, each on opposite sides of the great trunk. Or else they could pool their efforts and use a two-man saw, which, by its very construction, *required two men working in harmony*—one pushing, one pulling. A balance of Yin-Yang. Very Chinese.

Once the great tree (the Japanese) was felled, there would be plenty of time to divide up the firewood, with plenty to go around.

Ultimately, Mao and Chiang agreed to this—temporary—Communist/Nationalist alliance and Chiang was freed.

As Mao and Zhou watched Chiang leaving, Mao commented, "As prudent and practical as this temporary alliance might be, we both know that, as soon as the Japanese are defeated, Chiang will turn on us."

Zhou nodded agreement, smiling, "Any time an enemy helps you cut down a bothersome tree, thank him. But just make sure that tree falls in *his* direction!"

It took another nine years of bloody fighting before the Chinese alliance defeated the invading Japanese, after which, in very short order, the Chinese Nationalists and Communists were once again tearing at each other's throats.

In 1949, the "tree" finally fell on top of Chiang as he and his Nationalists were driven out of mainland China and forced to seek refuge on the isle of Formosa (Taiwan).

THE STEEL OF THE SILK GENERALS

All generals must be adept at the use of "steel," literally wielding weapons of steel, from swords to tanks and IcBMs, as well as possessing nerves of steel.

What separates "only adequate" generals from "accomplished" masters of war is the ability to not only wield "steel" but also, when called for, to possess the ability to entrap and wrap your enemy up in "silk"—to plant fear and doubt in his mind, to entice him forward—toward seeming gain . . . before then springing sudden defeat on him!

Though no stranger to "steel," Sun Tzu was the ultimate "silk" general. His strategy proved its worth during China's Warring States Period. As the name implies, this was a time of chaos and cruelty, ambition and atrocity, yet a time that nonetheless stimulated not only the Chinese art of war but also Chinese culture as a whole.

Such is ever the nature of struggle and strife. Shades of Nietzsche! What doesn't destroy us makes us stronger! The heavier the burden, the more the muscle grows. The more unforgiving the whetstone, the better the blade benefits. The harder the times, the more hardy the heroes have to be. The fall of Rome, the Crusades, the Civil War, World Wars I and II . . . and 9/11. Tumultuous times test our *mettle* . . . and our *metal,* our "steel" and often our "silk."

One such period of tribulation in China's history followed the fall of the Han Dynasty in 220 B.C.E., when China split into the warring kingdoms of Shu, Wu, and Wei.

K'ung Ming The daring darling of this "Three Kingdoms Period" was K'ung Ming, (a.k.a. Chuko Liang), a wily young warrior who outwitted and outlasted most of his senior rivals to become a renowned general and scholar in later years. Part Patton, part Scarlet Pimpernel, an obvious student of Sun Tzu, K'ung Ming's life was immortalized in Kuan Chung's 1400s epic novel *A Tale of Three Kingdoms.*

One of K'ung Ming's earliest triumphs (when he was not even yet a general), was against another notable strategist, Wei general Cao Cao, when Wei invaded Shu. (More on Cao Cao in a minute.)

In expectation of the next day's battle, Shu and Wei armies camped on opposite sides of a wide river.

When ten thousand arrows scheduled to be delivered to the Shu army failed to arrive, the commander of Shu was ready to retreat until a young Shu warrior named K'ung Ming came up with an audacious plan to acquire the arrows needed: That night, as a thick fog rolled in, blanketing both sides of the river, Wei sentries were suddenly alarmed by the obvious sound of boats crossing the river. Believing that Shu forces were attempting a surprise attack, all the Wei archers began firing blindly into the thick fog in the direction of the sound of the approaching enemy boats, exhausting all their arrows before their commander Cao Cao could stop them.

The cursing on the Wei side of the river began when the fog cleared enough for the Wei archers to watch Shu troops pulling back their unmanned boats, linked together with rope, each boat piled high with bales of straw, now bristling with ten thousand *reusable* arrows "donated" by their enemy!

This ploy was not a matter of chance on K'ung Ming's part; rather, it was a matter of prior study. Remember: Chance favors the prepared mind.

In anticipation of fording the river K'ung Ming had studied its currents and—like any warrior worth his salt—was already an accomplished meteorologist and so had anticipated the night's coming fog.

Most important, though still young, K'ung Ming already knew human nature: Listening to the noisy enemy camp, K'ung Ming recalled Sun Tzu's observation that: "When the enemy's night camp is noisy, it is because he is fearful" *(The Art of War,* IX: 36).

K'ung Ming's ploy also echoes another of Sun Tzu's commands: "A wise general's troops feed on the enemy."

Promoted for his ingenuity, K'ung Ming was put in command of a small force sent to prepare the defense of the walled city of Hsi. Yet no sooner did K'ung Ming arrive at Hsi than he learned that a large Wei force commanded by General Ssuma Yi (a famed commander in his own right) was on their way to take the city. Realizing there was no possibility enough Shu reinforcements would arrive in time, K'ung Ming inexplicably ordered what few troops he had into the hills as he prepared to meet the enemy alone!

When Ssuma Yi and his army arrived, they were shocked to discover the gates of Hsi wide open. On closer examination, they spied K'ung Ming sitting atop the city's wide wall, dressed not in armor but in a silk robe, playing the lute for a pair of giggling courtesans.

Alarmed, suspecting a trap designed to lure him into what only *appeared* to be an *undefended* city, Ssuma Yi immediately ordered his army to leave the Hsi area immediately.

K'ung Ming smiled as he watched the Wei army head off into the hills, where he knew they would have to break down their ranks in order to pass through a narrow canyon . . . where K'ung Ming's own smaller force was already hiding in ambush!*

Unfortunately for the kingdom of Shu, K'ung Ming was not commanding Shu forces when a Wu commander tricked the Shu commander by dressing condemned prisoners up in Wu uniforms and making them cut their own throats, successfully terrorizing and routing the Shu army. (See Lung and Prowant, 2001:38)

For a long time it seemed no one could challenge wunderkind K'ung Ming head to head except Cao Cao.

Cao Cao (also written Ts'ao Ts'ao) He was the most famous general of the Three Kingdoms Period. Living from 155 to 220, he was not only the contemporary of K'ung Ming but his rival and equal.

Like Sun Tzu before him, Cao Cao preferred to avoid bloodshed, fighting only as a last resort. When conflict was unavoidable, Cao Cao declared that one must "Let your enemy create your victory."

To accomplish this, Cao Cao's main maxim was clear:

> Nothing is constant in war save deception and cunning. Herein lies the true Way.

Cao Cao was quick to point out that there is no one hard-and-fast rule for accomplishing victory since the dynamics of war have no constant:

> Just as water has no constant form, so too war has no constant dynamic. As water adapts to each vase, so too those adept at war adopt an attitude of flexibility, thus adapting to flux and circumstance. So much of this cannot be known in advance but must be judged on the spot with a practiced eye.

---

*A variation of following Sun Tzu's advice to "Always leave an enemy a way out" is that you can leave them a way out, straight into your ambush!

Cao Cao was famed and feared for arriving at the battlefield before his enemies ever suspected his army was on the move. In this respect, Cao Cao shared the philosophy of Confederate Civil War General Nathan Bedford Forrest, who, when pressed for the "secret" of his winning battle after battle, snapped: "It's whoever arrives *first* with the *most!*"

Likewise, Cao Cao's philosophy was simple:

> Make a show of being far away . . . then march with all haste to arrive before the enemy even suspects you are on the move! Choosing a circuitous route that gives the illusion it requires a great distance to travel, even when you start out after the enemy does, so long as you calculate correctly, you can still arrive before your enemy.

Cao Cao was renowned for arriving first with the most, so much so that a superstition soon sprang up among his (ever-dwindling!) circle of enemies: "Never speak Cao Cao's name lest that old dragon appear!"

When actual warfare was unavoidable, Cao Cao did his best to acquire as much information on his enemies as possible, employing *Lin Kuei* (Chinese "ninja") spies to gather intelligence, while sending agents provocateur to sow dissent and confusion in the enemy's ranks.

Cao Cao followed Chinese traditions and etiquette when it came to combat. But when circumstance and happenstance demanded, he could just as quickly discard the accepted chivalry of Chinese combat in favor of unorthodox, unexpected, and some would say "underhanded" maneuvers designed to bring him swift victory. For example, although Cao Cao tells us, "Do not call up your army in bitter winter nor in blistering summer, since it is too much of a hardship on the common people," he himself successfully attacked the state of Wu in the dead of winter.

Another time, however, Cao Cao literally signed his own death warrant after he accidentally tramped down a farmer's crops after having given his marching men express orders to leave farmland unmolested. Only after much pleading—and a near mutiny by his troops—Cao Cao finally gave in and instead cut off his hair as punishment.*

Cao Cao used his mastery of strategy and seduction not only on his ene-

---

*Cutting off one's hair in ancient China was a serious punishment, since many Chinese wore their hair long in a queue in the belief that, upon their deaths, the gods or the Celestial Buddha would pull them up to heaven by their pigtail.

mies but also, when need be, on his own troops: Once, Cao Cao discovered that his army's supply of grain had been allowed to run dangerously low. Immediately he called for his quartermaster, Wang Hou. "There is something I need from you," Cao Cao told Wang Hou. "Something necessary to reassure the men that we have not neglected them." "Whatever my Lord needs, I will gladly give," Wang bowed.

Without another word, Cao Cao drew his sword and decapitated Wang Hou! He then placed Wang's head on a pole and under it placed a sign which simply read: "Wang Hou, Granary Officer." In this way Cao Cao's troops saw that the officer they believed responsible for their hunger had been punished by their beloved and benevolent General.

Whereas a bad craftsman always blames his tools, Cao Cao was an accomplished general who understood the importance of respecting your tools of the trade. Cao Cao's craft and trade was war, his loyal troops the tools of his trade.

Of course, Cao Cao saved his best tricks for his enemies: playing on their weaknesses, or, as he once wrote: "I let my enemies create my victories."

For example, finding his smaller force trapped in a narrow canyon, larger armies of his enemies at both ends, Cao Cao had his men dig holes into the side of the canyon walls. Leaving half his men hiding inside these holes, he boldly advanced to attack the enemy at the far end of the canyon.

Seeing Cao Cao's advance, the enemy force behind him quickly rushed into the canyon, intent on attacking his exposed rear. But no sooner had they unknowingly passed the men Cao Cao had hidden inside the canyon walls than those men fell in behind them and attacked the advancing enemy's rear! When this happened, Cao Cao suddenly wheeled around, crushing the trapped enemy between the two halves of his forces.

The enemy at the far end of the canyon was so stunned by this literal turnabout of fortune that not only did they fail to rally to the aid of their trapped allies but also fled in panic.

According to Cao Cao, there are *five virtues* a general must possess: Wisdom, Integrity, Compassion, Courage, and Severity. Compare these with Sun Tzu's *Art of War,* chapter I: 7.

These are the five virtues. Thus, the negative attributes we want to look for (and eventually find a way to exploit!) in our adversaries are their opposites. (See Figure 18, opposite.)

Like all true warriors, Cao Cao was himself both steel and silk, a man of action as well as a man of letters. Cao Cao's credits reach far beyond the bat-

THE FIVE VIRTUES

WISDOM	Ignorance (Lack of intelligence—both kinds!)
INTEGRITY	Treachery (He betrays his principles, those around him betray him!)
COMPASSION	Ruthlessness/selfishness/hatred
COURAGE	Cowardice/fear (one of the five "F.L.A.G.S."
SEVERITY	Sympathy (another one of the five "F.L.A.G.S.")

Figure 18.

tlefield. For example, he stands accused of "rewriting" Sun Tzu's *Ping-Fa,* and at least gets the credit for breaking Sun Tzu's *Art of War* down into its present thirteen chapters. He is also credited with creating a martial art called "Iron Wall kung fu" based on the practical lessons he learned on the battlefield,

Eventually Cao Cao was proclaimed "The Martial King" for his undisputed mastery of the art of war and became King of the Wei state. Later his son would become emperor and declare his father *T'ai Tzu* ("Respected Founder") of the Wei Dynasty.

The Three Principles When studying strategy in general and Chinese strategists like Sun Tzu, K'ung Ming, and Cao Cao in particular, we can easily isolate three recurring principles: *system and setting, balance,* and *correspondence.*

- *System and setting.* In any situation, circumstances must be viewed as a whole. We must see the big picture. Failure to focus on the big picture leaves us the victims of trivial events that drain our energies, wasting us, getting us wasted.

This means not only seeing how events are unfolding (system) but also the background (setting) against which those events are playing out.

From a practical seduction perspective, there's a big difference between trying to catch a woman's eye at a wedding reception and at a funeral! Likewise, different rules apply in a barroom as opposed to a laundromat or grocery store.

Seeing the big picture can also mean having to postpone our immediate gratification in favor of long-term gain; *waiting* when we would rather attack, *retreating* rather than pressing forward—be it verbal or violent, the battlefield or the bedroom.

Coming on "too strong" (and not just that aftershave you're wearing!) can startle and push away a potential lover, whereas, patiently—perhaps subtly—taking time to let her adjust to your presence will pay off in the long run. "The big picture," "the long run"—same thing.

Conversely, any time we can frivolously distract or otherwise bog down an adversary's resources with trivia, making him lose sight of the Big Picture by forcing him to deal with trivial (irritating) issues, we are well on our way to seizing the upper hand

- *Balance.* The universe is a naturally self-balancing system that rushes to fill a vacuum, mercilessly thinning out any species that hesitates, underestimates, or overpopulates.

In Chinese Taoism, this is yin-yang, balance.

Applying this to seduction: your potential love interest is likewise a "vacuum" needing to be filled . . . in other words, she (or he) needs something in their life—and your job is to convince them that *you* are that something that is missing from their life. In other words, you're just doing the universe a favor by helping it "rebalance" itself!

Come on *too strong,* and she's reaching for the mace. Come on *too shy* and you'll never get your foot in the door, let alone getting your (bleep) in her (bleepity-bleep-bleep)!

Listen twice as much as you talk, touch half as much as you'd like to. It all balances out in the end.

Traditional Chinese medicine uses this "need to balance" principle: a sick person either has too much of something, or else too little of something else. Simple addition or subtraction. The doctor either adds what is needed or else subtracts what is too abundant in the patient's life; redirecting the patient's bodily energy (chi) to or away from an affected area.

This same principle can be applied to strategy and seduction—military or mental, the battlefield or the bedroom.

Too much of my adversary is concentrated over there (either his physical troops or simply his focus of attention), so I distract him by making a motion or a noise over here, and he immediately sends part of his troops to check it out.

Judo is based on this very principle: He pushes, I pull. He pulls, I push. Either way, he fails. Or, as eighth-century Chinese strategist Li Chung put it:

Dodge left, strike right. Dodge right, strike left. Fake an attack forward to cover your retreat. Pretend retreat . . . before springing forward with ferocity!

Likewise, her attention is focused over there, and I need it focused over here, where I am.

- *Correspondence.* Japanese master samurai Yagu Munenori (1571–1646) taught that winning a battle by commanding a great army is no different from winning a sword fight in one-on-one combat. (As we will see in the section on Japan, Miyamoto Musashi taught that same principle.)

As above, so below. The rules governing the big also apply to the small and vice versa. Go on the assumption that all things are connected and at the very least you'll pay closer attention to life and life will pay closer attention to you.

While particular correspondences and connections might not immediately be apparent in all situations, they do exist, and discovering these hidden connections—a previously unknown weakness in an adversary, something you have in common with a lover—provides just the edge you need to overcome your adversary or get your new love interest to come on over. Find the connections in order to make the connections. Find things in common with the person you have "targeted" as your future baby's mama (or daddy, as the case may be).

Connect with her . . . in order to "connect" with her. Despite movies and romance novellas to the contrary, opposites don't attract.

These Three Principles apply to the art of seduction just as well as they do to strategy on the battlefield.

Ambush and Amour In Edgar Allan Poe's "The Cask of Amontillado" (1846) the "hero" of the story meets all four criteria required for staging a successful ambush:

- First, he *gathers intelligence* about his hated enemy, who doesn't suspect he's been targeted. Our hero learns his enemy fancies himself a connoisseur of fine wine.
- Second, *he prepares the ambush site beforehand,* baiting the trap with the perfect enticement: An entire barrel of the rare Amontillado wine his enemy covets has just been discovered! The only catch is its located deep inside catacombs far beneath the city.

- Next, *patiently* he lures his still unsuspecting prey *literally* deeper and deeper into his doom, down into those out-of-the-way catacombs.
- Finally, when the time finally comes to *spring the trap*—his enemy totally taken in, still distracted by greed and lust—our hero pounces!—executing his ambush *swiftly* and *surely.*

Having trapped his enemy with no hope of escape, our hero begins methodically—again *literally*—sealing his enemy's fate . . . by bricking him up inside a wall!

And, most important, the narrator of the story comes away from his successful ambush *unscathed* . . . and *unindicted!*

Poe's tale also gives us "The Two Rules of Revenge": First, your adversary has to know it's you who's brought about his defeat and downfall. Second, *you have to get away with it!*

The Craft of Confusion The craft of confusion hinges on our ability to deny our adversary accurate information. This means disguising our intent to do him dirty while providing him with plenty of distracting and disarming disinformation. Thus Sun Tzu's prime maxim: "All warfare is based on deception."

We hold the upper hand when our adversary doesn't see us coming or, better yet, when he (or she) counts us his confidant . . . right up to the moment we strike the telling blow. (Think Iago and Othello.)

Nature punishes the predictable. You have only one time to *bore* Mother Nature before she reaches for the remote and changes the channel—permanently!

Watch a magic trick enough times and, sooner or later, even a dumbass can figure it out.

Disguising your insidious intent means going about your business as if nothing is happening beforehand and afterward, as if nothing has happened. You're as surprised as everyone else in the office about what happened to "poor ol' Al."

When planning an operation, never draw attention to yourself by suddenly changing your routine. Instead, begin varying your routine and habits incrementally, far in advance. The further in advance of your target date, the better.

Sometimes, however, deliberately going out of your way to act strange, conducting activities outside your normal routine is a good way to distract an enemy away from your true objective. This is an especially good ploy when helping draw attention away from the activities of a coconspirator.

Practical seduction application? Use your wingman to distract her posse of cockblocking friends long enough for you to steal her away.

Disinformation throws a monkey wrench into our decision-making machinery. We (should!) make decisions based on "B.A.I."—best available information. However, if your intelligence gathering is flawed, or if someone *deliberately* feeds you false information, your decisions cannot but lead to disaster. (Yeah, he lied his ass off just to get a piece of yours!)

In this "Age of Information" it's becoming increasingly difficult to keep information out of the hands of our adversary, so the next best thing is to supply him with plenty of disinformation.

While you're trying to sell yourself to that blonde in sixty seconds, her (or his) girlfriend/buddy is already Googling you on her iPhone.

Thus, we prepare for battle while helping our adversary *un*-prepare. Sun Tzu 101:

> Long ago warriors knew to make themselves invulnerable while patiently anticipating the enemy's moment of vulnerability.

We accomplish this by feeding our adversary spurious information and skewed facts—either (1) firsthand, because they still foolishly trust us, (2) via a third party they trust, or (3) by planting revelations for them to brag about "discovering" all on their own.

The goal of disinformation is to get your adversary to show up to a gunfight with only a knife. The classic: your office rival shows up at the boss's *formal dress* birthday party wearing a toga because "someone" fed him an erroneous e-mail invitation to a "come-as-your-favorite-dumbass" *masquerade* party!

Get the other guy talking (digging his own grave!) and keep him talking—answering all your questions, providing you with invaluable intelligence. The more *he* talks, the more *you* know. Interrogation 101.

Study chapter 13 of Sun Tzu's *The Art of War* and, Book Three, chapter 2 in Machiavelli's *Discourses,* on how to turn *his* agents into *your* agents, and on how to entice him to embrace your point of view.

> Ethereal and subtle, the master strategist passes by without leaving a trace. Mysterious, like the way of Heaven, he passes

by without a sound. In this way master an enemy's fate.
(San Tzu)

SEDUCTION IN THE SHADOWS

From 1368 to 1644 China was ruled by the Ming Dynasty. In 1644, everything changed when China was conquered by the invading Manchu (a.k.a. Ching).

The Manchus succeeded in subjugating northern China, but in the south stiff resistance sprang up, rallying around a pirate leader named Coxinga. Outwardly, Coxinga threw his support behind the prince of T'ang as Emperor but, de facto, Coxinga ruled south China on both land and sea. Coxinga had spies and agents everywhere, including many criminal gangs and secret societies who threw in with him.

The coming of the Manchu changed how everyone did business, including China's many criminal and Freemason-like secret societies. According to Sterling Seagrave in his Black Science must-read *The Soong Dynasty* (1985):

> There have always been such secret societies [in China], piratical bands, and esoteric sects. But until the seventeenth century, they were fragmented and iconoclastic. The year of the Manchu conquest, 1644, was a watershed. After that a new network of secret societies spread across the landscape, dedicated to unhorsing the Manchus. (p. 72)

Monks and Mystery Men

You probably don't think of "holy" monks and monasteries when you think about seduction. But maybe you should.

Every history ever written on Asian martial arts always mentions the pivotal part played by the Shaolin monks. The twenty-eighth Indian Buddhist patriarch Bodhidharma (Tamo) is credited with founding the Shaolin Order; its original monastery was located in the Songhan Mountains in Henan Province, China.

Bodhidharma traveled from his native India in 520 C.E. to what was then a Taoist monastery near Foochow, where, after meditating for nine years staring at a wall, he had a revelation, out of which he formed Zen Buddhism.

What Bodhidharma taught was called *Dyana* ("meditation") in India. In China this sitting meditation technique was called *Shan* (Ch'an), a word that means meditation but which is also a play on *Shan* ("mountain") because a monk sitting upright and still in meditation takes on the shape of a mountain. In Japan, Ch'an is written "Zen."

Zen grew out of a fusion of indigenous Chinese Taoism and Indian Buddhism—both of which have a long and curious history of studying—and practicing—*sex* as a means toward both enlightenment and immortality.

As part of his system Bodhidharma taught the monks a form of Indian martial arts designed to help strengthen them for staying awake during marathon meditation sessions. Originally known as "Eighteen-Hands of Lo-han" *(Lo-Han* being another name for "monks"), he taught these "kung fu" exercises only for "medicinal purposes" . . . and never intended they should ever be used to kick serious ass. Or so the legend goes. He is therefore honored in Asian martial arts circles as "the (Grand) Father of the martial arts."

Part of this martial arts training included exercises known as *Xi sui jing* ("bone and marrow washing") and *Yi ji jing* ("muscle and tendon change").

As the years passed, several Shaolin monasteries, including the one at Foochow, fell out of imperial favor and were literally burned to the ground on the orders of the reigning emperor—only to win favor again and be rebuilt by a subsequent emperor. For example, during the Tang Dynasty (618–906), Shaolin came to the rescue of Emperor Li Shimin, who rewarded his saviors by casting a three-sided ("triad") imperial seal honoring their order. It is from this three-sided emblem that the dread Triads, the so-called Chinese "mafia," would one day take its name.

By the time of the Ming Dynasty (1368–1644) Shaolin had over three thousand warrior-monks. Like everybody else, the Shaolin Order was greatly affected by the Manchu conquest in 1644:

> Coxinga's resistance movement included a powerful spy system and underground. After his death, his underground fragmented. But 128 militant Buddhist monks, who were part of the resistance, held out against the Manchu army at the Shaolin monastery near Foochow. They were unusually skilled at the martial art that is now called Kung Fu. A traitor betrayed them to the Manchus, and only 18 escaped.
>
> One by one, the heroic monks were tracked down until only 5 remained. These 5 Kung Fu masters became the nucleus of a new anti-Manchu resistance, which was organized along the lines of the ancient sects and pirate guilds of

classical China. It was given the name Hung League after the first Ming Emperor, Hung Wu. (Ibid., 73)

This Hung League's rally cry was *"Fan ch'ing fu Ming,"* "Down with the Ching, up with the Ming!"

Ironic that the Shaolin Order of "peaceful" Buddhist monks should give birth to the Hung League, which, in turn, would give birth to every cut-throat Chinese criminal secret society that was to follow, including the ruthless Chinese Triad "mafia"!

As already mentioned, secret societies had a long tradition in China, long before the Manchu conquest of 1644. These secretive organizations were divided into two types: (1) *religious-motivated* groups (*Chiao*), and (2) *political and/or criminally motivated* secret societies (*Hui*).

Some were both. For example, in the pre-Manchu period, the most active secret society, the White Lotus Society, straddled the fence between religion and politics, once described as "originally a militant, messianic Buddhist order" (Hucker, 1975).

After the Manchu invasion, secret society activity, both Chiao and Hui, increased as unrest intensified, especially following the death of Coxinga in 1662. Throughout the 1700s, up into the first half of the nineteenth century, uprisings continued.

Even before the Shaolin Order was scattered to the four winds, Shaolin "secrets" of martial arts and "mysticism" (i.e., strategy and seduction) had already begun spilling out into the world at large.

Originally, for teaching purposes, this Brotherhood of Bodhidharma organized their knowledge into three training "Halls" that overlapped and complemented one another: *Ying Gong, Chi Gong,* and *Jing Gong.*

- *Ying Gong*: "Body toughening", consisted of calisthenics and yogalike exercises designed to strengthen the body. These were those exercises originally taught by Bodhidharma in order to help the Shaolin brothers stay awake during marathon meditation sessions. The focus was/is on strengthening the body *outwardly,* in order that the student could withstand the rigors of monastery life and/or survive in a physical threat situation when called upon to do so.
- *Chi Gong*: "Internal training" strengthened the internal organs and helped increase the student's overall "balance," both inside and out. These exercises purified and cleansed the internal organs and systems of the body, increasing overall health. Chi Gong also helped the

practitioner reduce stress, relax, and cultivate "chi" energy. Once a student had mastered the basics of Chi Gong, they graduated to Tai Chi *(Dai Qi Quan)* exercises—taught first as calming and balancing exercises, only later at a more advanced level was the more mature student shown the martial arts application.

- *Jing Gong:* "Senses training" is designed to increase a student's overall awareness through using their five senses fully. At this level, the student's previous forging of a *strong body-mind connection and awareness* is expanded. As a result, the student's adroitness of mind expands exponentially as the student masters first his own mind, and then develops the power to master the minds of others through strategy and seduction.

Secrets of the Black Lotus

"Even the most beautiful woman in the world, if she stands beside a lake will frighten the fish, and if she walks through the woods the deer will be startled and flee."
—Ancient Chinese saying

In December 1898, the wives of the seven major Western ambassadors to China received an invitation from the sixty-three-year-old Manchu Empress Dowager Tzu-Hsi, who was hosting a banquet in their honor in her Forbidden City palace

By the 1890s the West had begun to carve up "the weak man of Asia," as they referred to China. Realizing that facing down these Western "invaders" with stubborn "steel" was not an option, Chinese strategists began adopting a "silk" attitude.

The Empress Dowager took power earlier in 1898 after her twenty-seven-year-old reform-minded nephew had suddenly—mysteriously—taken ill.

The empress was not reform-minded, nor was she as disposed as her nephew to placate the Western powers. Point in fact, the empress' nephew had conspired to arrest and possibly assassinate his aunt. Discovering the plot, she had turned the tables, arresting him first and forcing him (under threat of death) to give up his throne. But then, in an effort to save face, she created the convenient fiction that he had taken ill.

A tiny woman, she was also a wily woman with a cruel streak who had risen from obscurity to become the concubine of a previous emperor and had then managed over the years to accumulate great power until she became the most feared person in China (Greene, 2001:267).

On this night, she ordered the Western diplomats' wives brought to the Forbidden City in splendid sedan chairs carried by impressive-looking court eunuchs in dazzling uniforms.

At the Audience Hall the wives were greeted by various Chinese princes and princesses, as well as other royalty, all in their best dress.

The wives were first served tea in the most delicate of porcelain cups, and then they were escorted into the presence of the empress, seated high on her jewel-encrusted Dragon Throne. Seated below her on a smaller throne was her pale—silent (probably drugged!)—nephew.

Uncharacteristically, breaking Chinese tradition, the empress shook the hand of each woman. As she did so, an attendant eunuch handed her a large gold ring set with a large pearl, which she slipped on each woman's hand.

The wives were then escorted through a grand, ornate archway into another room, deeper within the palace, where they again took tea, before they were led into a banquet hall.

Here the empress sat in a chair of yellow satin facing west—yellow being the royal color.

She spoke to them for a while through a translator. Then she again took the hand of each woman one by one and repeated, "One family, all one family."

The women then watched a special performance in the Imperial theatre. Finally the empress received them one last time with one more round of tea. This time, the empress first touched the tea to her own lips and took a sip, then lifted the tea cup on the other side to each of their lips, repeating, "One family, all one family."

Finally the women were given more gifts before being returned to their homes in sedan chairs.

As intended, the ambassadors' wives all gave glowing reports about the empress to their husbands, who, in turn, passed these favorable impressions along to their respective governments, quelling fears about the "evil" intentions of the empress.

On the basest level, we can see this little "get-together" as an attempt to create a little positive PR designed to convince Westerners that the empress wasn't all that bad. And it succeeded.

However, those few familiar with Chinese secret society rituals will instantly recognize this display for what it was: a Black Lotus initiation ceremony!

From early on in their history, Chinese Triads used various recognition signals to help identify themselves to one another in public without attracting undue attention. The best known of these rituals was the subtle arrangement of teacups on a table. Depending on the number of cups, how much tea was left in each, and the juxtaposition of the cups in relation to one another and in relation to where they were placed on the table (together, apart, aligned with the four directions, etc.) Triad members could convey complicated messages to one another.

Likewise, the ritual sharing of tea (a sign of trust and brotherhood) was an intricate part of all such ceremonies.

As with the Triads, so too with The Black Lotus.

What Greene (2001:269) refers to as "the little drama with the sharing of the teacups" was an elaborately staged seduction.

Whether these diplomats' wives were consciously aware of it or not, they had just been initiated into the Black Lotus—from the empress' point of view, a great honor. Consider:

- The women were carried to the ceremony in sedan chairs, likewise, the Black Lotus initiate is ritually carried into the initiation hall— symbolic of a sacrificial victim being carried to the altar for slaughter ("death" of former self).
- That handshake, so uncharacteristically Chinese, served a dual purpose. First, a gesture from the empress showing that she was open to "Western ways," i.e., handshaking rather than a traditional Asian bow. More importantly, special handshakes (such as those used by Freemasons and others) can allow an adept to gauge the other person's pulse, sweating—truthfulness! (Lung, 2007:120)
- Three rounds of tea, the final culminating in the empress actually sharing a sip of tea from the same cup as her guests, a sign of being full brothers, or in this case sisters, in the secret society.
- The giving of gold rings, single pearl on top—symbolizing a flawless pearl (disciple) afloat on a sea of gold (greed), symbol of the Black Lotus!

It has oft been argued (mostly by women) that "history" is just that: *his-story*, that the womanly gender has been woefully underrepresented in history. While this may be true overall, when it comes to plying the Black Science, female adepts are not hard to come by—both East and West.

The Bible, for instance, is full of scheming wives, witches, wenches, and women warriors beginning with Eve* ("I was framed!"), down through that horny Egyptian wife who tried to jump Joseph's bones; from dauntless Deborah and dazzling Esther, to that bad-to-the-jaw-bone-of-an-ass barber Delilah. There's king-wooing Bathsheba, headhunting Salome, and Jezebel, whose name has become synonymous with the kind of woman you definitely don't want to take home to Mother!

Outside religious mythology, we find naughty nautical entrepreneur Helen of Troy; toxic Lucrezia Borgia; Elizabeth, the "Virgin Queen" (though Sir Francis Drake and Shakespeare might have something to say about that!); equine enthusiast Catherine the Great; and Hillary Clinton—who tried to ride a jackass into the White House *twice!*

In the East as well there were—are—women both noteworthy and notorious, seductive and seditious.

The ideals of the Eastern beauty—the Japanese geisha, the Chinese concubine—will forever fascinate the fantasy bone of the West. While we cannot help but be captivated by their beauty, there are all too many historical glimpses as well of the will and wile—and, yes, wickedness—lying just below the surface, venom behind the veil, steel beneath the silk.

In fiction, there's the Middle Eastern melodic-voiced bride Scheherazade of *1001 Arabian Nights,* mesmerizing her husband with her tales. Further east, one of the most dreadful cults ever spawned, the dreaded *Thuggee* of India, were brazen killers who worshipped not a burly war-god, but rather the black-tongued, fierce-eyed bitch-goddess Kali. (See Lung, 1995.)

Then there's the insightful twelfth-century female Tantric Master Mahadeviyakka already mentioned. Another Indian mover and shaker, twentieth-century Indira Gandhi, ruled willfully and well, until her woeful assassination in 1984.

The Chinese had their classical heroine Mulan (yeah, that 1998 Disney cartoon was based on a real woman), as well as scores of twentieth-century Red Guard women warriors. Madame Mao we've already mentioned.

---

*Some "Lost Books of the Bible" maintain that Adam had a wife *before* Eve named Lilith, whom Adam cast out of the Garden of Eden and who went on to become—literally—the mother of all demons, vampires, and every other bloodsucker and succubus that haunts the night.

And while we always hear about the "Brothers" of Shaolin, that Order had a nuns' branch as well. In fact it was a Shaolin Buddhist nun who taught runaway bride Yim Wing Chun the art of Shaolin kung fu boxing, allowing her to fight her way out of a forced marriage. Today there is a martial art that still bears her name: *Wing Chun,* the art that launched Bruce Lee's career.

Like Wing Chun, the martial art and the woman, women in China (as perhaps women everywhere) learned to master the concept of *Shun,* which literally means "compliance" but which implies "going with the flow," being at one with the great t'ai chi universal order.

Knowing they couldn't fight a superior force, one possessing superior strength, these sisters adopted the philosophy of "give way in order to get your way," the judo principle.

Chinese women didn't need Sun Tzu to tell them: "When strong, appear weak."

Shaolin nuns took Sun Tzu's philosophy, the fighting arts they had learned inside the monastery, and everything else they could carry as they fled along with everyone else from the 1644 Manchu invasion.

And like their brother monks, those nuns who survived the Manchu massacre of Shaolin are credited with (or else stand accused of) having founded their own Triad—the Black Lotus—a secret society carrying on a tradition begun long ago by other Chinese women:

> "There had long been a female secret society in China, with branches throughout the rest of Asia, organized for the exclusive purpose of assassinating or otherwise punishing men."
> (Seagrave, 1985.261)

It's true that various Triads already had female members, or at least female auxiliaries, and that they often used female agents is well known. That a separate Triad—actually several loosely linked female Triads—existed (and are rumored to still exist in China and in other parts of Asia), is not that widely known or even admitted by those who do know.* While most trace the existence of this secretive sisterhood to the fall of Shaolin, other experts argue the Black Lotus (but one of many names it has been called—other include "Celestial Sisters," the "Ever-Empty Cup," the "Silk Toush," and "The Silk-Wrapped Blade") had its true origin far before the founding and falling of Shaolin. These researchers find hints, allegations,

---

*"Those who know, do not speak. Those who speak, do not know."

and veiled references to the existence of such a sisterhood stretching far back into China's history, with influences flowing both to and from all other parts of Asia.

Some researchers have traced at least elements of Black Lotus philosophy and mythology back to India, linking the Chinese secret society with the special all-female bodyguard created to protect fourth-century B.C.E. Indian Emperor Chandragupta. (See India Section)

Others are content to trace the origins of the Black Lotus back to the master of all strategists, Sun Tzu (a.k.a. Sun Wu, 544 B.C.E.–496).

The tale is told of how after spending years learning what was wrong with Chinese war strategies of the time, young Sun Wu presented himself before King Ho Lu of the kingdom of Wu, declaring that he had devised a new, quicker and more effective way of training troops. Sun Wu humbly requested an officer's commission and a "small" army of his own so as to be able to prove his new tactics.

Ho Lu was amused by this young warrior's bold claims and challenged Sun Wu as to whether or not his new training and tactics could be used to train *any* troops? When Sun Wu confidently replied "Yes," Ho Lu presented Sun Wu with a group of his giggling royal concubines "You have one month to train these women to be soldiers. If your methods are all that miraculous, you should have no problem doing so," Ho Lu told Sun Wu.

Without protest, Sun Wu bowed, "I shall do so not in one month, but in one week!"

Having gathered the women aside, Sun Wu handed each of them a spear and arranged them into ranks. He then proceeded to drill them, "March forward, left, right . . ." However, every time Sun Wu gave an order, the women would only giggle all the more.

Finally Sun Wu asked the women, "Who is the King's favorite among you?" In response the most beautiful concubine stepped forward, still giggling.

Without another word, Sun Wu decapitated her with a single stroke of his sword!

Within one week, as promised, Sun Wu had trained the remaining women so well that Ho Lu made them his personal bodyguard and made Sun Wu (now "Sun Tzu," Master Sun) his number-one general!

Those researchers with a decidedly more "occult" bent have gone so far as to accuse the sisterhood of supernatural origins, something the Black Lotus did (does) nothing to discourage. Thus, in the same way China's Moshuh Nanren "ninja" never discouraged the belief they were descended from Lin Kuei, "forest demons," so, too, Black Lotus sisters never discouraged tales tracing them back to, and placing them in league with, the much feared clans of I'zi-bu (Caibu) . . . vampires!

Pronounced T'zee-boo, T'zi-bu, Caibu bloodsuckers like Western vampires, they are "psychic vampires" who live off the life force of others. Indeed, the name literally means "taking the essence of another."* Caibu are more comparable to the Western succubi—demons who seduce men by appearing in the guise of beautiful women.**

That beliefs linking the Black Lotus to supernatural goings-on would be perpetuated (outside of sisterhood propaganda, that is) testifies to the suspicion and fear with which common folk viewed even the mere existence of such a secretive order.

Perhaps the most ancient tale told of the origins of The Black Lotus sisterhood traces them back to the ancient Chinese goddess Nuwa, a goddess who once repaired a great hole in the sky (perhaps a reference to an eclipse?).

To this day, a statue of goddess Nuwa is said to occupy a sacred niche in all Black Lotus sanctuaries.

The story is also told (as a cautionary tale for men) of how the first emperor of China once gazed upon a beautiful statue of Nuwa and fantasized about having sex with her. In response, the statute suddenly came to life and spit on him, causing a hideous growth to sprout on his face that remained for forty-nine days. (See *Tales of Emperor Qin Shihuag* by Yuan and Xiao [Foreign Language Press, Beijing, 1997].)

Mount Li was sacred to Nuwa and remains so to The Black Lotus, often being listed as the society's place of origin.

That this Black Lotus sisterhood existed prior to Shaolin is likely, given China's proclivity for secret societies in general. But the truth as to whether the Black Lotus originated in China or was imported from elsewhere may forever remain obscured behind a silken black curtain of coy and convoluted cunning and craft.

---

*See *Mind Control* (2006: 244) for a more detailed discussion of T'zi-bu and their connection to the Moshuh Nanren "ninja" of China.

**Lest we discriminate, there are iccubi who perform pretty much the same services for women.

We do know for a fact that similar secretive sororities have thrived in Japan for centuries. Whether these were influenced by—or may in fact be legitimate branches of—the Black Lotus must forever remain shrouded in mystery.

We do know Shinobi Ninja clans fielded *kuniochi,* female agents every bit as deadly as their male counterparts. Likewise, Yakuza also employ(ed) women—agents, prostitutes, perhaps your cleaning lady!—to gather information, to leave the right door unlocked at the right time, perhaps to slip a little something extra in your morning tea or martini.

Japan's "Floating World" of the geisha was/is also an exclusive sorority adept at keeping their own feline confidences, purring pleasantries while lapping up the confessions—dreams and (mis)deeds—of their clients.

And then there are the *Miko.*

The Chinese phrase *Shen-tao,* meaning "spirit way," becomes Shinto when written in the same characters in Japanese. Shinto ("Way of the Gods") is the ancestor-worshipping state religion of Japan whose roots can be traced back to ancient Asian animism and shamanism.

Shen-tao originally referred to spirits and to spirit worship. Like so many things Chinese, Shen-tao was eventually adapted to fit Japanese sensibilities.

That Japan owes much of its early development to China is well documented. Japan's bureaucracy, much of its religious thought (particularly Buddhism), and many of its arts and crafts came from China. Political intrigue, already a Chinese specialty, also found its way to Japan, or some say, *had* its way with Japan!

For example, prior to the sixth century, the ruler of the Yamato was only a local warlord, wielding power over a bunch of contentious clans. But during the sixth century, reaping the bounty of seeds secretly sown centuries before, the Yamato succeeded in dominating all the other clans and ultimately uniting them into a single kingdom.

Before long the Yamato king had adopted a new title, taken from the Chinese: *Ten'o*—"Heavenly Emperor"!

Let's back up a little, since most experts agree that the foundations for this Yamato unification had been laid three centuries earlier. In the third century C.E., the crown of the Yamato leader had been seized by a woman named Himiko. Sometimes written Pimiko, or simply Miko, Himiko was a powerful shaman, believed by friend and foe alike to possess magical powers (a belief she did everything she could to encourage). Somewhere between casting sinister spells with her left hand and wielding a sharp sword in her right, Himiko became the undisputed leader of the Yamato, becoming Japan's blend of Boudicca and Joan of Arc.

In fact, some suspect the meteoric rise of the Yamato to have been a plot by Black Lotus backers to take advantage of Japanese belief in the magical power of their Miko to set up a rival (counterbalance) to the Chinese Imperial Court—allowing them, in effect, to rule Japan by proxy. Others go so far as accusing Himiko herself of having been a member of the Black Lotus, and perhaps a Chinese agent provocateur.

Not only did she become ruler of the Yamato and materfamilias of the Imperial lineage, she also became the spiritual founder and inspiration for a secretive shamanistic sisterhood whose name derives from her name: Himiko-Miko!

Today "Miko" are Japanese female shamans and psychics who possess knowledge of *Kagaku,* "The Ancient Learning," believed to be a form of powerful nature magic.

Some Miko are *itako* (a.k.a. *ichiko),* often-blind spirit mediums, human oracles *(takusen)* through which *kami* (nature spirits) and the spirits of the dead instruct the living.

It's not hard to see how even a minor Miko oracle might all too easily influence events—alliances, state marriages, even whether or not a clan or a country should would go to war. In fact, similar allegations of having been a Chinese agent provocateur have been lodged against Japan's first ninja, Otomo Shinobi, spy and confidant to Prince Shotoku during his sixth-century war of succession.

Miko still exist today in parts of Japan. For example, it is a local custom that all women in Okinawa upon reaching thirty are initiated as *nanchu* (the equivalent of miko) in a solemn ceremony called *izaiho* held every twelve years around the middle of November by the old lunar calendar.

Whether the Miko of Japan and similar sisterhoods scattered throughout Asia—some serene, some sinister—were birthed by the scheming of the Black Lotus depends on whose scroll you read. Some maintain that the Miko and other feminine Asian fellowships influenced the origin, development, and diffusion of the Black Lotus.

Whatever the truth of their origins, one thing remains constant: the overall art of strategy and tactics employed by all such successful sisterhoods.

And that art is, first and foremost, truly the Art of Seduction. To accomplish this, the Black Lotus concentrated on the three Shaolin disciplines of Ying Gong, Jing Gong, and Chi Gong to perfect body and mind, to balance yin and yang.

These three disciplines were practiced to varying degrees by different cadre depending on individual mind-set and collective motivation: For the more physical minded, for practical reasons, there was an emphasis on Ying Gong—"steel" body toughening and Shaolin kung fu fighting technique. The more cerebrally oriented preferred to follow the wise Buddha's Chi Gong observation that "Your best weapon is in your enemy's mind." Thus, all secret societies try to wrap themselves in a "silk" cloak of mystery. This is done to discourage scrutiny and for protection—*Reputation spills less blood*!

Like many shadowy groups, the Black Lotus were believed by outsiders to possess mystical powers. Some of this belief came from outsiders' own superstitious fear, while other such tales were the result of pure propaganda and self-promotion on the part of the Black Lotus PR department.

Cultivating superstitious awe and/or promising to bestow supernatural powers on the worthy was/is a marvelous cult recruiting tool. Still today, cults promise to teach recruits how to "open their third eye" and unleash their "hidden mystic powers."

In the East, shadow-knights like the Assassins, India's Thuggee, China's Lin Kuei, and Japan's ninja all knew the advantage of playing on their enemies' superstitions, of feeding their foes malarkey about their possessing magical powers to shape-shift, walk through walls, and of being able to kill with "The Death Touch" (Lung, 1998).

The Chinese Boxer rebels of 1900 used dazzling displays of Shaolin-based martial arts, sleight-of-hand magic, and techniques of hypnosis and mind manipulation to terrorize enemies and pull in recruits.

More often than not the "magical powers" exhibited by such cadre were simply a full use of a person's abilities which—to the indolent and inattentive—appeared magical.

ZIZHI-DAO: THE ART OF CONTROL

That which is decent in Japan is indecent in Rome, and what is fashionable in Paris is not so in Peking.
—Voltaire

Every gigolo knows the more in control you are, the better lover you are. Likewise every general knows the more control he has over the battlefield—and over himself—the greater his odds of winning. As on the battlefield, so in the bedroom.

Zizhi-dao (pronounced dzee-gee-dow) in Chinese means "The Art of Control." "Control" refers to *external* control of our lives (by fortune, fate, gods, and governments). But Zizhi-dao also applies to the amount of *personal* control we exert over our lives, which is directly dependent upon the amount of *attention* we give ourselves and our environment.

Gaining more personal control over our lives means (1) taking more responsibility, as well as (2) disciplining and (3) challenging ourselves both physically and mentally before our environment and/or our adversaries do:

> *Test yourself with fire and ice, sand and sea, bile and blood, before*
> *your enemies do.*
> **—Hannibal Barca**

In the East, control over your physical health and safety is often accomplished by mastering one of the many martial arts. In China, what we in the West call kung fu is called *"wu shu"* (war art). Kung fu (sometimes written *gung fu* or even *gong fu*) actually means both "hard work" and the "mastery" that comes from that hard work. Kung fu thus applies to *mental* arts as well—both the mental control (discipline) we exercise over ourselves and the influence (cunning and force of will) we use as strategy and seduction.

To successfully influence and overshadow another's mind—whether a military foe (through our use of propaganda and strategy), a mugger on the street, some authority trying to grill us concerning our whereabouts on the night in question, or that fine filly at the bar, we use what the Chinese call *"gancui"* (pronounced *gang-kway)* which literally translated means "to penetrate neatly and completely," to "get inside the head" of our target.

Getting inside an adversary's head means trying to figure out where he's "coming from" (his likes, dislikes, fears, etc.) and then jamming disturbing and doubt-ridden thoughts, images, and paralyzing emotions (like fear and lust) directly into his brain. No matter if you're facing an adversary on a physical battlefield or a battlefield of the mind; the principles of victory remain the same. So, too, from the battlefield to the bedroom.

Black Lotus teachers first taught their students to control their own minds—"to develop minds like water" before teaching them *Ping-Fa* strategy designed to help them control the minds of others.

Zizhi-dao, when applied specifically to mind penetration, is also known as *I-Hsing,* the "Mind Fist" (not be confused with the respected Chinese martial art *Hsinq-I).*

Hsing-I kung fu (a.k.a. *Yueh Fei Ch'uan),* founded by Chinese military hero Yueh Fei during the Sung Dynasty (960–1280 C.E.), is a formidable fighting style of *kung fu wu shu* that emphasizes grace and economy of movement, with powerful straight-line fist attacks.

Sun Yat Sen (Sun Wen), architect of the 1911 revolution and first (and last) president of the short-lived Chinese Republic, was a master of Hsing-I. And, judging by his masterful juggling of the volatile politics and the various fiery personalities contending for control of China during those explosive times, Sun Yat Sen must also have been an initiate if not an adept at the mental art of I-Hsing.

I-Hsing, the mental art of the Mind Fist, is often studied hand in hand with Hsing-I, the more physical side of the equation. The balance of healthy mind/healthy body is respected in both East and West.

It was Chinese *Hsi Hao* mind-manipulation techniques being used on Western Korean War POWs that turned "brainwashing" into a household word in the West. Many of these techniques were believed to be derived from (or at least associated with) this ancient art of I-Hsing.

Down through China's colorful history, various cadre have used a vast array of mind-control techniques—some to gain control over self, some to rule over others; some for the betterment of their fellows, some for the debasement of their fellows. These tactics and techniques range from the profound self-mastery secrets of ancient Taoist immortals, to tactics of intrigue and intimidation wielded by Moshuh Nanren "ninja," through masterful strategies from accomplished generals like Sun Tzu and Cao Cao, down to twentieth-century skullduggery by secret societies and criminal cadre of every ilk.

Six Senses: Ying Gong and Jing Gong

There are even senses that are never used.
—Voltaire

With self-mastery of your own mind soon comes (the temptation of) mastering the minds of others. There are thus thin lines between magic, mysticism, and true mind control. Whereas the first two can all too easily be faked, true mind control requires first exorcising our own demons before learning to exercise the demons inside our adversary's head!

Like many who find their succor in the shadows, the Black Lotus realized that if their enemies believed they possessed a "sixth sense" that included abilities of mind reading and mind control, such belief would create an added layer of hesitation between them and their enemies.

Developing the full use of your five given senses makes it appear to our more indolent, ignorant, and superstition-prone adversaries that we possess a magical "sixth sense"—ESP, if you will. Thus the Chinese motto: "Sow five, harvest six," meaning that mastery of our five given senses will grant us use of that elusive "sixth" sense.

Many Black Lotus techniques for mind control and manipulation have been lost or still remain hidden to outsiders. Fortunately, many other of their techniques have been revealed and preserved.

So far twenty-first-century scientific discoveries have only served to prove what ancient Taoist masters, Shaolin priests, and Black Lotus adepts intuited about the potential—the powers!—to be gleaned by giving our five senses our full attention.

Nothing will benefit us more than actually devoting the time and attention it takes to actually develop our own mind. We begin by making our initial goal the full mastering of our mundane five senses. And if along the way during our struggle up the food chain we inexplicably discover ourselves with the ability to "hear" other peoples' thoughts, to bend them to our bidding through our "intense" mesmerizing gaze alone, and if objects suddenly start levitating around the room . . . well, I'm sure we'll never ever be tempted into using such special mind powers for *selfish, evil, twisted* gain . . . Heh-heh-heh.

It's a simple formula: *Sensation* leads to *Recognition,* which in turn leads to *Thought* and *Action:*

Sensation ⟶ Recognition ⟶ Thought/Action.

The trouble is, in between what our senses encounter (sensations) and what our brain actually ends up taking in (recognizes and decides to think about) are:

- *Physical diseases or defects* in our senses that prevent this second stage from taking place (e.g., hearing loss, varying degrees of blindness)

- *Psychological detours and defects* that can interfere with what messages our brain sends to the rest of our body

If you've read *Mind Manipulation* (2002), *Mind Control* (2006), *Mind Penetration* (2007), and/or *Mind Fist* (2008), or if you've at least managed to stay awake during the first half of *this* book, then you know most people can't trust their everyday senses. However we can gain more mastery—perhaps even complete mastery—over our senses. At the very least, we should aim to make our senses our servants, rather than our remaining a slave to them.

According to Dr. Anthony Zaffuto, author of *Alphagenics: How to Use Your Brain Waves to Improve Your Life,* the key to gaining full control (full awareness) of your senses is to, (1) close off all sensory input, and then, (2) focus and concentrate all your attention on one sense at a time (Zaffuto, 1974:31). This is the same method used for centuries by mind masters and mystics of the East, the basis for all mind-control disciplines (e.g., meditation and self-hypnosis), which were taught to students first at Shaolin, and then by Black Lotus cadre as part of their overall Jing Gong training.

In order for us today in the West to gain better control of our senses, it's first important to understand that despite popular belief and pop psychology to the contrary, there's no such thing as "multitasking." Your mind can only consciously concentrate on one thing at a time. Our goal is therefore to train (program and reprogram) our mind to switch back and forth seamlessly, and to race along the myriad of synaptic connections within our brain (1) faster and (2) with more direction and purpose in order to (3) process incoming sense information as effortlessly, expediently, and efficiently as possible.

Why bother to "master" your senses? First, for protection. The more aware you are of your surroundings, the better your odds of outwitting, outlasting, outfighting your adversaries. And the only way to be more aware of your surroundings is to increase the attention you give your surroundings via your senses: seeing, hearing, smelling, tasting, and touching your environment.

Sun Tzu's "Know yourself, know your enemy, and know your environment" can all be satisfied by simply paying more attention to our five senses.

Mastering our senses makes us more "at one" with our surroundings—upping our odds of finding shelter, weapons, and food when survival calls for it . . . and a Frisbee mate when "Little Willie needs to go for a walk" (wink-wink).

In a battlefield situation, being more aware of the environment can mean the difference between life and death. In other words, a fuller use of your senses enriches our life, be it on the battlefield or in the bedroom.

But if survivin' and thrivin' aren't good enough reasons for mastering your senses, what if we told you it would improve your sex life? Ah! Now that we have your *full* attention . . .

It's no secret that many of China's Jing Gong practices derived from Indian yoga.

Left-handed Tantra adepts practiced "sensory awareness" exercises that allowed them to direct their prana (breath/vital energy) to different parts of their bodies. This is similar to the way a Chinese chi-master can direct his chi-flow simply by willpower alone. This ability to direct prana/chi flow greatly enhances any experience, but especially sexual pleasure.

Let's face it: For most men, untrained in the arts of lovemaking, sex is a dick thing. In other words, their orgasm is 99 percent centered in their penis. They are most sensitive (literally) to sensations (pleasure) generated from contact between the glans (head) of their penis as it rubs against something—anything! For most men, therefore, "sex" consists simply of finding something—again, *anything!*—to rub the head of the penis against (or preferably, *inside*) that will produce the maximum amount of friction to stimulate their penis. They do so until the sensation actually becomes too "painful." You see the human brain has a hard time distinguishing extreme pleasure from extreme pain since both are simply sensory overload.

At the point at which this stimulus overload can no longer be tolerated, the brain releases massive amounts of painkilling endorphins ("happy chemicals") directly into the bloodstream. The resulting "orgasm" (release from pain) is then felt throughout the body. But most men concentrate this orgasm in their penis, since that's the "tool" that took them there.

Male tantra disciples first learn to prolong/delay their orgasm—the longer the buildup, the more intense the orgasm, right? (Any teenager realizes that after just his first wet dream!)

But step two in tantric sex training is learning to move the locus (area of concentration) of the orgasm to other areas of the body. In other words, rather than concentrating the orgasm only in the penis (sex organ), the tantric master can achieve an orgasm in any of the other eight remaining Nine Gates.

This is possible because recent scientific discoveries have determined that, since all physical sensation is first channeled (filtered) through the brain, *all orgasms take place in the brain.* Thus the brain is our ultimate sex organ!

Seems Western science is just now catching up with what ancient tantric masters already knew: that by learning to control the flow of your consciousness (focus and concentration), you can have an orgasm centered in any part of your body. No need to imagine the possibilities—we're going to teach you all about them!

By the way, focus and concentration are not synonymous. *Focus* refers to our "tightening" one of our senses (or our overall mind), sharpening it to a pinpoint of attention directed at a singular, particular thought or object. Sometimes we call this "lusting."

Concentration means holding that captured thought or object with our mind and within our mind (focused sense) for some period of time. Think of it this way: *focus* is how we thrust the blade . . . *concentration* is how we twist it in the wound!

An increase in our overall focus and concentration is both the way in which we strengthen our senses and the by-product of doing so. Thus, mastering our five senses literally begins and ends with focusing and concentrating on each of our senses in turn:

> ***Eyes given to see are not always open.***
> **—Voltaire**

Opening the Eye-Gate Open any book on optical illusions and, in short order, you'll realize you can never trust your eyes again! But actually it's your brain you can't trust, because it is the gatekeeper and interpreter of what your eyes take in.

The brain always chooses the easiest and quickest path to identifying something. Only later, when the brain is sure the object poses no danger, does it relax and return for a second, closer, look. This explains why you jumped that time you thought you saw a dangerous snake in the grass, but it turned out to be a piece of harmless garden hose.

Sometimes we "see" things that aren't there. Other times our *untrained* brain misses things—important, possibly dangerous things that are right in front of our face. So it's not like we're starting from square one in trying to improve our senses . . . we're actually starting from a *deficit* position!

We need to train ourselves to "see" better and comprehend better what we are seeing. That is why all too often would-be seducers "look" at a woman (or at a man), ogling her without actually "seeing" her body language. Likewise, on the battlefield, if we only see what our enemy wants us to see, before long we might not be seeing anything . . . ever again!

Begin by studying every optical illusion book you can get your hands on—especially, Al Seckel's *Incredible Visual Illusions,* Chartwell Books, 2005. Learn how magic tricks work. Go to live magic shows and expect to be tricked because you *are* going to be tricked. Practice catching the ol' switcheroo, the misdirection. (Stop staring at the "lovely assistant" in the skimpy tights. That's where the magician wants you to look, dummy!)

Consider this: At a live magic show you expect to be fooled and you're watching intently for the "trick" . . . and you *still* get fooled. How much easier is it to fool a person when they're *not* watching out for it? Not expecting it out on the street or in your place of business? On the battlefield? In the bedroom? You need to take the same attitude you cultivated at the magic show back out into the real world: You *are* going to be tricked. So watch for it. Train your eyes (and your brain) to see trouble coming. Paranoia can be profitable.

Here's a couple of Jing Gong eye-strengthening exercises to start with. Actually, they're more attention-strengthening exercises:

- *Object-Spotting Exercise:* Have a friend place a couple dozen small, everyday objects on a table between you. Now close your eyes while he adds or removes or otherwise rearranges these objects. Opening your eyes, try to determine what's different.

This exercise helps train your eyes (brain) to better spot what's missing or what's "out of place" or when a novel variable has been added to the landscape. (Cheater's hint: With your eyes closed, listen carefully and you will be able to approximate where on the table your friend changes things. This helps train your sense of hearing.)

- *Shape-Spotting Exercise:* Walk down the street or through a park during the day and try to spot all the objects shaped like circles. Later walk the same path and look for square shapes. Now try triangles—harder, huh? How about diamond shapes? Harder still. Retrace your route at different times of the day. Shadows look different in the morning than at high noon, than they do in the afternoon. What about at twilight, and again at night? Notice how varying degrees of light and shadow—chiaroscuro—play tricks on your eyes.

In the dark, new shapes—islands of light and circles of shadow—appear where none existed during the day. These shadows can hide a person standing just inside a doorway or trick the eyes into seeing false doorways—safe havens where none truly exist. Your eyes are dazzled and confused by the changes and, as your mind struggles to "make sense" of contradictory information your adversary closes in . . .

What you thought was a trash can turns out to be a squatting homeless man. Those two trees over there? Perhaps one is that stranger you saw earlier in the day, but in the dark his silhouette resembles just another tree . . .

Study to survive. Survive to thrive.

- Mind's Eye Exercise: Concentrate on Figure 15 (page 81) for a full minute. Now close your eyes and practice holding the "after-image" in your mind's eye for as long as possible. Don't be discouraged when the image eventually fades. That's normal. The goal is to keep the afterimage in your mind's eye for longer periods of time.

In India, this is called a yantra. Yantra range from the simplest—a dot, or circle—to incredibly complex images known as "mandalas." In practical use this kind of exercise trains your eyes to keep more complicated images (such as a park scene) in your mind's eye for longer periods of time, giving your mind a chance to file away its initial impressions and (re)examine the scene more closely for potential danger and/or opportunity.

Opening the Nose-Gate Our sense of smell is too often ignored. How frequently have we literally been led around by our nose, manipulated by unseen forces that can influence our mood without our being aware of it? Experts tell us that our sense of smell is one of the strongest triggers for memories.

Through the years our olfactory sense has been targeted and twisted by military attacks, merchandising assaults, and out-and-out mind-control ploys meant to manipulate our mood and master our mind. And, in one way or another, all of these sucker punches to our proboscis have landed right on the button.

Armies have designed weapons that specifically target our sense of smell. For example, ancient Chinese soldiers used "stink bombs" to unnerve their enemies (Seagrave, 1985:180). Today the U.S. military, looking for nonlethal crowd-control alternatives, has developed a noxious-smelling "puke gas" that when dispersed over an unruly crowd makes rioters vomit, urinate, and defecate on themselves.

Special Forces soldiers eat only indigenous foods prior to penetrating deeply into enemy-held territory where, even at night, their body odor (sweat, flatulence, feces, even their urine) can smell of "foreign" food, alerting an enemy (in tune with *his* senses!) to their presence.

In the modern war on terrorism, beyond drug- and bomb-sniffing dogs, individuals can be now identified by their distinctive body odor, since each of us exudes a combination of body chemicals as unique as a fingerprint *(BusinessWeek,* August 8, 2005:55).

Madison Avenue has been leading us around by the nose for decades. Smells are used to first draw us into stores and then "encourage" us to buy more while we're there.

Nike paid for a study that concluded that most people will buy more shoes (and be willing to pay a higher price for those shoes) if the room smells like flowers. Likewise, the Las Vegas Hilton gambling casino found that its patrons spent 50 percent more time playing slot machines when the air around them was doused with a floral scent. The stronger the fragance, the longer individuals gambled. This even works in real estate, where the smell of fresh-baked bread and cookies (giving potential buyers a "homey" feeling) increases sales (ibid.).

To make matters worse, advertisers have discovered that by pairing the right packaging label to the right smell they can seduce the eye and the nose simultaneously. Storming two of the city's Nine-Gates at once . . . good battle plan! (If you're heading out to pick up a date tonight, take note.)

Another recent study shows that identical scents smell different from one another, depending on the type of labeling used. Thus, if a smell is paired with a pleasant-looking label, it will be perceived as a more pleasant smell overall than the same scent when paired with a more negative, less attractive label. It's not hard to figure out that our expectations influence how our brain perceives a smell. Research bears this out. Brain scans taken during this particular study reveal that the person's initial reaction to the labels—positive or negative—affected how blood flowed to the test subjects' olfactory processing areas.

Above and beyond getting us to buy stuff we don't need, recent research into how we react to our sense of smell has led to several revelations, some of which might benefit us, all of which might be used against us:

- *Keeping us more alert:* The smell of peppermint or cinnamon can increase alertness, helping keep drivers awake. This according to a Wheeling Jesuit University study. *(Men's Health,* May 2006:36)

- *Improving our memory:* Smells that act as memory aids include rosemary oil, basil, lemon, and sandalwood—which increase both contemplation and creative thought.
- *Making us more successful:* People whose clothes smell of pine are perceived by others as being more successful, more intelligent, sociable, sanitary, and attractive than those whose clothes smell like lemon, onion, or smoke. *(Psychology Today,* September/October 2005:32)
- *Making us more sociable and trusting:* In research done at the University of Zurich, after test subjects sniffed oxytocin (a hormone associated with female lactation and social bonding and interaction) they were 20 percent more likely to trust strangers with their money. *(Scientific American,* August 2005:26)
- *Improving your sex life:* Research has shown that between ages eight and sixteen, girls begin to dislike the odor of male sweat. Likewise, a recent survey of adult females found that women overwhelmingly agree that a man's body odor is more important than his appearance. *(Psychology Today,* September/October 2005:32).
- *Men also have noses:* A recent study rated unattractive women 20 percent more favorably when the room was spritzed with pleasant fragrance. (Ibid.)
- *Built-in sex detector:* Some researchers believe that we're born with an inborn olfactory sense that may act as a steering mechanism guiding men and women to members of the opposite sex (Bayer, 1987:34).

Recall from *Mind Control* (2006), in the chapter on "The Art of Seduction," that when a woman is interested in you and/or aroused by you it may seem that the air between the two of you seems "thicker," as your nose subconsciously picks up on an increase in her sexual pheromones, the same way you "smell" rain coming. Such human pheromones can now be bought off the shelf and are increasingly being added to perfumes and colognes. In addition, many scents found in nature have been proven to affect us sexually. Sandalwood, for example, is considered an aphrodisiac by Hindu yogis. (Much more on natural—and a couple *unnatural!*—aphrodisiacs in the section on Sexual Feng Shui.)

Sexual feng shui tip #1: Prior to an important meeting, douse the meeting room with scents designed to relax the person(s) you will be negotiating with. If that person happens to be a woman, depending on your agenda, you might also consider using artificial sexual pheromones. (Review "Kama Sutra Karma.")

Evil strategy tip No. 666: Prior to your business rival attending an important meeting, saturate his clothing with foul-smelling odors designed to be triggered by body heat. Or spray liberal amounts of a woman's perfume in his car, or onto his clothing, where his wife is sure to smell them because . . .

It's no secret women have more sensitive noses than men, so this ploy works even if you fold only a small amount of "the other woman's" perfume inside one of his handkerchiefs.

Here's a couple of exercises for honing your sense of smell:

- *Practice smelling:* Fill your memory banks with different smells. Allow a friend to blindfold you and then try to identify different scents they place under your nose. As with the taste exercise that follows, this can easily be used as a titillating game. (Who says sex can't be educational?)

- *The Z-E-N-Rose Exercise:* Both a meditation and a way to increase your awareness of your sense of smell. When we smell something pleasant, a rose for instance, we draw our breath in to its fullest. Nostrils flared, we draw the air to the bottom of our lungs. This is how you should breathe when you're meditating.

Most meditation techniques call for you to "Sit in a comfortable, quiet place" . . . yeah, good luck finding a place like that these days! This Z-E-N-Rose meditation you can do anywhere. A nice quiet place is great, if you have such a luxury. Filling your meditation spot with incense and other calming scents is also good. Real roses? Even better.

Now take a minute to *think* about your breathing. Close your eyes (if in an appropriate place to do so) and take in a full, deep breath, imagine you're smelling a large rose, trying to draw as much of its delicious fragrance as deep as possible into the *bottom* of your lungs.

As you breathe in, mentally repeat the letter "Z" (as in "getting your Z's"). Hold this "Z" breath for a few seconds before exhaling. As you exhale, think "E" (for "exhale"). Gently force all the breath from your lungs.

Now breathe in another slow, deep "rose" breath as you mentally recite "N" (as in "breathing *in,*" get it?). Or think about how an "N" is just another "Z" relaxing on its side.

As you breathe out this time, mentally say "ONE" . . .

Continue this breathing exercise, repeating "Z-E-N" as you breathe in, out, and in again. At the completion of each cycle of three breaths count "one," then "two," "three," and finally "four."

That's all there is to it. Takes you three, four minutes, tops. Of course, you can do it longer if you'd like, if circumstances permit. Just start the exercise over once you complete "four."

And if you concentrate on your "rose breathing," before long don't be surprised if you actually begin *smelling* a pleasant roselike fragrance. This will be your proof that you have moved into a more relaxed state where the mind has created the smell from the image of the rose you have successfully held in your mind. Calmer mind, stronger senses. Stronger senses, stronger mind.

Learn to meditate (1) to reduce stress, (2) in order to "center" yourself for more self-control, and (3) to increase your overall awareness, especially sense awareness.

A recent study at Massachusetts General Hospital concluded that forty minutes of meditation a day appears to thicken parts of the cerebral cortex. This is the part of the brain involved in attention and sensory processing (reported in *Psychology Today,* September/October 2006:74).

> We should pay attention to the ability of odors to affect our mood and concentration, since they take the most direct path to the brain of all stimuli perceived by our senses. Bad odors could obviously cause inattention. But also remember that positive odors such as the smell of flowers, of your favorite perfume or cologne, or of fresh baking can help set a positive mood. (Tony Jeary, *Life is a Series of Presentations,* 2004)

Opening the Ear-Gate The smallest bones in our body, the tiny bones in our ears, do one of the biggest jobs. "Hearing" is actually those tiny bones in our ears vibrating in response to sound waves.

When the Native American put his ear to the rail, listening for the iron horse, he wasn't "hearing" so much as "feeling" vibrations. The same is true with the old woodsman's trick of sticking a knife into the ground to "hear" someone approaching.

Old-fashioned safecrackers didn't really "listen" for the sound of tumblers falling, they instead "felt" the tumblers clicking in place through their fingertips (hence the old movie cliché of a safecracker "sharpening" his fingertips on sandpaper).

Ever see an Indian-Hindu snake charmer blowing on his flute, making his pet snake dance? First of all, since a snake doesn't have ears to actually hear the sound of the flute; the music is for the benefit of the audience. The snake is actually "charmed" by the gentle swaying of the fakir and the tapping of the fakir's foot, which the snake "hears" vibrating through the ground.

Human capacity to hear changes over time, and not just in old age. For example, the cochlea in the ear begins to "dull" after age twenty-five. As a result, "kids" can hear at least one frequency we know of that older people can't. A British department store successfully isolated this juvenile frequency and used it to pipe "uncomfortable" (subliminal) music into the store aimed at discouraging kids from loitering *(Good Morning America,* ABC News, June 13, 2006).

In the same way our eyes see many things that we don't consciously register, so too our ears pick up many more sounds than we are ever consciously aware of. That's because our brain sorts through and prioritizes what it considers immediately important stimuli (sights and sounds), ignoring the rest. This explains the "Cocktail Party Effect" when, in a crowded noisy room, we still can hear someone casually speaking our name from halfway across the room. That's because our name is important to us and our brain takes immediate notice whenever it's spoken.

Sexual feng shui tip #2: When meeting people, especially for the first time, always smile and repeat their name, adding a flattering comment about their name's origin (study!) or about how pleasant sounding the name is. It also helps to mention some famous person having a similar name (yeah, more study!). People like hearing their own name. So it stands to reason they will like someone who says their name often, while smiling, always in a flattering, interested-in-you-as-a-person way.

- *Listening to music:* Pick one instrument in an orchestra or band and concentrate on it. Try to isolate the drum, for instance. Then do it again for the guitar, then the keyboard. This is easy to do with loud rock music, harder with more subtle arrangements. Orchestral music is excellent for this exercise, since it tends more toward the subtle and complex.
- *Practice isolating sounds:* We can more easily home in on conversations at the next table over.
- *Learn to lip-read:* It's not technically "hearing," but it will improve your powers of concentration.
- *The farthest-away-sound meditation:* Begin by first using your Z-E-N-Rose exercise to relax yourself. Having accomplished this,

now close your eyes and *really* listen to the sounds around you. After a few minutes, gently "push" your thoughts further outward, as if "a circle of sound" is expanding out from you on all sides. Listen for the farther-away sounds—sounds outside the room you're in, perhaps outside your house.

When doing this exercise outside, on your porch or in the park, listen first for birds in the area, then those farther away, and then farthest away. Perhaps you'll hear that squirrel over there playing in the fall leaves, or else scratching his way up a tree. Extending your listening farther . . . now you hear that jet high up in the sky, and a subtle sound of the wind picking up. (You should also be able to feel this breeze on your skin, and perhaps smell the rain coming.)

Opening the Tongue-Gate You wouldn't expect imperial Chinese poison tasters to have had much of a retirement plan. The truth of the matter is many of them were experts in their craft, able to tell with just the minutest taste whether something was safe for the emperor to partake of. Of course these masters also used their eyes and their sense of smell to augment their talented tongues.

Those poison tasters not so adept and adroit of tongue didn't live long enough to complain to the chef. Some such poison tasters took small amounts of known poisons over the years, slowly immunizing themselves against commonly used poisons.

Let's improve your sense of taste:

- *Blindfold taste test:* This exercise is similar to the exercise we did to improve our sense of smell. Blindfold yourself and have a friend give you small amounts of food—and other nontoxic materials—to taste. Note the texture of these foods, not just the taste.

Sexual feng shui tip #3: With the right person, this taste exercise makes great foreplay!

Opening the Skin-Gate Your skin is your largest organ.

Human skin is so sensitive we can feel the weather changing (air pressure, increase of moisture in the air, etc.). We can also feel a potential lover's body heat increase along with their interest and arousal. In return, we show our interest through our sense of touch: by smiling and lightly touching her arm—she may touch your leg. When someone touches us in this way, we feel flattered, comfortable with them, and like we are more attractive. Recall from *Mind Control* (2006), in "The Art of Seduction," that the quickest way to her heart is through touching the "sweet spot" on the inside of her elbow. (Works on him as well!)

Detectives (and that nosy guy on *Cheaters*) can spy someone's passing or their presence by sweat left on a doorknob, by heat left on a chair, or by feeling the hood of a car to tell if the engine has recently been running.

Chinese masters of traditional Chinese medicine can diagnose a person's overall health simply by feeling the patient's pulse and/or by using their hands to determine the person's chi flow. In much the same way, a Western doctor might feel a patient for blood flow to an extremity (coolness and rigidity in the limb are indications of poor circulation).

Chi masters can not only diagnose disease but also ferret out psychological stress by touch—recognizing tension and/or spasms, tics, and twitches in muscles.

This is not as hard to do as it sounds. I'll bet you can already tell when someone is anxious or scared just from their sweaty palm and/or from the slight tremble you feel when shaking their hand. Some secret societies, Freemasons and the International Finder for instance, have special handshake grasps that allow them to feel the pulse of the other person, in order to tell if the other person is unduly tense or even lying.

Modern-day magicians and "mentalists" who specialize in "mind reading" are actually only adept at "muscle reading" the tension in a person's shoulder, arm, or hand while that person is being asked a question.

Contact sports and other physically demanding arts require participants to become more sensitive to touch. Ballroom dancers use their "body-sense" of touch to feel their partner's every move, as do martial artists, especially those who specialize in close-in fighting (e.g., judo, aikido, Wing Chun), arts that require students to instantly react to an opponent's shifting position, intuiting by touch the subtle shift of balance, a settling of their opponent's weight, in preparation for an attempted takedown.

During the Middle Ages, Shinobi ninja, anticipating having to fight enemies in the pitch dark, would strip themselves naked so that whenever they touched clothing, they instantly knew it was an enemy.

Here's how you improve your sense of touch:

- *Learn and regularly practice tai chi and chi gong:* When "dancing" your hands through the air during these exercises, imagine you are pushing your hands through warm water. Feel the air slightly resisting your skin.

Practice tai chi and chi gong while up to your neck in water.

- *Go-Ju Exercise:* (Japanese for "hard and soft") Carry a small hard object, a rock or marble for instance, in your right pocket and a soft object, a small piece of fur or wool, or one of those rubber-squiggly balls in your left pocket. When feeling stressed out, slip your hand in your left-hand pocket and squeeze the soft object several times.

Conversely, when feeling like you need a burst of energy, or when you feel the need to "center" yourself, slip your hand into your right pocket and grind the rock or other hard object into the palm of your hand.

Think this sounds like too simple an exercise? Think again. The mind operates on very simple signals. Merely rubbing your hand across something soft makes your mind identify and record the experience, and in the process of identifying and categorizing the object in your hand, your brain sifts through other objects in its files labeled "hard" or "soft," thus just one squeeze of such an object causing a dozen images of "hard" or "soft" to race across the mind, helping establish, or reestablish, a calmer or else more energized and determined mind-set.

> *Restless man's mind is so strongly shaken in the grip of the senses . . . Truly I think the wind is no wilder.*
>
> *—Bhagavad-Gita*

ASP: The Hidden Gate (Making Sense of the Sixth Sense)

Having increased our awareness of the five senses, it will often seem to others, and sometimes even to ourselves, as if we have access to a sixth sense—ESP—simply because we now have "sensory acuity"—we've become more attuned to picking up on the unconscious clues and cues given off by others:

- Fluctuations and hesitations in their speech,
- Feeling their body tremble,
- Seeing their goose bumps,
- Noting their sweaty palms when we shake their hand,
- "Smelling" pheromones of lust—or fear!—exuding from their pores.

Our five senses now work for us rather than against us. Now let's take our awareness of our five senses to the next (deeper) level!

Wouldn't it be great if we could actually read an adversary's (or a lover's) mind to know what they were thinking and planning, perhaps before they even knew it themselves?

A 2006 survey published in *USA Today* asked adults what "superpower" they would most like to have: 1 percent said they'd like to be able to walk through walls; 11 percent wanted to be able to turn invisible; another 15 percent dreamed of having the ability to fly. But the number-one "superpower" most people chose—28 percent of those surveyed—was *the power to read minds.*

According to recent scientific findings, acquiring the ability to "read minds" may not be as far-fetched as it first sounds. But we're not talking about ESP (extrasensory perception). We're talking *ASP—Additional Sensory Perception.*

Noted psychic researcher Ingo Swann puts it this way:

> We are talking about whether the bio-human possesses additional receptors for organizing information that exceeds the local limits of the five physical senses. This he does with the help of at least seventeen more different types of senses that have been identified by biologists and neurologists.

Swann goes on to associate these "additional receptors" with the powers sought by Indian yogis. (See "Remote Viewing as One of Sidhas," Ingo Swann, January 10 1996, InterNet, in Victorian, 2000.)

You can do this.

ASP begins with the full use of our five senses, something you've already been learning, right? Since you have mastered your five senses, people around you are beginning to wonder if you don't already possess extrasensory perception. You da man! Or da wo-man . . . or, still just a little gender confused. But either way, those around you have begun to suspect you are a force to be reckoned with! You have no reason to tell them different!

Recent discoveries about how our five senses gather information, and more importantly how we process that information to the fullest extent of our five senses—and beyond!—prove ASP is possible.

For example, people who have lost their sight can often still "see," possessing the ability to "perceive" the movement, color, and shape of objects around them. This "spooky sense" (as it's sometimes called), also known as "blindsight," occurs when the eye takes in images that somehow bypass the (damaged or cut-off) primary visual cortex (the part of the brain that sifts through data from our sense of sight). That's right: even though we're not consciously aware we are "seeing" such images, other parts of the brain subconsciously respond to this "shadow information" without waiting for it to be processed through normal channels.

One theory is that "blindsight" is a good thing, preventing the brain from going into "sensory overload" by "filtering" the vast amounts of information coming into the brain via the eyes. Thus, at any given moment, our brains are receiving—and responding to—not only conscious "sensory" information but also a subconscious, "extrasensory," flow of data as well. As a result:

> The unconscious flow of information . . . allows us to change
> our behavior and make decisions without ever quite knowing
> why we did. (Kruglinsky, 2006:13)

Thus we find ourselves unconsciously making decisions, adjusting our behavior to fit information that we are not consciously aware we are receiving. (Yeah, this does sound a lot like subliminal suggestion!)

People often think they "predict" something is going to happen—a disaster, for instance—and congratulate themselves for being "psychic" when, in reality, it wasn't ESP, it was ASP—an additional focused use of their already existing five senses. Seeing us act or react to this unseen ASP information, others will be awed, believing us to have ESP.

I'm sure you can already see the advantage in allowing an adversary (and even a lover) to go right on believing something like that.

Let them go right on believing that you have ESP. You have science on your side. According to author Ker Than, a recently discovered natural process might give the impression we possess ESP. "Mirror neurons" buried deep inside your skull are specialized brain cells that "read the minds of others" and know their intentions. These mirror neuron brain cells fire in response to the "reflection" of another person. For example, when you watch a coworker lift his cup to take a drink, the mirror neurons in your brain activate just like they would if it was you lifting your cup to take a drink. Neuroscientists believe these mirror neurons are what make us feel empathy and compassion for other human beings and cite research showing that autistic boys' mirror neurons fail to fire in this way, and that may account for an autistic child's lack of social interaction and communication skills (*Psychology Today,* August 2005:26).

Recall from our India section that some Hindus equate the "sixth sense" with the use of the heart chakra (feeling and compassion), which we might also think of as simply being empathic, which brings us right back around to those recently discovered "mirror neurons."

*　　　*　　　*

As Western science continues to uncover new information about how the brain works, or at the very least continues to find credence and correlation with the wisdom intuited by Asian mind-masters of long ago, we may one day find that all of us do indeed possess some sort of ESP—*"Extra*-Senses Potential."* But until then, we need to put effort into developing the first five, if only to show ourselves worthy of possessing a sixth! Until then, let's see what we can do to develop that "sixth sense" on our own:

- First, repeat the exercises for the eyes, the ears, the nose, and your senses of touch and taste.
- And then repeat them again!

Sensory Modes One final way in which we can use our knowledge of the five (or is that six?) senses is to learn to discern which of the five senses others are dominated by. While we all use our senses to varying degrees, we still each tend to favor one sense over the others.

This unconscious preference is often reflected in our conscious choice of entertainment—going to a movie (seeing) versus going to a classical music concert (hearing), versus going to a dance (touching), versus going to a fine restaurant (tasting, sniffing the wine), and in our chosen hobbies and careers:

- A taste-oriented person might be right at home working as a chef. Ah, but they could also like working with their hands (touch-oriented) which is also used a lot in cooking.
- Though we usually associate teachers with talking, those dominated by the sense of hearing actually make the best teachers, since they can better determine a student's individual needs by really listening to better determine their students' "sense modality."
- Likewise, we associate artists with the sense of sight, but what about all those sculptors and carvers dominated by the sense of touch?

Be mindful not to too quickly stereotype a person into one of these five sensory modes since people sometimes use more than one sensory mode of talking, just as we all use different senses from situation to situation.

Determining which sensory modality dominates a person is part of what's called neurolinguistic programming (NLP), a concept near and dear to the heart of those of us here at "The Black Science Institute."

NLP was popularized in the 1980s by motivational speaker Tony Robbins *(Unlimited Power)*, although the concept was known to the Chinese a few thousand years earlier. (See "Getting Some Chinese Face" chapter later in this book).

Two fellows at the University of California at Santa Cruz, Richard Bandler (a language expert) and John Grinder (a computer programmer), get the credit for the (modern-day) discovery of NLP, which they originally created for use in psychiatric therapy, to help therapists better recognize the particular sensory modality their patients were using to process (interpret) the world around them: visual (sight), auditory (hearing), or kinesthetic (touching, tasting: physical contact).

Once the therapists recognized the patient's sensory modality, the therapist could then adjust ("mirror") that sense modality by choosing their own words, body language, even breathing pattern to match the patient's, making the patient more relaxed and more receptive to therapy.

More on "Mirroring and Matching" in the section on Sexual Feng-Shui.

Most often we can discern a person's dominating sense mode simply by the words and phrases with which they choose to express themselves. (See Figure 19, opposite.)

- A sight-oriented person might remark: "I see what you're trying to say." Whereas a tactile-touch oriented might phrase the same thing, "I feel you! I'd like to touch base with you on that again."
- A touch-oriented person might have to look your proposal over but, if you study them carefully, you'll notice them literally "fondling" the folder, rubbing their hands over the cover, perhaps even bouncing it up and down in their hands, literally "weighing" your proposal.
- A taste-oriented person can be caught "smacking" or licking their lips or gums, even grinding their teeth (look at their jaw tensing), as they mull over your idea.
- A hearing-oriented person might ask questions like, "What did so-and-so say about this idea?" or "What's the word around the office?" or "What's the scuttlebutt on the grapevine?"

Once we figure out which of the five sense modes (or three "sense modalities") dominates our target person, we can then craft our overall demeanor (speech, body language), to fit them, in order to better schmooze or kiss ass.*

---

*Black Science adage number 411: "It's not kissin' ass so long as you realize you're kissin' ass. In which case . . . it's *strategy!*"

VERBAL PHRASES THAT BETRAY US

WATCHERS	LISTENERS	TOUCHERS

WATCHERS	LISTENERS	TOUCHERS
Clear (cut)	Pay attention to . . .	Hits the nail on the head
Vague	Silence	A feel (for business, etc.)
Flash (of inspiration)	Attuned to . . .	Slip this by you
Imaginative	Question	Run this by you
Enlighten	Afterthought	Make contact with
Photographic memory	Give an earful	Fits the bill
"It just dawned on me . . ."	"Sounds good to me."	Turn (around/over)
"It appears to me . . ."	"Music to my ears."	Sway the jury
Beyond a shadow of a doubt	Clear as a bell	Smooth operator
Bird's eye view	Hold your tongue	Fast-paced
Eye-to-eye	Rings a bell	Shaky
Face-to-face	"To tell the truth . . ."	Topsy-turvy
Paint a picture	Make music together	Underhanded
"See to it that . . ."	Word-for-word	Get the upper hand
"Look into . . ."	"My ears are burning."	Up/down
Drawing a blank	Voice (an objection)	"Hot under the collar"
"I see through you . . ."	Voice (an opinion)	Dirty (evil)
Patterns emerging	Buzzing (gossip)	Chilly (reception)
Bright future	Screaming headlines	Foot in the door
Up front	Give me your ear . . .	Get a handle on
"Behind the eight-ball"	"That clicks for me."	Get a load of this
Well-defined	In a manner of speaking	"Touch base with you"
Tall order	"Can we talk?"	Boils down to
Glowing report	"Let me hear your opinion."	All washed up
In person	"I hear what you're saying.	Come to grips with
One-on-one		Calm, cool, collected
Vision (ary)		Walking on thin ice
"I see what you're saying."		Treading water
		Pain in the ass
		Cool under pressure
		Pull some strings
		"Hold your horses."
		"I feel you."

Figure 19.

You can also use your knowledge of a rival's dominant sensory mode to toss a stumbling block in front of them.

For someone who is "seeing" oriented, arrange for them to have to listen to lengthy, boring audiotapes.

Once you peg his sensory mode type, it is a simple matter to craft a counterstrategy or seduction, either using their dominant sensory mode to attract him or else deliberately counter with a sensory mode designed to repel and trip him up.

Mind Like Water: Frozen, Fluid, or Freed?

Steadfast as Earth, await the enemy's movement. When he moves,
flow into him like Water striking, consume him like Fire!
—T'ai Li'ang, 374 B.C.E.

Confucianism, Buddhism, and Taoism are the big three in the history of Chinese religious thought, each having been influenced by the other two. Confucius and Lao Tzu, the founder of Taoism, were sixth-century BCE contemporaries although accounts and legends differ as to whether the two actually ever met.

Legend has it that Lao Tzu, "the Old Dragon," disappeared at the end of his life shortly after writing his *Tao Te Ching*. Some say he headed for India, where he became the tutor for Prince Siddhartha, who was himself destined to become the "Buddha." A thousand years later, Bodhidharma repaid the compliment by taking his particular (some say peculiar) brand of Buddhism from his native India to Shaolin, where it blended with indigenous Taoism to create Zen Buddhism.

While embracing Buddhism, the brothers (and sisters) of Shaolin still retained many Taoist concepts they found compatible with Bodhidharma's Buddhism—the two religions had more similarities than differences. Among these similarities was their use of water as a metaphor and teaching tool.

Recall that, in the Taoist universe, everything exists within the Tao and the Tao exists within all things. There is nothing but Tao in all the universe. Even our thoughts when trying to comprehend the nature of Tao are still Tao:

The Tao that can be spoken of is not true Tao. (*Tao Te Ching*)

Things around us appear to be different from one another but this is an illusion because Tao is always the same—everywhere, always, and perfect. Tao resembles "The Force" in the movie *Star Wars*—all-powerful, yet impersonal, available to Luke Skywalker and Darth Vader alike; all-powerful, with no preference save that which *we* project onto it. And that's where our problems start.

According to Taoism, we humans perceive things imperfectly, seeing our world as composed of warring opposites (hot-cold, light-darkness) when in fact there is only the one Tao. So instead of seeing Tao as a singular, unchangeable circle, we see it as divided, ever-changing "yin-yang." We then go on to further divide up these yin-yang "opposites" depending on whether we perceive them as rising ("ascending") or in decline ("descending"). This, in turn, gives to the five elements of which all things in the physical universe are composed. (See Figure 20, page 142.)

While most Westerners readily recognize the black-and-white "yin-yang" as the symbol for Taoism, Water is actually the symbol the Taoist "Immortals" (masters) used most often when attempting to explain transcendent Taoist concepts to minds still trapped by three dimensions.

Water is the ultimate shape-shifter. This is why it is often used as the ideal to strive for in the martial arts. Higher-level adepts give up stiff, harsh movements in order to "flow like water," adopting more natural, graceful movement that allows them to more easily "blend" with their opponent (as opposed to always meeting force with force). This higher level of training is especially apparent in such martial arts as tai chi (Dai Qi) and aikido.

Not surprisingly, this idea of water is also applied by Taoists to the *mental dynamics* of human beings as well.

Taoist Immortals have made this simple for us still-stuck-in-the-mud folks by comparing the three dominant human mental states or attitudes to the three states of water: frozen, fluid, and freed. And while each of us is dominated personality-wise by one of these states, we are still free to use the other states:

> **Frozen** *(Ice):* Water in its fixed, solid form, appears to be unworkable. Yet under a firm, disciplined hand ice can be sculpted to represent any form. Likewise, human beings dominated by an "ice" attitude are fixed, and in extremis, stubborn in outlook and conservative in output.

On the positive side—seduction-wise, "frozen" people aren't the sharpest tools in the box. Imagination isn't their strong suit. So when explaining things to the "Iceman" or the "Ice Princess" stick to the K.I.S.S. principle: "Keep it simple, stupid!"

THE THREE ATTITUDES OF WATER

Shape	Essence	Attitude	Strategy to Use
Frozen *(ICE)*	Solid, fixed, appears unworkable.	Positive: Dependable, predictable. Negative: Unimaginative, unreasonable, stubborn *in extremis.* Cold and conservative toward others.	Ally: K.I.S.S. when talking to him. Simple and straightforward. Adversary: Encourage his stubbornness, encourage him to stay on the defensive.
Fluid—Yin *(STILL WATER)*	Potential, reactive to changes in "the weather" and circumstances.	Positive: Adaptable, patient. Negative: Hesitant, Overly cautious. Suspicious.	Ally: Negotiate with him. Keep him on a "need-to-know" basis. Adversary: Feed his paranoia.
Fluid—Yang *(MOVING WATER)*	Active, flowing rushing, forceful.	Positive: Persistent. Negative: Impulsive, Liberal toward others. Tepid. Cautious but Tolerant.	Negotiate with him while planning your Pearl Harbor. If he is attacking, use the judo principle to make him overextend himself. As he rushes forward, funnel him into your container.
Freed *(STEAM & CLOUDS)*	Ephemeral	Positive: Curious, playful, innovative when focused. Negative: ADD—short attention span. Unfocused, undecided. Has trouble committing himself. Seeks form, easily led.	Ally: Help him to focus on your cause. Give him small concise missions, one at a time. Adversary: Encourage his confusion, fog, and fugue. Put him under pressure until he explodes from frustration.

Figure 20.

This "Ice" type of personality secretly desires guidance, direction, and reassurance, but responds best when they think your idea is "their" idea.

Ice is difficult, even treacherous, to navigate but, with patience, it can be put to good use. So, too, are ice-dominated people. They are as loyal as they are stubborn; they are tough nuts to crack, but it's well worth the effort to get to the sweet meat within.

These types are what Sun Tzu referred to as "expendable agents," usually good for only one thing, dependable for only one mission and then only while under constant surveillance and/or supervision. Consider a spear made of ice: It can work just as well as a "real" spear, only to melt and eventually evaporate soon after. Expendable, but useful—perhaps vital—to the immediate need.

"Frozen people" often hesitate too long, missing out on timely opportunities.

When enlisting the aid of an ice-bound ally, it may be necessary to "light a fire under his ass" just to get him to loosen up and get moving. Beware, though, ice heated too quickly turns to steam and disappears into the clouds.

Being slow to act is something we want to encourage (strategy-wise) in our adversaries. However, when it comes to seduction, the quicker we can get her (or him) to see things our way the better our chances to "score." Thus the hustlers' adage: Study long, study wrong! Or to paraphrase Sun Tzu: Swift victory has never been associated with long delays.

> **Fluid** (water) is either "resting" or "rushing." Resting water–dominated people make perfect actors, gigolos, spies, and assassins. They are patient, inwardly balanced, and liberal in attitude and adaptability, ready to flow into any container, fill any void. They are the "stem cells" of strategy and seduction.

They are persistent, which always pays off in the end—the same way single drops of water during the infamous "Chinese water torture" steadily drip-drip-drip onto a victim's forehead until the victim either "breaks" or goes insane.

Nature forms hard sedimentary rock as well as stalactites and stalagmites this way, a few drops of water at a time. But once formed, those rocks are as hard as . . . well, stone.

Chameleons capable of color shifts at a moment's notice, Machiavelli and Charles Manson come to mind when thinking of "resting water" personalities, as do other cult leaders and longtime political survivors.

Striking a balance, being able to "shape-shift" at will, never allowing yourself to be "trapped" (and thus vulnerable) in a fixed form (like ice), or doomed to simply disappear into the background (like steam), gives us the advantage over those less adept at adapting.

"Rushing" water eventually overcomes everything in its way, either through dynamic action (impact/force of will/"steel") or else through persistent attrition (wearing down/negotiation/"silk").

Those dominated by a rushing-water personality make the best artists (Michelangelo), patient guerrilla fighters (Mao Tse Tung), and attentive lovers (Don Juan, Casanova). That's because (1) they don't take "no" for an answer, (2) nor are they likely to bow under to critics and, most important (3) like water they rush to fill any vacuum, molding themselves perfectly to the container at hand.

> **Freed** (Steam and clouds) water is ephemeral, undecided and unfocused, yet carries within it the potential of becoming either fluid or ice. Steam-dominated people are hot tempered and can explode under pressure. Stress is not their friend. Anger can be their downfall, but so can hesitation, as they have a short attention span. Thus they sometimes err on the side of taking too long to make a decision or else they make a decision on the spur of the moment without regard to future consequences, either of which can spell disaster on both the battlefield and in the bedroom.

It's impossible to pin a "steam person" down—who can catch steam in their fist? Who can lasso a cloud?

They can be innovative—often because they never took the time to learn what isn't possible in the first place. Thomas Edison is an example of this type.

They are full of ideas and plans, but lack the focus and sometimes lack the commitment to carry through their visions.

Negatively, the steam-cloud person is confused and undecided as to which way to go. Like the Iceman, this individual sometimes hesitates too long. Hesitation = death. But unlike Iceman, Steam-boy (or girl) doesn't hesitate out of an inability to process information at a reasonable rate; rather, steam people often have too many ideas floating around inside their heads at

CHINA: THE TAO OF SEDUCTION

one time. Short attention span, remember? Leonardo da Vinci was a steam-boy. For all his genius, for every magnificent work of art and invention attributed to him, there were a dozen of his masterpieces left unfinished, scores of his inventions never built, left unrealized. For steam people, the ideas can come so fast they often never actually get around to completing any of them. Such people have their heads too far "in the clouds" and are often of little "earthly" use.

Steam people need somebody to help them settle down, to coalesce and condense their ideas . . . *Be* that somebody.

It is a truism that a general must monitor a battle constantly, adjusting his plans at an instant's notice. A steam-dominated commander will change his mind and his plans—arbitrarily—a dozen times, until he loses the confidence of his own men.

Confronting a steam-dominated adversary, encourage his confusion, his indecision. And never forget that he is anger prone, and remember, that anger is one of "The Five Warning F.L.A.G.S."

We use these three attitudes of water in two main ways:

- Draw our adversary out of his dominant comfort zone, weakening and confusing him further before finally trapping him in unfamiliar territory and untenable ground where his dominant personality trait becomes the liability that ultimately dooms him.
- Or note the "weaknesses" inherent in each of these states, and in our adversary, and then reinforce and exploit those weaknesses to our advantage.

Ping-Fa Strategy

No destiny but that which we whittle with our own will, craft with
our own cunning.
—Duke Falthor Metalstorm

Having first cleansed the body of weakness in order to make it strong, having then awakened the senses through Jing Gong, Black Lotus disciples (those who survived this far!) now advanced to the "Hall" of Ping-Fa strategy.

When we speak of Sun Tzu's "Ping-Fa" (Art of War), we are referring specifically to a written opus, a master's text. But Ping-Fa also refers to the craft and the cunning, mind-set, machinations, and maneuverings it takes to survive and thrive an intense challenge situation: whether that "challenge" is an enemy army across the way eyeing your army, or that fine filly giving you the eye from across the room.

The Black Lotus had an eight-point system for teaching strategy, a comprehensive system that had its inspiration in the Pa-Kua "Eight-Trigrams" practice that was first a philosophy, then later a martial-art style developed by Taoist alchemists at the Yu-hau shan monastery.

The martial art of Pa-Kua uses open hand strikes paired with circling-around footwork that forces an opponent to constantly shift his position, denying him a firm stance from which to launch counterstrikes. In other words, you keep your opponent off balance at all times. Black Lotus Ping-Fa strategy is built on this same principle, only it's your adversary's (or lover's) mind you keep off balance.

This strategy values (1) astute observation, (2) realistic evaluation, (3) succinct application, and, if need be, (4) reassessment of a failed plan. In this way ancient Ping-Fa strategy is similar to the typical Western problem-solving model: (1) clearly *define* the problem, (2) *brainstorm* possible solutions, (3) *prioritize* possible solutions in order of their best chance of success, (4) *implement* prioritized solutions, and (5) *adjust* as needed, compensating for shifting realities, factoring in any points of weakness or failure as they become obvious.

Compare these with the eight steps of Ping-Fa strategy. (See Figure 21.)

- *Chou* ("to measure"). Before embarking on any campaign, mission, or business venture, we must first "measure" two variables: *Xing* and *Shih* (pronounced *shing* and *she*), another way of saying circumstance and flux.

Xing is the arrow. Shih is the drawn bow.

Xing is the outward appearance of a thing, a person, or a situation—the way it "appears" to be.

In the case of a person, Xing is the proper, public face they show to the world.

Shih is the inner essence of a thing, a person, or a situation, the potential (stored) energy within. In the case of a person, Shih is their real face, the one they keep hidden from the world. Expose this face and you expose a person for what they truly are. (See "Getting Some Chinese Face.")

Shih is the inner dynamic, the inherent power of something. This includes all the possible outcomes to a given situation.

PING-FA STRATEGY

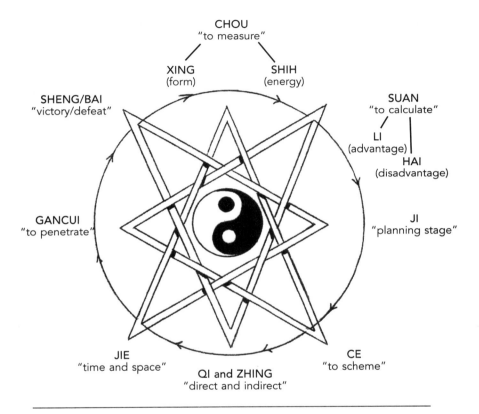

Figure 21.

When "measuring" people, Shih reminds us of Sun Tzu's "Know your enemy." But Shih also reminds us of the second part of Sun Tzu's teaching, ". . . and know yourself." In any given situation, we must first "measure" (1) the potential of ourselves. Then assess (2) our adversary and (3) our immediate surroundings, where our strategy or seduction will be carried out: Do our resources (and our ruthlessness) coincide with reality?

Based upon his past actions, what is our adversary capable of? What is the current situation? Is this the right time and place to attempt this particular strategy?

What's her body language telling you? Is she ripe for seduction?

All these must realistically be weighed—measured *(chou)*—before we continue crafting our strategy.

- *Suan* ("to calculate"), is composed of *Li* and *Hai,* gain versus loss.

Li is "advantage," all that we have to gain if we are successful in our strategy or seduction. Hai is "disadvantage" or "risk," all the things precious (our time, money, reputation, life!) we have just placed in the line of fire, into the uncertain hands of Fate. Hai is the cost we are willing to pay to achieve Li.

Gamblers' math: Big risk = Big reward. Gigolos' math: She can't say "yes" if you never ask.

- *Ji* ("planning"). Having measured our own worth as well as the worthlessness of our adversary, having then calculated what we are willing to risk in order to gain a thousandfold, we now come to the planning stage of our operation.

How to get our idea off the drawing board and into the bank, or how to get her behind off that bar stool and into bed?

Consult with former and current experts in the field—be they generals or gigolos. Balance the quickest route against the path of least resistance. Perform "mock operations," mirroring the real thing as realistically as possible. This means practicing your lines of attack and/or your pickup lines in advance.

Sexual feng shui tip #4: Don't bother practicing your "smooth" pickup lines with your bros. What your buddies and even your wingman might think are "Bitchin!" pickup lines will probably sound lame to the ladies. Instead, ask for advice from your sister or your female friends—*never* from Mom (That's just sad!)

- *Ce* ("to scheme"). Having laid out your plan—your routes of approach, you now need to think about what your target (adversary or lover) is thinking.

Whereas Ji, "planning," focuses on "necessities" in life (those things we have to have in order for a plan to succeed), Ce, "scheming," is where you start tweaking your plan, in order to turn a ho-hum layup into a slam dunk.

Beware. Your adversary has eyes and spies, too. Right now he's scheming how to counter your scheming. And so you have to make counterschemes for his counterschemes. As on the battlefield, so in the bedroom, from the chessboard to the headboard.

Ce (scheming) also involves any camouflage, cunning, and conciliatory gestures you use to reassure your adversary that you're not up to something. Ce is the distraction before the extraction!

Remember hearing about all those full-size wooden planes, tanks, and other equipment—complete phony airports and fake army bases replete with straw soldiers—that were set up along the English coast to confuse Hitler's spies just prior to the D-day invasion? That's a good example of Ce—scheming. (Stuffing that rolled-up sock into your briefs? Not a good example of Ce—!)

- *Zheng* and *Qi* ("direct and indirect" a.k.a. written *Cheng/Chi* and *Xing/Shih*). At this stage we are forced to look at both sides of the coin, and listen to counterargument and naysaying we don't want to hear.

It would be nice if we could foresee every possible contingency and map out our strategies and seductions accordingly—being right every time. Not gonna happen. Some of the greatest military minds in history have both won and lost great battles based purely on "shit happens."

Likewise, love has been won and lost based simply on a slip of the tongue . . . and where it is you happen to slip that tongue!

Every criminal knows that no man's smart enough to be his own lawyer. That's why every great leader surrounds himself with a posse composed of people who are not afraid to tell the boss when they think he's messing up. In other words, you need a good wingman or, better yet, a whole posse of wingmen, to watch your back and to tell you when you're screwing up.

Mao Ze Dong had Zhou Enlai. Bill had Hillary. Now Hillary's got Bill.

Zheng and Qi also apply to how we gather up our forces and to how we deploy those forces.

There are direct (Zheng) strategies we can use, straightforward counterattacks of equal or greater force meeting our adversary mano a mano, face-to-face on the field of battle. But that's not always practical even if we do know ourselves to be evenly matched to our opponent. Thus, never go toe-to-toe with an opponent unless you know you are in the superior position—and, even then, don't be overconfident.

Qi refers to those indirect "guerrilla" tactics we adopt when we know our adversary has superior numbers, superior firepower, or holds a superior defensive position.

In such an event, we "play the Che,"* nipping at his heels. Mao was also a master of this type of strategy.

On the battlefield we slowly, secretly, unsuspected, gather our forces, increasing our worth and power incrementally, so as not to arouse suspicion; building up our reserves, biding our time until the time is right to strike. Recall how Kou Chien outfoxed rival Fu Chai by rebuilding his "steel" in secret (having made sure beforehand to send a seductive "silk" distraction his foe's way).

As in strategy, so in seduction: we ply her (or him) with patience and petting before we pounce! When one big business plots the "hostile takeover" of another company, before revealing their intent, they quietly start buying up shares of the targeted company—buying these shares secretly through third parties, so as not to prematurely alert their intended target.

This is no different from the secret army training and the slow, subtle shifting of resources Hitler accomplished prior to launching World War II; successfully rebuilding Germany's military might right under the noses of those who should have been watching him the closest.

Of course, you don't have to choose between using one or the other, Zhing or Qi. In any conflict or campaign, a good general uses both direct and indirect—steel and silk—tactics.

In his *Art of War* Sun Tzu not only teaches how a general moves his conventional (Zheng) troops from place to place but also stresses the importance of a wise general employing plenty of unconventional (Qi) forces: fast-moving special forces and spies.

In our seductions, we likewise use surprise: an unexpected gesture of tenderness, a small gift, whatever it takes to help us stand out from the crowd.

Always have your WIT about you. W.I.T.—"Whatever It Takes" to make it happen. Make this your mantra and always make sure this is the kind of wit people ascribe to you, and not the 3 other kinds of wit: half-, nit- and dim-!

W.I.T. = MASAKATSU! Remember?

---

*Ernesto "Che" Guevara (1928–1967) revolutionary and guerrilla warfare expert.

- *Jie* ("timing and space"). The best product in the world won't sell if the people aren't ready for it. It's all about timing—right place, right time to trip up and trap your target.

Maybe she's ready for "rebound" sex, maybe she just wants to be left alone.

Jie also means "space," reminding us to take note of the distances between things, people, and destinations.

Give her "space" and you'll come off looking "sensitive." Chicks dig sensitive.

In Asian martial arts students must master "bridging the gap," closing the distance between them and their opponent as quickly as possible, to take that opponent out of the fight as economically as possible. Take this same attitude with you into all your strategies and seductions.

- *Gancui* (pronounced gang-kway, literally "to penetrate neatly and completely") means getting inside your enemy's head in order to (1) know what he's thinking, and (2) tell him what he should be thinking.

Gancui requires penetrating deeply and completely. When we strike, we give it all we got. No half-assin'. In Japanese karate, they call this *Ikken Hisatsu*, "To kill with one blow." And while we may not be using a physical "steel" strike to bring down our opponent, when striking with our silk-covered "Mind Fist" the same rules apply.

You should take this Gancui attitude with you into all your undertakings.

- *Sheng* and *Bai* ("victory or defeat"). In the end we win or lose. But it's not always that simple. There's a thing called a "Pyrrhic victory," a win that costs you too much to win. (It's like saying "The operation was a success . . . but the patient died!" or like staying in a toxic relationship just because the sex is so darn good.)

A victory that depletes your resources leaves both you and your defeated adversary vulnerable to attack by a third party who has been waiting patiently for you and the first adversary to cut each other down to a size he can swallow. Of course, this is a great opportunity, provided you are that patient and ruthless third party!

During any military campaign, setbacks and stumbling blocks magically appear that couldn't possibly have been anticipated during the Ji-planning and Ce-scheming stages. By the same token, sudden serendipitous advantages can also appear out of nowhere. If not grasped immediately, these opportunities will evaporate just as quickly as they appeared.

After any "mission" comes the "debriefing," when you toast your victory, reliving how that victory was brought about, or else reviewing what didn't work.

> A first taste of defeat, though bitter, goes far to prepare your palate for future feasts. (Hannibal Barca, *The 99 Truths*)

If you've lost out, you damn sure want to figure out what the hell went wrong. And, even when you win victory, instead of resting on your laurels, you need to immediately turn to measuring *Chou* again, honing your strategy, stockpiling your energies, readying yourself for the next challenge.

The Five Movers

> *God hath given you one face and you make for yourselves another:*
> *you jig, you amble, and you lisp, and nickname God's creatures,*
> *and you make your wantonness your ignorance. Go to, I'll not more*
> *on't; it hath made me mad.*
> **—Hamlet**

The brain was the battlefield of the Black Lotus. For therein will always lay the strength of such sisterhoods: Men, everywhere, in all times, underestimate women.

Underestimating your opponent is the flip side of a very fatal Janus-faced coin. The reverse being overestimating yourself. Know yourself . . . know your enemy.

Rather than dealing with opponents on a physical level, Black Lotus adepts attacked a man where he was weakest—between the legs!—which just happens to be controlled by what's between his ears.

We are all susceptible to our emotions, emotions that can change in the blink—or seductive wink—of an eye.

In Japan, Miko and other women whose livelihood—indeed, their very lives!—depended on their ability to placate and please their gentlemen callers mastered the art of Ninjo,* "human emotion," in particular, "empathy"— feeling what another is feeling.

---

*Not to be confused with "Ninpo," a synonym for ninjitsu, the art of the ninja.

This means feeling sympathy for another person, offering them generosity.

But on a deeper, darker level, Ninjo refers to feeling out (intuiting) what another person is thinking by how they talk, how they walk, their body language.

The art of Ninjo is thus the study of human emotions: *Gojo-Goyoku*, the "Five Movers," a.k.a. the "Five Warning F.L.A.G.S." Fear, Lust, Anger, Greed, and Sympathy.

All human interaction is based on these emotions. Figuring out how to tap into another person's emotions is just another way of "hitting their buttons" or "yankin' their chain."

It's just simple yin-yang: If we like someone, if we are attracted to them, we'll want to be around them more, do business with them, perhaps fall in love with them . . . or at least tumble into bed with them. In all human interaction, emotion is the key. Remember in *Mind Control* (2006) we pointed out that if you want to have a chance at hitting her "G-spot," you have to first hit her "E-spot"—"E" for emotions.

Everybody's got their emotional buttons, everybody's got their price. As soon as you go thinking you're the exception, you've placed yourself in the worst kind of danger.

They say you catch more flies with honey than with vinegar. But what about bullshit? Flies are attracted to bullshit, too!

These Universal Five Movers (Weaknesses) are known in the West as well, at least to the Immortal Bard:

> FEAR: "Of all base passions, fear is the most accurs'd." *(King Henry VI)*
>
> LUST: "And careless lust stirs up a desperate courage." *(Venus and Adonis)*
>
> ANGER: "Never anger made good guard for itself." *(Antony and Cleopatra)*
>
> GREED: "See, sons, what things you are! How quickly nature falls into revolt when gold becomes her object!" *(King Henry IV)*
>
> SYMPATHY: "Of pity is the virtue of law, and none but tyrants use it cruelly." *(Timon of Athens)*

In his book *Street Ninja* (1995), Dirk Skinner explains modern applications of Gojo-Goyoku by urban survivalists seeking to add another weapon to their defensive arsenal, as well as by unsavory characters seeking to manipulate others. For example, modern-day criminals use female assistants to distract their victims in much the same way female ninja first distracted and then dispatched foes by appealing to their lust. Likewise, modern con men seek out that little bit of greed in us all, and/or play on sympathy.

On the flip side, Skinner shows how a mugging victim can fake a heart attack and cause a mugger (who's only after money) to flee in fear he'll be charged with murder. Skinner also shows how anger ploys can be used in self-defense to make even a professional fighter commit amateur mistakes.

Each of the Gojo-Goyoku has its positive aspect as well as its negative side. For example dosha (anger) is negative and self-defeating. But *righteous* anger—anger expressed over an injustice—is "good" anger.

Chinese strategist General Tu Hsing knew how to use anger to his advantage. After seizing a large cache of booty, Hsing's troops were weakened by greed and lost their desire to fight. To remedy this, Tu Hsing secretly sent agents to burn his own men's barracks and the treasure they'd stored there. The wily general then blamed the fire on enemy spies, turning his men's greed to anger, a deficit into an asset.

It is important to keep in mind that these Five Feelings can be either friends or foes. For example, *kisha* can manifest as negative obsessive lust or as positive passion. Likewise, fear can paralyze us into inaction or galvanize us to flight or fight.

Sung Dynasty strategist Ch'en Hao knew how to use the Five Weaknesses, attacking an enemy with greed (rakusha) while throwing in a healthy dose of lust (kisha) to further unnerve the foe:

> Entice an enemy with young boys and maidens to distract him, offer jade and fine silk to draw out his greed.

Sung Dynasty strategist Chang Yu also pointed out how emotional shortcomings could bring down an enemy:

> To control a foe, first *anger* him, then *confuse* him, then *teach him fear* without rest. Thus he loses his will to fight, thus he loses his ability to plan.

This sounds like something we should study:

Rakusha (Greed) Ploys Sun Tzu says the sure way to control an enemy is by appealing to his greedy nature; entice him with something he is certain to want (an easy victory) and with promises of easy gain. Likewise, Tu Mu points out how potential traitors can be swayed by appeals to their greed and licentiousness.

Confidence men have always counted on their victims not reporting having been swindled. First, the victim doesn't want to look as foolish as he feels for having been duped. Second, he doesn't want to look greedy, even though greed—desire for a fast buck—is what put him in the con man's clutches in the first place.

Like all the Five Movers, greed can be deadly. For example, the classic wartime ploy of scattering booby-trapped "souvenirs" (swords or other weapons), in the path of advancing troops.

Chinese astrology warns that people born under the sign of the Snake never let an opportunity slip, and are thus prime candidates for any too-good-to-be-true offer mind-slayers wave in front of their faces. (See "The 12 Animal Passions," next)

For our own self-defense, when tempted by the lure of easy gain, we would do well to remember the ancient Chinese adage:

> "Under fragrant bait there is certain to be found a hooked fish."

Dosha (Anger) Ploys Tu Mu illustrated the cost of uncontrolled anger by relating the story of the wily general who, rather than sending his enemy counterpart the traditional exchange of prebattle wine between equals, instead sent the rival general a pot of piss! In a rage, the pissed-off general imprudently ordered his men to attack a heavily defended stronghold, decimating his command.

Whether in a major battlefield engagement, in one-to-one martial-arts combat, or when engaged in high-stakes negotiations, seeding anger in an adversary's mind clouds his reason, opening the way to his defeat.

Kojiro Okinaga, one of Miyamoto Musashi's early teachers, instructed the young Musashi: "Goad your foe into attacking before he is ready, and you will always gain the advantage over him." Musashi never forgot this instruction, using the strategy to his advantage on many occasions.

Mind-slayers know that a single word spoken at the right time or a single gesture can incite an otherwise calm and calculating foe into making a reckless mistake: "Anger his general and confuse him." Sun Tzu (I:22)

There is a Zen story that seems apropos:

> A samurai asks a master monk to teach him about heaven and hell. The monk immediately slaps the samurai! Enraged, the samurai draws his sword and chases the monk around the

room, intent on killing him. Finally cornering the monk, the samurai—face still contorted in rage—raises his sword for the killing blow . . . "That!" says the calm monk, pointing to the samurai's anger-flushed face, "is hell!" In a flash, anger flees from the samurai's face, replaced by confusion. "And that," declares the monk triumphantly, "is Heaven."

Perhaps the best example of this is the true story of "The Forty-seven Ronin."

In 1701, Lord Kira, the shogun's master of ceremonies, knowing his longtime enemy Daimyo Asano to be a man easily brought to anger, deliberately provoked Lord Asano into drawing his sword on the shogun's grounds—a capital offense. For this breach of etiquette, Lord Asano was ordered to commit seppuku (ritual suicide).

At the time, Lord Asano had forty-seven samurai retainers. As was the custom of the time, many thought that at least some of Lord Asano's forty-seven knights would commit hara-kiri and follow their master into the void. At the very least, to save "face" and guard their honor, many believed the forty-seven should have launched a suicidal attack against the vastly superior number of samurai guarding Lord Kira. But it appeared their fear of dying prevented any of the forty-seven from doing so. Instead the forty-seven chose to become ronin, "masterless" samurai—men without a purpose.

For two years thereafter wherever one of these forty-seven ronin went in Japan, they were reviled as the scum of the earth. Fathers pointed the forty-seven out to their sons as examples of how not to be, of what happens when samurai lose their honor.

Then, on the second anniversary of their master's death, all forty-seven ronin secretly gathered outside Lord Kira's residence and boldly breached its walls. Caught by surprise, Lord Kira's samurai fell beneath the blades of the ronin. The following dawn, the forty-seven ronin placed Lord Kira's head on Lord Asano's grave and then, one by one, all forty-seven committed hara-kiri, finally joining their lord in the void.

Those 730 days during which the forty-seven ronin pretended to be fearful of death, fearful of the hated Lord Kira, must have been the hardest of their lives. Yet their strategy succeeded.

Kyosha (Fear) Ploys When we think of using fear against our enemies, we inevitably think of making an enemy fear us. After all, as the old adage says: "Reputation often spills less blood."

In 518 B.C.E., when the armies of Wu and Ch'u met, the commander of the Wu, realizing that the Ch'u forces were all too eager for battle, ordered three thousand condemned men brought from Wu prisons. Since they were already condemned to death, the commander of the Wu promised these men that their families would be well cared for after their deaths provided they performed one final task for the Wu commander. When all three thousand agreed, the Wu commander had the prisoners dressed in Wu uniforms and placed in front of his troops, directly across the battlefield and in full view of the eager Ch'u troops. The Wu Commander then sent a message to the Ch'u telling them to watch closely as the Wu commander demonstrated the loyalty and determination of his troops.

At a prearranged signal, all three thousand condemned men cut their own throats! Believing these to be real Wu troops, Ch'u forces fled in terror.

Sinan, leader of the infamous Syrian branch of the medieval *Hashishins* (assassins) used a similar ploy, ordering his fanatical warriors to commit suicide in full view of visiting dignitaries in order to intimidate those guests into paying "tribute."

A second way to use fear is to make enemies think we fear them:

> *Pretend inferiority and encourage an enemy's arrogance.*
> **—Sun Tzu**

According to Tu Mu, one can only feign weakness and fear effectively by being extremely strong. Thus instead of sending his enemy, Emperor T'ai Wu of Wei, the traditional complement of wine before equals met in battle, his enemy Sung General Tsang Chih sent him a pot full of piss! Enraged, T'ai Wu attacked in anger, besieging T'ang's well-fortified city, losing half his troops.

It is classic guerrilla strategy for a small force to take potshots at a larger enemy force and then flee, feigning fear, drawing the pursuing enemy into an ambush. Custer learned this the hard way, as did U.S. troops in Vietnam.

> **Three-fourths of the people you will ever meet are thirsting for sympathy. Give it to them, and they will love you.**
> **—Dale Carnegie**

Aisha (Sympathy) Ploys You're standing at a bus stop and the person next to you drops an object. Being the kindhearted person you are, you instinctively reach down to help pick up the object for them . . . and receive a knee to the face for your trouble. The purposely butterfingered mugger takes your wallet and flees. You have just fallen victim to a "sympathy" ploy.

Criminals and con men are adept at using sympathy ploys (a.k.a. "Good Samaritan traps") to cause us to stop to help that "stranded" motorist along that deserted stretch of road, or cause us to open our doors to a lost traveler just needing to use the phone.

Sometimes the cost of falling for a sympathy ploy is high. For example, serial killer Ted Bundy wore a fake cast on his arm in order to elicit the sympathy of unsuspecting women he'd targeted.

Another sympathy shortcoming is the fear of hurting others. Accomplished word-wizards have a variety of ploys they use to make us hold our tongues in order to avoid offending another person—our silence being our implicit approval.

Sun Tzu maintained that having a fear of too many casualties is a fatal flaw in a general.

Tu Mu also warns that too much sympathy for your own troops leads to shortsightedness.

We know that both lust and greed can lead to recklessness. Yet no less fatal is allowing excessive concern or misplaced sympathy to cause us to hesitate when called upon to do the right thing—right now!

Kisha (Lust) Ploys The Bible is full of tales where lust for tail always came to a bad end:

- Joseph cast into prison after spurning the lust of the wife of his Egyptian master.
- Lust clouding his better judgment, Samson got screwed by Delilah.

What Musashi called *attitude,* Black Science calls "posture." Studying your own posture, as well as that of your adversary, is as important to us in today's world as it was in Musashi's time.

"Posture" includes how we sit, stand, fold our arms—all the subtle and subconscious twitches, tics, and "tells" of our body that all too often betray a person's true feelings and intent, as well as the "masks" we wear.

Often we deliberately try to adopt a posture designed to disguise our true intent and feelings. Unfortunately, our body language just as often betrays us.

So much about our body posture—from minor fidgeting, to flight or fight—is beyond our control, whether because we are unaware of these reactions or because we are too lazy to make the effort needed to master them.

Other body reactions we can learn to control, even activities we'd swear we have no conscious control over:

- Indian yogis can control their heart rates. Recall from our discussion on Tibet how lamas use techniques called tumo to deliberately raise their body temperature, allowing them to endure extremes of cold.
- Deep-cover spies train with biofeedback and self-hypnosis to learn to control body responses during intense interrogation—even beating lie-detector tests.
- Accomplished actors, con men, and spoiled children can cry on cue.
- And most of us can deliberately make our lips smile, even if our unsmiling eyes give away the fact we're faking it! (Remember: Always squint and "crinkle the crows-feet" around your eyes when sporting a "genuine" fake smile.)

Fortunately, so far as our Black Science mind control is concerned, natural reactions like sweating when anxious, blushing in embarrassment, and nervous laughter at funerals are beyond most people's ability to control.

Just by looking, most of us can easily tell if another person is in a good or bad mood, nervous, or otherwise stressed out. (See Figure 22, page 160.)

- King David's lust causes him to arrange the death of Uriah, so he can bed the dead man's wife.

It has been said that lust is simply greed with genitals attached.

From frustrated lust is born jealousy. *Othello* testifies to know how easily lust can be manipulated into jealousy by an unscrupulous Black Science adept.

Realizing that all of us are susceptible to these Five Movers, ninja *sennin* learned to guard their own mind castles from such strategies. They realized, as we must, how vital it is we exorcise our own emotional demons before attempting to incite the emotions of others, lest we—too late!—discover that the hunter has become the hunted!

Mindfulness of our own feelings and a realistic assessment of our own emotional strengths and weaknesses can help us better guard ourselves against mental frustration welling up within and from arrows of emotional manipulation aimed at us from those attempting to storm our mind castle.

MOOD SPOTTING

	GOOD MOOD	STRESSED/BAD MOOD	DECEPTIVE
MOUTH	Full smile (teeth visible)	Lips only smile. Quick smile if at all.	Nervous licking of lips, trembling biting of lips.
EYES	Wide and alert, good eye contact.	Eyes narrowed looks away. Conversely: Eyes may be wide and pupils dilated if frightened.	Eyes darting. Rubbing eyes with fingers. Avoids eye contact.
HANDS	Hands open, fingers loose and expressive.	Clenched. White knuckled.	Rubbing hands together. Playing with objects.
ARMS	Loose. Wide "friendly" gestures..	Crossed. Closed off.	Hands in pocket (also denotes nervousness). Elbows close to body.
SITTING	Relaxed	On edge of seat	Shifting
FEET	Wide stance, tipping back on heels. "Boxed" facing, shoulder-to-shoulder aligned.	Feet close together. Side towards you.	Shifting. Foot scraping floor. Tapping floor.
BREATHING	Regular, deep, "belly breathing"	Irregular, short "chest" breaths	Short "chest" breaths (facilitates "fast talking")
MUSCLES	Relaxed	Stiff	Stiff/twitching

Figure 22.

GETTING SOME CHINESE FACE

Miyamoto Musashi used the word *attitude* to refer to the way a samurai held his sword and to the overall stance one took when facing down an adversary. Master Musashi also taught we should make our combat attitude the same as our everyday attitude. Like samurai on the battlefield, we must always be alert and prepared to deal with danger—whether an actual physical attack or psychological intrustion into our mental space.

Likewise we should be able to carry the calm and relaxed attitude we have out in our everyday life out into the stressful world at large. Musashi knew what he was asking and was astute enough a student of human nature to realize that we "carry ourselves" differently at work than at home than at church.

In other words, we all wear different "faces"—*masks*—for different situations.

T'-zi-bu: Chinese Vampires

Japanese ninja can be traced back to tactics, techniques, and training taken from Chinese Moshuh Nanren (Lung and Prowant, 2000). Yet even among lions, there are always to be found lions with longer teeth, sharper claws.

Master strategists and interrogators for the Moshuh Nanren were called "T-zi-bu," which literally means "Taking another's life-force for one's own." In other words, a "vampire"!

Noshuh Nanren (themselves sometimes referred to as Lin Kuei, "demons") employed T-zi-bu operatives for a variety of tasks, but they seem to have originated as female agents adept at stroking secrets from foes (paging Delilah!) since the name originally implied a form of sexual vampirism, similar to medieval Western legends of a succubus (demons appearing in the guise of beautiful women who suck the life out of sleeping men).

Some researchers point to these Moshuh Nanren female "vampires" as a possible origin for the Black Lotus sisterhood. While undoubtedly some T-zi-bu agents may have pulled double duty (working as both Moshuh Nanren and being Black Lotus initiates), and whereas dispossessed T-zi-bu may have found sanctuary within the Black Lotus, the actual origins of the Black Lotus obviously go even further back in Chinese history.

True T-zi-bu (pronounced T-zee-boo, sometimes spelled Caibu) were masters (and mistresses) of gathering information, not only via the Moshuh Nanren's extensive spy network(s), but also by targeting individuals using what has been called Dim Mak Hsing.

Whereas the "death touch" art is said to have originated in India as a purely physical art (known in Sanskrit as *Varma adi,* "striking at vital spots," or simply *Marman,* "death spots"), the *Dim Mak* of the Moshuh Nanren had both the physical component as well as a psychological (Hsing) component.

T-zi-bu psychological ploys are based in the *Pakua* "eight Trigrams" (see Lung and Prowant, 2001). These "eight Trigrams" can be (and have been) applied to physical combat (e.g., Pakua Boxing created by Taoist alchemist Yu-hau Shan, employing circular movements and open hand strikes) and to Black Science ploys meant to undermine an interrogatee's resistance, sabotage a negotiator from getting the upper hand, or soften up an opponent by planting doubt in his mind. (See Figure 23, opposite.)

The Twelve Animal Passions

Astrology has always been popular throughout the East. Practiced in China in ancient times, it was still thriving in the thirteenth century when Marco Polo met scores of wizards who used a variety of fortune-telling, the most popular being horoscopes.

Asian astrology is based on the longest chronological record in history, the Chinese lunar calendar, a cycle of which is completed every sixty years. This is further broken down into five subcycles of twelve years each. Our current sixty-year cycle began in 1984. February 7, 2008 marked the Chinese New Year, opening the year of the Rat, 4706.

According to legend, the emperor of heaven (later identified with Buddha) sent invitations out to all animals inviting them to a great feast, but only twelve beasts obeyed him by answering the summons. These twelve beasts were in turn rewarded by the Emperor, who named one year of the twelve-year cycle after each of them: Rat, Ox, Tiger, Rabbit, Dragon, Snake, Horse, Sheep, Monkey, Cock, Dog, and Pig.

Over centuries of observation, Chinese astrologers recorded the tendencies of persons born in each year and determined that the animal ruling the year in which we are born has a profound influence on both our personality and potentiality. Your birth sign is "the animal which hides in your heart." Understanding your "birth beast" gives you insight into yourself and helps you avoid disaster by advising you the best times to act and the best times to refrain from acting.

Chinese astrology eventually spread throughout the Far East. When Chi-

T'ZI-BU EIGHT TRIGRAMS PLOYS

CHINESE NAME	PHYSICAL PART	CONTROLS	MIND PLOY
Ch 'ien	HEAD	HEAD	Attack his mind using the five F.L.A.G.S. (Fear, Lust, Anger, Greed, and Sympathy)
Kan	EARS	KIDNEYS	Upset and undermine your foe with gossip and disinformation
Ken	HANDS	NECK	Attack him through his job, coworkers, his boss. Uncover past deeds
Chen	FEET	Left side of abdomen	Question his motivation, make him doubt his chosen path in life. Incite his *spleen* (ill will and malice)
Sun	BUTTOCKS	SPINE (from the first segment of the coccyx up to the seventh vertebra)	Excite his lusts, especially his sexual desire
Li	EYES	HEAD (again) THE SENSES	Dazzle him with illusion confuse him with the play of **shadows**. Turn his black-and-white world gray. (See *Ninja Shadowhand*, Lung and Prowant, Citadel, 2004)
K'un	ABDOMEN	Midsection of ABDOMEN	Attack his appetites both (physical (addictions) and psychological (lusts, fetishes, and phobias) Unbalance him (Tan Tlen)
Tui	MOUTH	Right side of the ABDOMEN	Incite his ill temper (gall) by putting words in his mouth. Make him choke on his own words.

Figure 23.

nese astrology was first introduced to Japan, Shinobi ninja immediately recognized it as a valuable tool and weapon. From the ninja *sennin's* mastery of Chinese astrology came the ninja art of *junishi-do-justu,* cataloging valuable clues for undermining the seemingly impenetrable walls of a foe's mind castle.

Today, at sunset on the streets of Tokyo, sidewalk fortune-tellers known as *ekisha* set up booths. Dressed in black kimonos, these mysterious individuals use astrology, palmistry, and consult the *I Ching* (Chinese Book of Changes) to tell the fates of passersby. Many ekisha trace themselves and their arcane craft back to medieval ninja sennin.

Master strategists and seducers throughout the Far East, and not just in Japan, employ the ancient art of Chinese astrology to determine a person's overall temperament as well as that person's weakest time of the day, when they are most susceptible to physical attack and mental manipulation.

For strategists, an adversary's birth year reveals information about that adversary's personality, insight that can be used when plotting strategy (for example when a adversary is the weakest and thus most vulnerable to attack). Study of astrology also warns the strategist of their own inherent times of weakness, when they should refrain from action, times when an adversary— also versed in astrology—might target them!

Each of these yearly animal "totems" has a strongest and weakest time of the day, corresponding to a period of two Western hours. For example, for a person born under the sign of the Cock the strongest period of the day is from 5 P.M. to 7 P.M. Moving toward this period, in ascendancy, the Cock steadily gains in strength. Moving away from this prime time, toward its 11 A.M. to 1 P.M. latency period, the cock becomes weaker and more vulnerable to both physical and mental assault.

Seductionists employing this method also take into consideration their target's weakest time of day in order to determine when the target will be most susceptible to the power of suggestion.

Another factor is whether or not your adversary is surrounded by conflicting and counterproductive (toxic) birth beasts that suck away his energy (rather than complementing birth beasts that might strengthen him). A Cock, for example, will have trouble working with or marrying someone born under a Horse sign.

Medieval ninja diligently studied the inherent weaknesses associated with each birth-totem of Chinese astrology. Thus, when infiltrating a female kuniochi agent into an enemy court, ninja strategists would pick an agent whose birth beast made her compatible with, and thus inherently attractive to, the targeted foe.

Let's take a look at these "Birth Beasts":

- **The Rat** is an ambitious hard worker who refuses to ask for help or take charity. Thus his pride cometh before his fall. The Rat seldom makes lasting friendships. He (or she) has a small circle of friends.

- **The Ox** is a complainer. Pretending to sympathize with him gets you closer to him. The Ox tries to live up to the expectations of others. Show him a way to do this (building up his confidence), or make him doubt that he is accomplishing this (undermining his confidence), and you'll have the Ox's undivided attention.

- **The Tiger** is candid to the point of being rude, restless, rebellious, and suspicious. The Tiger keeps his promises and becomes angry with those who do not. Feeling betrayed, he may react violently.

- **The Rabbit** is kind and sensitive, making him the perfect patsy for sympathy ploys. The Rabbit becomes frustrated and doesn't think straight when inconvenienced. He hates to fight, and is thus too prone to compromise. Rabbits are shy, yet are good in business and handle money well. A business venture that "needs" his expertise will get the Rabbit to open his door every time. For all their business savvy, Rabbits believe in luck. Take off his foot and make his luck your own. A windfall becomes the Rabbit's downfall.

- **The Dragon** thinks he's above the law. Eccentric (like the Cock) the Dragon expects admiration. Dragon has an explosive temper, and is passionate about nature and his health. So energetic, like a fire which is continuously fanned higher and higher, Dragons often burn out early in life.

Martial arts great Bruce Lee was born in 1940, year of the Dragon at the hour of the Dragon, making him a "Double Dragon," a very powerful celestial sign in the East. A restless, noisy, and temperamental child, the Bruce Lee the world came to admire was in every way a Dragon personality: passionate about health (to the point of being eccentric), in many ways he felt himself above the law in the way he casually revealed many forbidden Eastern martial-arts secrets to the West (for which, many believe, he was killed).

- **The Snake** is attracted by physical beauty. Susceptible to "the finer things" in life, vain and high-tempered, a Snake-dominated personality is a prime candidate for lust-seduction ploys. As a result, a Snake (male or female) will be putty in the hands of a kuniochi. A vain Snake (male or female) can be trapped with promises of the fountain of youth.

Do not underestimate the Snake; they can be calculating and ruthless. Snakes are poor gamblers (and superstitious). And one of the Snake's biggest failing's is that they can't let an opportunity pass. Snakes look for love in all the wrong places—and usually find it!

- **The Horse** likes to be the center of attention and needs people. Get close to the Horse by posing as an adoring fan. Ostenatious and impatient, champing at the bit, the Horse often suffers from restlessness and insomnia. They don't take to the bridle and saddle well, but once "broken" serve loyally.

- **The Sheep** is timid and prefers anonymity. They are quick to defend the underdog, making them suckers to sympathy ploys. The Sheep doesn't take personal criticism well. As a result, Sheep let pressure build up and when the Sheep finally does explode, it is with inappropriate anger. Remember *Rams* are sheep, too.

On the battlefield we attack the Sheep in small increments, increasing the pressure little by little until the Sheep explodes and, in a rage, makes a fatal mistake. To seduce a sheep, tease, in order to pull the wool over their eyes.

- **The Monkey** is always full of plans and always looking for someone to tell those plans to. Give the Monkey your ear. Innovators and inventors, Monkeys are nonetheless easily discouraged and confused, and thus open to anyone (such as a mind-slayer) who acts like he knows the answer.

- **The Cock** has a strong point when it comes to being punctual. However, that same punctuality—or predictability—makes a Cock more vulnerable to anyone spying at his path through life. On the battlefield a predictable enemy is a godsend. In the bedroom a predictable cock is asked to go more times than it's asked to come.

Combative, eccentric, often selfish, Cocks like the public eye. Look closely. They may be secretly insecure and in need of constant bolstering—opening the door for the insincere praise of a "sympathetic" seducer.

The cock is a perfectionist who can't admit to being wrong and is thus easily trapped by the manipulator who can first make the Cock appear wrong and then provides him a way out of being wrong. This two-pronged ploy follows classic Chinese strategy. Says Tu Mu:

> Trap an already trapped foe twice by offering him a clear road
> to safety, creating the possibility for life where there was only
> the determination of death. Having done so, strike!

- **The Dog** is loyal to a fault, that fault being that, in extremis, dog people are born followers, and easily led astray by others. Dogs are generous, making them prime targets for donation scams, especially from religious hucksters who use "plain talk."

- **The Pig** lives for today and has a (dangerous) "fatalistic" streak. Home-loving (which can lead to laziness) and family-oriented, Pigs marry early and, as a result, are prone to marital strife.

Your order of birth and your birth beast can have positive and negative influences on your life. These two factors are predispositions, not predestination, and point only to innate tendencies that once aware of, we are free to embrace or reject.

Nothing illustrates this better than the story of master strategist Miyamoto Musashi (though, in telling this tale Chinese will often substitute Sun Tzu's name, Indian adepts swear it was Kautilya . . . well, you get the idea!):

> On the eve of a great battle, Miyamoto Musashi noticed that
> the (samurai lord) with whom he'd taken service seemed distressed and unable to focus on the coming battle.

Asked what was the matter, the lord told Musashi that his favorite astrologer had predicted that he, the lord, would soon die!

Shocked by this, Musashi immediately called for the astrologer. When the astrologer presented himself, Musashi confronted him.

"Where do you get this information that our lord will soon die!" Musashi demanded.

"All is written in the stars," the astrologer smiled.

"And when do the stars say you will die?" Musashi asked.

"The stars predict that I will live a long life, find fame and fortune, and have many offspring!" the wizard proclaimed confidently.

Musashi's sword separated the wizard's head from his shoulders.

Tossing the head of the astrologer at the feet of the shocked lord, Musashi explained, "If a man is unable to predict his own fate what hope has he of predicting the fate of others?"*

During World War II, British intelligence maintained an Occult Bureau with astrologers on staff, all because it was well known that Hitler and many other Nazi bigwigs believed in astrology. This Occult Bureau used astrologers to figure out what Hitler's astrologers were telling him on any given day, hence how the dictator might be expected to act.

So it doesn't matter if we don't believe in astrology, but it helps to know if our foe—or that babe at the bar—does. (See chinesezodiac.com.)

Whether we think astrology is a crock or not matters only insofar as it can be made to work to our advantage.

Siang Mien: Face-Reading 101

The human face contains a world of secrets.
—Henry Linn

---

*The headless wizard was later discovered to have been a ninja spy planted in the lord's court to unnerve him.

When it comes to strategy, East or West, China's Sun Tzu is the acknowledged master.

Most students of Sun Tzu are more familiar with his masterpiece *Ping-Fa,* "Art of War" but Sun Tzu's first book was *Prime Principles of Victory,* a treatise concentrating on deceit. So Sun Tzu literally "wrote the book" (actually two books) on mastering strategy.

There were, of course, other strategists before Sun Tzu, most of whom he undoubtedly studied. But after Sun Tzu, all subsequent strategists (and seducers) would be compared to him.

Unfortunately, Sun Tzu is a lot like the weather: everybody talks about it, too few actually do anything about it. It's the age-old problem of "appreciation" versus "application."

Philosophy, be it meditative or military, battlefield or bedroom, is easy to talk about, hard to apply practically. But finding practical applications today for ancient wisdoms is what will make us the masters of tomorrow.

Let's try an example:

> When you have surrounded your enemy, you must leave him
> a way of escape. Never press an enemy at bay. (Sun Tzu,
> chapter VII:31–32)

In combat, this means that desperate men, trapped with no way out, will fight to the death. Therefore, on the battlefield always give your opponent a way out, a way to withdraw with honor. In China this is referred to as saving face, "face" being a synonym in the East for honor, dignity, and status. The opposite is *Tiu Lien,* "to lose face."

The same principle applies in the West. For example, in an argument even when a person knows they're 100 percent wrong, even when they realize you've trapped them in an indefensible position, they may still stubbornly hold their ground for fear of "losing face," being made to look foolish, or, in today's jargon, fear of being "punked out."

Now, rather than browbeating and belittling them (unless this was your intent all along!), graciously leave them a clear avenue of escape, one that allows them to retain their dignity and save face.

They may be so relieved by your show of mercy that you will turn them into an ally. Or, at the very least, they will have learned to fear you and not challenge you again.

Likewise, always allow your lover to save face and face might not be the only thing you get back in return!

One way to help yourself save face is by better learning to read other peoples' faces.

By now you should have no doubt that increasing your ability to read the interest, intent, and intrigue written on another's face can spell the difference in your saving face on the battlefield and maybe getting some face in the bedroom.

Not the easiest of tasks considering we routinely use as many as three thousand different expressions each day!

In wartime, anticipating the movement of ten thousand enemy troops comes down to correctly reading the face of a single individual, that of the enemy commander, or in reading the truthfulness on the face of a captured spy or enemy traitor. (See *Theatre of Hell: Dr. Lung's Complete Guide to Torture*, 2003.)

Whether trying to read the faces sitting around the Saturday-night Texas hold 'em table, or the face of the lawyer across from you at the negotiation table, whether your goal is to get your adversary to drop his guard, or just getting some fine filly to lower her standards, being able to read the tells and twitches on another's face can certainly come in handy. (See Figure 24.)

Chinese physiognomy takes the skill of face-reading seriously, taking it a step further, claiming to be able to tell not only a person's personality just by looking at the shape and features of their face, but also to be able to determine that person's past, present, and perhaps even their future destiny. That's because one's face changes with one's mind:

- Good deeds and good intentions bring about positive changes in your *joss* (luck, fate, karma) and this will be reflected in your face.
- Bad deeds and malicious intentions cause correspondingly unfortunate changes that will also show up on your face.

Siang Mien, the Chinese "art of face-reading," goes back thousands of years and is one of the oldest professions in China. Though banned along with other feudal "superstitions" when the Communists came to power, face-reading has remained popular in China down to the present day. In fact, despite the ban, it was common knowledge that high-ranking Communists, including Mao Zedong himself, remained firm believers in the art.

So far as strategy and seduction are concerned, it doesn't matter whether you personally believe in the art of face-reading or not. So long as whomever you are dealing with believes in it, it will affect you. Those believing in this system might use it to prejudge you, to stereotype you the minute you walk through the door from something as simple as the shape of your face.

PERFECTING YOUR POKER FACE

SIGNS OF . . .

1. OPENNESS:	Arms spread wide, legs not crossed. Coat unbuttoned.
2. COOPERATION: (Negotiations)	Sitting on the edge of his chair, leaning forward, attentive. Unbuttoning his coat. Nodding. Rubbing chin in consideration.
3. CONFIDENCE:	Hands and fingers "steepled." Fingers in pockets with thumbs exposed. Hands grasp labels of coat. Back straight. Hands behind back, clasped (i.e. hiding an "ace-in-the-hole").
4. CONSIDERING: (Evaluating)	Rubbing chin (wise man stroking beard while he thinks about something). Cleaning glasses (so he can "see" more clearly). Finger tapping nose ("I like the way this smells."). Filling his pipe (He's already decided to take the offer and is preparing to "relax," or begins fiddling with a cigar, ready to "celebrate" the deal.).
5. DEFENSIVENESS:	Arms and legs crossed, pointing fingers. "Karate-chop" gestures with stiff hand. Fast movements with hands (afraid slower movements will betray him).
6. WORRY: (Nervousness)	Fidgeting. Playing with objects. Clearing throat repeatedly. Pulling on his ear. Wiping his nose (doesn't like the way this "smells").
7. SUSPICION:	Arms crossed protecting chest (heart). Sideways glances. Standing more than 5 feet away (out of arm's reach). Coat remains buttoned (for fast getaway). Rubbing eyes (to "clear" his vision and get a better look/keep an eye on you).
8. INSECURITY: (Lack of confidence)	Hands in pocket (afraid he'll accidently "break" something). Playing with/chewing on pen, etc. (surrogate nipple). One thumb holds down (covers) the other (keeping "little" brother out of trouble). Jiggling money (ready to "pay" his way out of trouble). Playing with his keys (ready to start the car and go home, back to his "comfort zone."
9. FRUSTRATION: (Irritation)	Hands keep making fists. Wringing hands (to relieve tension). Rubbing hands through hair (seeking to stimulate inspiration). Rubbing the back of his neck (to relieve tension). Taking short "noisy" sighing breaths. Making "tsk" sound and sucking in air through his teeth.
10. FEAR:	Quiver and hesitation in voice. He makes his silhouette "smaller" by slouching, putting his hands in his pocket, crossing his arms and legs (see Defensive). Avoids eye contact.

Figure 24.

According to Siang Mien, the left side of the human face is yang (male, conscious), while the right side is yin (female, subconscious). As a result, the two halves are not always in agreement. By obscuring one side of a person's face, you can see when the two sides are not in agreement (for example, one side will actually look like it is slightly frowning), indicating that, at the very least, that person has doubts about what they are saying.

Quick face-reading tip #1: You already know you can spot a laughing liar when his eyes don't match his smiling lips. By using your thumb (or a playing card) to surreptitiously block out the lower part of his face—his smiling mouth—you can see if his eyes match his lips. Works great at the poker table to help spot the other guy bluffing.

Quick face-reading tip #2: Pay attention to the lower part of the face, since false "social emotions" tend to be expressed through the lower half of the face, while our more sincere "primary emotions" are more likely to be expressed on the upper part of the face, especially around the eyes.

Gui Gu-Tze, author of the classic face-reading text *Xiang Bian Wei Mang* (250 B.C.E.), is considered the "Father of Chinese face-reading." Gui Gu-Tze was also a great philosopher and teacher. One of his students was Sun Bin, a direct descendent of Sun Tzu and author of *The Lost Art of War.*

Gui Gu-Tze collected his data from personal observation, calculation, from foreign sources, and from ancient texts on face-reading imported from places like Tibet and India. For example, the *Kama Sutra* instructs in the art of knowing the character of a man from his features. (See section called "Kama Sutra Karma." See also Lung and Prowant, 2001.)

Two respected Chinese (pseudo)sciences are also known to have influenced Gui Gu-Tze:

> *I-Ching,* an ancient system of divination traced back to the twelfth century B.C.E., called possibly the oldest book in the world (Linn, 1999:9), and
>
> *Wu-hsing,* the Taoist theory of the "Five Elements" (see Lung and Prowant, 2001:31).

According to *Wu-hsing,* all things and situations are constructed from five "elements": Fire, Water, Earth, Wood (also called Void), and Metal (also called Wind). In each instance, one of these elements is dominant. These elements either complement or cancel out one another. (See Figure 25.)

As to the future of face-reading, it remains alive and well throughout the East:

TAKING THEM AT FACE VALUE

	FIRE	METAL	WOOD	WATER	EARTH
SHAPE:	Pointed	Square	Long	Round	Thick
KEY:	Proriety (Justice)	Rightiousness	Kindness	Intelligence	Reliability
ORGAN:	Forehead	Eye	Ears	Mouth	Nose
SENSE:	Thought	Sight	Hearing	Touch	Scent
COLOR:	Red	White	Green	Black	Yellow
MEDICAL:	Heart	Lung	Liver	Kidney	Spleen
ATTITUDE:	Consumes (like fire)	Cuts Off (like metal)	Builds (like wood)	Flows (like water)	Endures (like earth)
FLAWS:	Hot-headed, ambitious, can be cruel	Short-tempered, calculating, outspoken.	Sympathetic, overly generous.	Opportunistic, unscrupulous	Secretive, desire for power.
STRENGTH:	Ambitious, physical courage	Born leaders, outspoken.	Generous, sympathetic.	Born businessmen. Quick and eager.	Calm, easy-going. Trustworthy.

Figure 25.

Without a doubt, the fascinating art of face reading will continue to play a significant role in the political, social, cultural, and personal events in China for a promising future in the personnel and strategic decision-making processes of both private corporations and government agencies throughout the world." (Linn, 1999:8)

Any chance face-reading might fall out of favor in this technological age? No way. As popular as ever in the East, face-reading continues to grow in popularity in the West, where computer software has already been developed that blends the ancient art of face-reading with modern high-tech biometrics.

For example, a recent report published in *The Journal of Evolution and Human Behavior* speculates that facial structure and features can say a lot about sexual and relationship traits.

Seven hundred men and women were polled. Seventy-two percent correctly guessed the person's sexual attitudes based on facial features. Woman judged other women who had casual sexual tendencies to be more beautiful.

According to the study, done at Durham University, girls with large doe eyes are more likely to be interested in a one-night stand.

Conversely, men couldn't always tell which women were more strongly interested in short-term sex.

The lead author of the study feels these facial recognition techniques and preferences stem from evolution because they allow women to tell which men will make good fathers, while men can figure out what kind of woman will "let him in." *(American Curves* July 2007:23)

More on face-reading in the section on "sexual feng shui." (See Figure 26.)

To pay attention to what someone does not do is often more
important than noting what he does.
—*The Method of Zen,* **Eugen Herrigel, 1974**

GENDER-BENDERS

Animals don't do sexual identity. They just do sex.
—**Sociologist Eric Anderson** (*Scientific American Mind,* **July 2008**)

A modern Chinese tale of seduction: When Shi Pei Pu met Bernard Bouriscout, a young diplomat assigned to the French embassy, at a party in China in 1964, the two struck up an immediate friendship and (as Bouriscout later admitted) the Frenchman found himself queerly attracted to the petite Chinese man: This disturbed Bouriscout somewhat since he did not consider himself homosexual.

The two quickly became friends and, over time, Shi Pei Pu confided to Bouriscout that "he" was actually a "she," that she only pretended to be a man. It seems male children were more highly valued in China, so as a child she had been forced to live as a boy.

Bouriscout was fascinated (and a little relieved) and Shi Pei Pu quickly grasped on to the young man's lust for intrigue and adventure to further entice him.

Won over by Shi Pei Pu's story, Bouriscout fell madly in love. They moved in together. They had sex . . .

Shi Pei Pu continued to dress like a man.

TAO

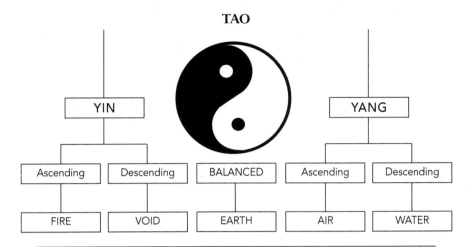

Figure 26.

In December 1965, despite his protestations, Bouriscout was recalled to Paris but, before they parted company, Shi Pei Pu announced she was pregnant with his child. A year later Pei Pu wrote Bouriscout saying she had given birth, and sending Bouriscout pictures of his son, "Bernard."

Bouriscout was overjoyed. The boy looked just like him.

Now even more obsessed to return to China, to the woman he loved and to his son, Bouriscout finally won another diplomatic posting to China in 1969. By this time, Mao's Cultural Revolution was in full swing, severely restricting the activities of "imperialist" foreigners in China.

In a desperate attempt to gain more access to Shi Pei Pu and his son by currying favor with Communist authorities, Bouriscout began stealing French government secrets for the Communists. He was repaid by finally being allowed to meet his son.

Bouriscout continued funneling secrets to the Communists until he was recalled to Paris again in 1972. Finally, after Herculean effort, he succeeded in getting permission from his Communist handlers for Shi Pei Pu and little Bernard to come to France.

But it was already too late for Bouriscout. Under suspicion for some time, in 1983 he was finally arrested by French authorities and charged with spying.

In an attempt to justify his actions, Bouriscout made a full confession, claiming he did it all for the love of his wife and son.

French investigators were confused about the "wife" part until Bouriscout explained that Shi Pei Pu, the "man" he was living with, was really a woman.

French authorities decided to examine the evidence a little closer. This included examining Shi Pei Pu a little closer . . .

Then it was Bouriscout's turn to be confused when French authorities showed him graphic proof that Shi Pei Pu, the woman pretending to be a man was, indeed, a man!

What the authorities had on their hands was a real life *Victor Victoria* (1982) stew, with a dash of *Yentl* (1983) and a pinch or two of *The Crying Game* (1992) thrown in for spice!

Accomplished Chinese actor and female impersonator (!) Shi Pei Pu had pretended to be a woman pretending to be a man all in order to seduce a naïve twenty-four-year old Frenchman into turning traitor. Under(the)cover(s) mission accomplished.

Even as he was being led away to prison, Bouriscout refused to believe his wife, the love of his life, the "mother" of his child, was a man.* (Obviously there's no translation into French or Chinese for the American adage "Always look under the hood.")

One might argue that Asians have a somewhat more enlightened view of such things . . . or perhaps just a more colorful history of such things?

In Japanese Kabuki theater men play all the roles, including the female parts—as it was in Shakespeare's day. Remember 1998's *Shakespeare in Love?* (By the way, the very word "drag" comes to us from that very Elizabethan stage, where it first appeared as stage direction for male actors "Dressed As Girls.")

In Kabuki, masters of such feminine impersonation are called *Onnagata,* and are much honored in Japan. The argument is that it doesn't take much for a male actor to play a man on stage, but it takes one helluva male actor to play a female convincingly.

So impressive was (and still is) the Onnagata art that, during medieval times, young ninja were often sent to study with such masters in anticipation of assignments where they might have to dress in drag in order to get close to a target. (See the section on "The Art of Disguise" in *The Nine Halls of Death,* Lung and Tucker, Citadel, 2007.)

Japanese author Yukio Mishima (committed seppuku ritual samurai sui-

---

*See *Liaison* by Joyce Wadler. (New York, Bantam Books, 1993.)

cide in November 1970) was once enamored of one such actor. Such things seem to be better understood in the East. In the West, there is inevitably scandal, ever since ancient times.

For example, Julius Caesar repeatedly had an affair with King Nicomedes of Bithynia while he (Caesar) was still a young man on military campaign in Asia Minor. Reportedly, Julius was the passive "bottom" in the affair, being dominated by the older man. Romans at the time accepted homosexuality, but expected men to remain a manly "top." (Terry Crowdy, *Military Misdemeanors*, Osprey Publications, 2007)

This scandal almost ended Caesar's political career before it even began. Roman author Suetonus Tranguillus went so far as nicknaming young Caesar "Queen of Bithynia," quipping that Caesar was "every woman's man and every man's woman"!

Fortunately (?) for Caesar, this early sexual scandal would pale in comparison to the world-shaking affair between him and Cleopatra.

Asians overall tend to view gender-benders, if not with acceptance, then at least with more understanding and tolerance.

As in the West, various Asian authorities disagree as to the origin of homosexuality, with most coming down on the nature side of the equation. Of course, to most Asians, nature can include reincarnation.

Buddhists tell of how once the Buddha was begging for alms in the city of Rajagriha (India) when two young boys, one named Virtue Victorious (Skt. *Jaya*) and the other Invincible (Skt. *Vijaya*) made him an offering of mud pies. So innocent and sincere was this offering that Buddha blessed them and as a result of the good karma generated by their act (and by the blessing of the Buddha) the two friends were later reincarnated as Indian King Ashoka and his consort-wife. (You may recall King Ashoka from our India section?)

Thus, to the Asian mind, lovers and friends often find one another again across many lifetimes—sometimes switching genders. As such, it is understandable that human attractions might not always remain simply one male, one female.

In India, at the time of the writing of the Kama Sutra, homosexuality was not only acknowledged but was commented on to some extent:

> A man should therefore pay regard to the place, to the time, and to the practice which is to be carried out, and also as to whether it is agreeable to his nature and to himself, and then

he may or may not practice these things according to circumstances. But after all, these things being done secretly, and the mind of the man being fickle, how can it be known what any person will do at any particular time and for any particular purpose? *(The Kama Sutra of Vatsyayana)*

and

The characteristics of manhood are said to consist of roughness, and impetuosity, while weakness, tenderness, sensibility, and an inclination to turn away from unpleasant things are distinguishing marks of womanhood. The excitement of passion, the peculiarities of habit may sometimes cause contrary results to appear, but these do not last long, and in the end the natural state is resumed. (Ibid.)

For those requiring a more detailed road map, chapter 12 of the Kama Sutra is devoted almost entirely to the practice (and perfection!) of Aurparishtaka, "mouth congress" (fellatio), especially as performed by eunuchs:

There are two kinds of eunuchs, those that are disguised as males, and those that are disguised as females.

Eunuchs disguised as females, imitate their dress, speech, gestures, tenderness, timidity, simplicity, softness and bashfulness. The acts that are done on the *jaghana* or middle parts of women are done in the mouth of these eunuchs, and this is called *Aurparishtaka*. These eunuchs derive their imaginable pleasure, and their livelihood from this kind of congress, and they lead the life of courtesans. So much concerning eunuchs disguised as females.

Eunuchs disguised as males, keep their desires secret, and when they wish to do anything they lead the life of shampooers.

Under the pretense of shampooing, an eunuch of this kind embraces and draws towards himself, the thighs of the man whom he is shampooing, and after this he touches the joints of the thighs and his *jaghana,* or central parts of the body. Then, if he finds the lingam of the man erect, he presses with his hands, and chaffs [i.e., teases and playfully scolds] him for getting into that stage [i.e., an erection]. If after this, and knowing his intention, the man does not tell the eunuch to proceed, then the latter does it of his own accord and begins the congress. If however, he is ordered by the man to do it, then he disputes with him, and only consents at last with difficulty.

The following eight things are [then] done by the eunuch, one after the other viz. the nominal congress; biting the sides; pressing outside; pressing inside; kissing; rubbing; "sucking a mango fruit"; swallowing up.

At the end of each of these, the eunuch expresses [i.e., feigns] his wish to stop, but when one of them is finished, the man desires him to do another. And after that is done, then the one that follows it, and so on.

In case you're understandably curious about exactly what all "sucking a mango fruit" entails, the Kama Sutra is more than happy to explain—and instruct:

When, in the same way, he puts the half of it into his mouth, and forcibly kisses and sucks it, it is called "sucking a mango fruit." (Ibid.)

Though ostensively written for eunuchs, ladies take note:

The Aurparishtaka is practiced also by unchaste and wanton women, female attendants and serving maids, i.e. those not married to anybody, but who live by shampooing.

The male servants of some men carry on the mouth congress with their masters. It is also practiced by some citizens who know each other well* among themselves. (Ibid.)

The author of the Kama Sutra was well aware that women have "needs" too—especially lonely women:

The women of the royal harem cannot see any men on account of their being strictly guarded; neither do they have their desires satisfied, because their only husband is common to many wives. For this reason, among themselves, they give pleasure to each other in various ways now described. Having dressed the daughters or their nurses, or their female friends,

---

*Well, if they didn't "know each well" *before,* they sure will now!

or their female attendants, like men, they accomplish their object by means of bulbs, roots, and fruits having the form of the lingam, or they lie down upon the statue of a male figure, in which the lingam is visible and erect.

Such women were not above the use of either skullduggery not encouraging a little cross-dressing on the side when necessity demanded:

By means of their female attendants, the ladies of the royal harem generally get men into their apartments in the disguise or dress of women. (Ibid.)

Speaking of cross-dressing . . .

Gaydar

"Gaydar" (gay + radar), is defined as the seemingly extrasensory ability to tell whether someone is gay or straight. Some seem to have it, some don't . . . some don't want to tell—so don't ask! Recent research however has taken away the air of mysticism surrounding "gaydar" by revealing that the reason some people have the power to literally sniff out another's sexuality is strongly rooted in biology.

At a 2005 experiment conducted at the University of Pennsylvania's Monell Chemical Senses Center volunteers were asked to sniff underarm sweat from donors of a variety of genders and sexual orientation. Findings:

- Gay men strongly preferred the odor of other gay men.
- Lesbians gravitated toward the smell of other lesbians.
- Straight women rated the odor of straight men higher than that of gay men.

In short, each group preferred the smell of their first-choice mates, indicating a scent-based ability to assess sexual orientation. Another similar study confirmed that gay men and lesbians can recognize and identify the odor of others who share their sexual preference, leading researchers to conclude that "This kind of scent-based gaydar enables gays to pinpoint potential partners instantly." ("Solving the Mystery of Gaydar," *Psychology Today* January/February 2008: 73. See also "The Hidden Power of Scent" by Josie Glaususz, *Scientific American Mind,* August/September 2008: 38–43.)

Likewise, researchers at Karolinska University in Sweden have identified a potential reason why gay men find the smell of other men so enticing. They found that androstenone (a steroid compound) excited brain areas that control sexual behavior in gay men but left the brains of straight men unaffected. Conclusion: "This suggests the chemical may be an integral part of the scent-driven signaling mechanism that attracts gay men to each other." (Ibid.)

Androstenone is found in both a man's sweat and semen and is believed to help put women in the mood by altering their levels of cortisol, a stress hormone (a stress hormone found in women's saliva). Smelling androstenone can induce significant changes in a woman's hormonal balance. (Glaususz, Ibid., 43)

Other tried-and-tested methods to determine which team you should be playing for:

- Your ring finger is longer than your index finger.
- The swirls of hair on the back of your head go counterclockwise rather than the "normal" clockwise.
- And you know the words to every Celine Dion song!

You do know that all children are conceived female, right? Somewhere along the womb-way some of us get an extra little squirt of testosterone and suddenly those ovaries decide to become testicles, while that already hard-to-find "little boy in the boat" grows up to be the hulking (you wish!) head of Mr. Willie.

In the same way it's been theorized that the prostate gland in men is just an "enlarged" version of the woman's G-spot . . . or vice versa. FYI: The prostate gland has hundreds of nerve endings and holds all your manly fluids (the testicles "only" hold your little wigglers; the prostate actually produces the viscous fluid, semen, that your little seamen swim around in).

As a result, many men—yeah, straight guys too—enjoy it when their lady friend lounges around a little on the back porch.

Yang-chi Cultivation

Yang is by nature weaker and more vulnerable to depletion than yin, and therefore it needs to be carefully nurtured, especially during intercourse.
—Reid (1989:278)

During any sexual union an exchange of yin and yang takes place, with the one partner "absorbing" the complementing/balancing chi essence of the other.

Some Taoist scholars maintain that essence is simply "lost" during homosexual acts (gay or lesbian) while others maintain that their identical chi signatures or vibrations merely exchange places with one another—no gain, no loss.

Other Taoists and Tantrists maintain that another man's yang essence can be absorbed during anal intercourse, with the chi essence of the "dominant" partner being absorbed via the prostate and/or absorbed via the porous tissue of the rectum.

Loss of chi-infused semen can be prevented (during either heterosexual or homosexual encounters) by applying firm pressure on the perineum (located between the base of the scrotum and the anus) as ejaculation approaches. This pressure can be applied either by the man himself, or by his sex partner.

Deep breathing in men helps massage the prostate, helping reabsorption of essential elements. More on the benefits of "semen retention" in the section on Sexual Feng Shui.

Two Taoist exercises designed to help gay men better prevent a drain of their yang essence, thereby (re)balancing their chi:

Yang Exercise One: Standing naked in direct sunlight, achieve an erection and orient the glans of your penis toward the sun. Concentrate on feeling the warmth penetrate the glans while alternately tensing and relaxing the muscles at the base of your penis (in effect, making your penis "jump"). This exercise both strengthens the base of the penis while simultaneously allowing you to process needed yang-chi directly from the sun.

Yang Exercise Two: Naked, assume a "dog" position on solid dirt, packed sand, on a natural wooden floor, or on a mat of grass or pure woven fabric. Arch your back up several times—stretching your spine—while simultaneously rolling your shoulders forward and then back, all the while, concentrating on the feel of your flat palms, knees, and the toes and balls of your feet pressing against the ground.

Both these yang exercises can be augmented by using the Z-E-N "Flower breathing" exercise you learned earlier.

What all sexual feng shui scholars agree on is that, in the same way that introducing any single element into a room (a vase of flowers, for instance) must be "balanced" against other objects and arrangements (concentrations of energy) already in the room in order to achieve maximum feng shui benefit, so too in sex in general, and homosexual sex in particular, the participants should consider the entire context of the act (time, place, personalities, emotional investment) and consider adding chi-stimulating activities (other than sex!) before and after the act itself. These can include such things as music, food, fabrics, lighting, and the use of various "mood-enhancing" scents.

A Little Homophobic Strategy

So let's say watching other men "prancing" around gives you the heebie-jeebies (or at least a real "queer" feeling) . . .

And while "Not that there's anything wrong with it, Jerry!" you just don't feel like pinch-hitting when it involves "that other team" . . .

And "those guys" are definitely, 100 percent, swear-to-Christ not the first miss-things that come to mind when you think about seduction, despite all that, remind yourself it's still good strategy to know what "the other team" has up their sleeves (let alone their dresses!).

It's kinda like our argument before concerning Chinese astrology: You may not personally believe that being born in the Year of the Cock has any true significance in your life, but that Hong Kong businessman you're trying to woo might believe that that Cock is very important . . .

We've all heard our buddy's excuses: "It was really dark in the bar . . . and, uh, I was really drunk. . . . No, I didn't notice her Adam's apple. . . . Well, you know some women just have naturally deep voices. . . . Anyway, by then I'd already paid for the room so I thought what the hell!"

Yeah. In this day and age it's easy to get fooled.

That's why you always "Measure twice, cut once."

You should realize that the same seduction strategies, tactics, and techniques that work male-on-female/female-on-male also work on gays and lesbians.

More important, whether for your personal "protection," or some private predilection you'd rather not talk about, keep in mind that gender-benders can use these techniques, too. . . .

Happy hunting. Watch your six!

So how is a dyed-in-the-wool, like-to-roll-in-the-hay-with-a-little-fur (and *only* fur!) kinda fella supposed to use all this gender-bender information to his advantage?

Curiously, there are two ways straight man have found to turn (or is that "bend"?) gender-bending to their dating advantage:

First, *"Faux-mosexuality,"* noun: defined as faking homosexuality in order to appear trendy. And, we should add "less threatening." Yeah, like Warren

Beatty's character in *Shampoo* (1975) and Tony Curtis's milksop in the classic *Some Like It Hot* (1939)—remember, *he* got Marilyn in the end!

A lot of women love hanging out with gay men, since they don't feel pressured or threatened. Also, there is always that politically incorrect, unspoken, hidden agenda wherein a woman thinks "One night in bed with me and I'll turn him straight!" Faux-mosexuality is touted by bands such as tATu and Turbonegro. (Boese, 2006:140)

Second, there's "Fake Fagging," verb: A heterosexual man pretending to be gay in order to pick up women, first gaining the woman's trust and friendship, and then flattering her vanity by claiming her beauty has converted him to heterosexuality. (Ibid.)

> *Honey, it's all drag!*
> **—RuPaul**

6

Vietnam

*Open battles are easy to record. All we need do is follow the noise
and count the bodies. What isn't as easily seen are the many
intrigues and hidden agendas playing out behind the black curtain,
masterful schemes and intricate skullduggery just as important to
the unfolding of history as are bullets and bayonets. Unfortunately,
all we inevitably end up with when trying to decipher the comings
and goings of crafty cabals, secret societies, and shadowy
government agencies is always the same: a dancing tendril of smoke
glimpsed behind us in a dark mirror, whispers and winks.*
—*Lost Fighting Arts of Vietnam* (Citadel, 2006)

The area where the Red river meets the Gulf of Tonkin was once part of the
Qin Empire of China called Xiangjun, "The Elephant District." Its people
were known as the south Yue people or Nan-Yue, which became Nam-Viet,
hence Vietnam.

Vietnam lies halfway between Indian and China along one of Asia's ancient
trade routes. This has been both boon and burden for the people of Vietnam.

In order to survive, the Vietnamese have been forced to master not only
the blade, bludgeon, and bomb but also Black Science.

What can't be taken by force can often be wrested away by skullduggery;
what can't be defended openly can often be supported via subterfuge. Where
strength fails, strategy often wins out.

The Vietnamese have spent the last two thousand years in constant warfare, fighting to expel one uninvited (invading) "guest" after another: Khmer, Chinese, French, Japanese, the French (again!) and, finally those overdressed and overly noisy Americans.

But not all pivotal battles are fought with blade and bullet on an open field. Indeed, many of the most important battles in Vietnam's history took place behind what has been called "a black curtain" of subterfuge, espionage, and policies penned with poison-dipped poniard.

One Vietnamese group that realized early on they might have to fight the French Foreign Legion one day and Freemasons the following day, bartering with European merchants today, getting the better of Japanese invaders tomorrow, was the Cao Dai.

Cao Dai means "High Tower," and it is a tower with "Nine Gates" . . .

Officially founded as a spiritualist movement in the 1920s, but with a spiritual/political blood-pulse going back centuries, in its day Cao Dai not only maintained a well-trained self-defense force but also fielded a wide-ranging network of intelligence operatives, the most adept of which were/are *O Nhm,* "Black Crows."

Cao Dai Black Crow agents are part mystic and magician, all ninja, adept at gathering intelligence and willing to use any method to accomplish his (or her) mission—from making spirits seem to appear, to making enemies disappear!

Black Crows are masters of *Am thi tinh,* the "art of suggestibility," Black Science practices intended to sow doubt and harvest fear in an enemy's mind.

Like Viet Cong guerrillas out in the bush, Black Crows were adept at stringing mental trip-wires and planting passion-dipped punji across the path of their intended victim. O Nhm knew that somewhere within the *That tinh,* the "Seven Passions" we all possess, could be found a weakness to successfully trip up any foe. Thus:

- Joy can be turned to sorrow.
- Sorrow can be dissipated by joy.
- Love made to doubt becomes jealousy and hate.
- Hate can be dispelled or at least confused by the appearance of love.
- Love and lust all too easily come disguised as one another.
- Lust can all too easily override fear (or common sense).
- What we fear we also hate. Yet people often use intense hate to hide secret lust . . . even from themselves.
- And anger can be used to either open our eyes (e.g., "righteous

anger" in response to injustice), or it can blind us by "feeding" emotions like hate and fear.

Black Crows' overall strategy is called *Giao Hoat*, "craft and cunning" and consists of five complementing and overlapping stages called "Jewels," which first aid an O Nhm agent in assessing a situation (or an individual) and then crafting an appropriate "approach strategy."

They are called "the Five Jewels" for the way in which they distract and dazzle the unwary, the same way real jewels so often do.

Understanding these Five Jewels provides us with a strategy and seduction roadmap taking us where we want to go—whether a quick victory on the battlefield or a quickie in the copy room.

The Five Jewels

- *Can nao* (lit. "war of nerves"), consists of *alertness* (realizing that a problem exists, preferably while the problem is still small) and the *patience* to calmly gather necessary intelligence before acting.

This takes us back to Problem Solving 101: clearly define the problem/goal/challenge; brainstorm possible scenarios leading to victory; prioritize best scenarios (based on currently available intelligence and resources; implement plan (with an eye toward adapting as changing circumstances demand).

This same sequence of steps holds true and leads to success whether your challenge is taking an enemy stronghold or taking some fine babe home at closing time.

- *Dom do* (lit. "to watch"). At this stage we watch: gather intelligence either through direct experience or else through agents.

Remember that intelligence is of two types: the innate kind you're born with and the gathered variety you glean by paying attention. Lack of the former can be made up for with more effort in acquiring the latter.

Martial artists have a saying: "The more you know, the better you throw" (fight). Farmers likewise say, "the more you know (about farming) the better you sow."

Would-be lovers would do well to learn from Farmer Brown, that is, if you're looking forward to sowing those wild seeds.

- *Coi mach* ("to evaluate"). At this stage we sift the intelligence gathered, separating wheat from chaff—something else learned from Farmer Brown.

- *Ngu quan* ("Five Weaknesses"), these are similar to the *Gojo-Goyoku* "Five Sense Weaknesses" strategy of Japanese Ninja, in turn derived from the Chinese Taoist *Wu Hsing;* one (or more) of the emotional "Warning F.L.A.G.S." (Fear, Lust, Anger, Greed, Sympathy) which dominates all of us at one time or another. (See Lung and Prowant, 2001)
- *Choc* (lit. "to draw out"). At this stage all the insight and intelligence gathered in the previous four stages come together into a "jewel" so dazzling it will literally "draw our enemy out" into the open. Thus this stage is also sometimes called *Lam me,* literally "to bewitch."

It has been said:

> In war, you use whatever works, no matter if that tool, tactic, or technique was crafted by friend or foe. The finest weapon is the one you pry from your dead enemy's hand. (Lung, *Lost Fighting Arts of Vietnam*)

We would only add to this that a true strategist/seductionist also prises such weapons directly from their target's troubled minds!

7

Japan: Silk and Steel

The heroes of ancient Japan love and die within their shells of silk and steel.

—Marguerite Yourcenar

INTRODUCTION: THE THREE TREASURES

Tenno-rei, the "imperial soul," is the Shinto belief that at his coronation each new Japanese emperor receives a cumulative, eternal "soul" that has, in turn, passed down through the entire historical line of emperors, beginning with the divine origin of the first emperor of Japan.

Also passed down from emperor to emperor are the *Sanshu no shinki,* the "Three Treasures": the sacred sword, the sacred mirror, and a sacred string of royal jewels.

According to myth and tradition, the Three Treasures were given to the Japanese imperial line by Amaterasu, deity-creator of the Japanese archipelago.

But the Sanshu no shinki are not just physical objects. It is believed these sacred objects exist simultaneously in three worlds: our physical world, the spiritual world that overshadows the physical, and the world of ideas (thought) that acts as a bridge between the first two.

As physical objects the Sanshu no shinki de facto exist in the physical world. As sacred spiritual objects they hold a special place in the mythology and ritual of the Shinto religion and represent the imperial identity. But there

189

is also a mental-level lesson to be learned from these three—a Black Science lesson.

As often as the future fate of Japan was decided on fields of bloody battle, with a shimmering stroke of samurai sword (or perhaps a ninja knife to the back!), just as often lives were lost and an empire won through intrigue within the imperial palace itself, where the rich and powerful samurai clans vied for the ear of the emperor—all the while plotting to replace him with one of their own.

"The *shoji* have eyes" has been a common saying since the founding of the Imperial Court. Shoji are those sliding doors found in traditional Japanese homes, opaque paper "walls" on wooden frames. A master intriguer was thus a "wet finger," alluding to the fact that one only had to wet a finger to poke an eyehole through this thin paper veneer in order to spy on whoever was on the other side.

In the same way that the Japanese borrowed much of their culture (writing, religion, martial arts, etc.) from China, so, too, it seems they borrowed many of their more masterful—albeit still despicable—techniques of court intrigue and cunning from their Chinese cousins.

Sun Tzu's *Ping-Fa* is well-known in Japan. Sun Tzu wrote in the fifth century B.C.E. but, as early as the Chou Period (twelfth century to seventh century B.C.E.), the *Shin Ching* ("Book of Songs") warned:

> You must guard well your idle words, for the walls have ears.

Strategist Kuan-Tzu (fourth century B.C.E.) echoes this same warning.

> In olden times we were warned 'The walls have ears.' This refers to vital intelligence overheard by someone other than The Emperor for whom that information was intended. One way this disaster comes about is through the wiles of the sly courtesan who uses her charms to lull the emperor into a lax mood, where she can then tickle such secrets from him. In the end, only her evil pimp benefits.

Of course, one need only look at the history of Rome, study Machiavelli, or simply read the Bible, for that matter, to be able to convincingly argue that Asian imperial courts have never had a monopoly when it comes to backbiting and backstabbing!

Whatever the shape of the keyhole, there's sure to be an eye to fit it!

The word *Mekura* literally means "blind" but refers more to those whose eyes are fine but who lack an "inner eye" for subtle and even esoteric under-standing, particularly when it comes to intrigue.

To get ahead—or at least to keep the head you had!—meant samurai had to develop this Mekura inner eye. But, since deliberate court intriguing, if caught, could cost them—and their whole family!—their heads, wily Japanese courtiers never spoke openly of their covert surveillance, conspir-acy, and corruption. Instead they used overly polite and subtle euphemisms, several taken from Noh theater (see section below).

Other times, intriguers used the "Three Treasures strategy," which gave intriguers the option of different "approaches" for pushing their enemy over the edge into the abyss, pulling them into a trap, or simply using numerous subtle ploys to ensnare their court rivals: Sword, Jewel, or Mirror.

The Sword Approach The sword is the "soul" *(kami)* of the samurai. One story tells that Susano the storm god slew a great dragon and found the sacred Imperial sword in its tail.*

The sword defends, it repulses the enemy. But all good swords cut both ways.

Using The Three Treasures "sword approach," we confront our adver-sary head-on. We push, and we keep pushing until he bends and ultimately breaks. We use our sword (symbol of intelligence and force) to instill fear and anger in him. Filled with fear, he will be paralyzed to raise his own sword against us. Or, just as deadly, we anger him into making rash moves, ill-advised maneuvers that place him at our mercy.

When it comes to using "the Sword Approach" in seduction, we take the direct approach. We're honest, upfront, and straightforward about our intentions—whether we're looking for a one-night stand, or for something a little more lasting.

Believe it or not, the direct approach often works. Tired of fending off an endless line of horny suitors, a woman often appreciates straightforward honesty and rewards same, especially if she's only out looking for a "booty call" herself.

The Jewel Approach A jewel-based strategy uses the opposite tack than does a sword-based approach. By its very nature a jewel dazzles, a hypnotiz-ing gem of many facets that inexorably draws us into it.

---

*The Shinobi ninja clans of medieval Japan trace themselves back to this same storm god. See Lung, *Ninja Craft,* Alpha Publication, 1997.

Rather than push like the sword, the jewel pulls, like a spider attracting us deeper and deeper into its web until escape is impossible.

A strategist employing jewel-based ("Machiavellian") thinking often allies himself with those of equal or greater power, an alliance guaranteed to strengthen his own prospects and increase his profits while setting the stage for his eventual dominance.

This kind of crafty covenant is preferable to having to play the "swordsman" and go toe-to-toe with an adversary you're not sure you can defeat in open battle.

Since our "jeweler" is trying to attract (pull) his target closer, he freely resorts to seduction and bribery. You'll no doubt recall our buddy "bribery" as one of the dreaded "Six Killer B's"? *(Mind Control, 2006)*

Jewelers invented "strange bedfellows" and "marriages of convenience." Indeed, a person dominated by this type of thinking would have no qualms about marrying for the money.

Symbolically, jewels have been used in the East to represent reincarnation (many lives, like gems hanging on the single string of the soul). Jewels have also been used to represent the chakras within the human body, physical and psychic power centers activated once our innate, but usually dormant, kundalini energy is awakened through the practices of yoga, meditation, tantric sex, and other physio-mystical disciplines. (See India section, see also Vietnam.)

The Mirror Approach When you can't overtly push (sword) or pull (jewel) an adversary (or love interest) into seeing things your way, you have to resort to a more cunning, mirror strategy. Using mirror strategy, we deflect criticism and discourage scrutiny—"Why bother with me? I'm so unimportant, so harmless." This is Sun Tzu 101: "When close, appear far. When strong, appear weak," all in order to cause your enemy to underestimate you, seeing you as no threat. (Read Robert Graves's *I, Claudius.*) In modern parlance this is called "rocking him to sleep," getting your target so relaxed they never sees your rock coming!

This approach also teaches us to "reflect" our adversary's attitude, pretending to agree with them, stalling them with negotiation, until the time is ripe to show your true face. We feign weakness in order to get our enemy to drop his guard.

This strategy is the essence of the spy's craft, the heart of the prostitute's art, and part and parcel of the professional politician's steaming pile of . . . polemic.

Mirror ploys require the greatest of weapons: patience. The 47 Ronin waited two years, pretending weakness, until they could successfully get revenge for the death of their lord.

Chinese Tongs were infamous for inviting their rivals to "peace" banquets, only to poison them (Seagrave, 1985). Another mirror patience ploy involved Chinese plotters feeding specially bred silkworms poison and using their toxic silk to make exquisite robes that would then be given as gifts to one's enemies. After the robes were worn for a while, the poison would slowly leach out of the fabric and into the wearers' skin, sickening and eventually killing them (Lung and Prowant, 2001).

In the Bible there's the story of how King David's son Absalom, unable to take immediate revenge against his brother Amnon for raping their sister Tamar, bided his time for two years. Finally, Absalom invited his brother to a banquet where the doors were then locked. After Amnon had gotten drunk on wine and feasted his fill, Absalom was finally able to feed this sexual predator his just desserts! (See 2 Samuel: 13.)

Across the centuries various cadre in Japan—samurai, ninja, even Yakuza gangsters—have used one, or all, of these strategies—the sword, the jewel, the mirror—to successfully seduce and, when need be, slay their adversaries.

SAMURAI SLY

When you cannot be deceived by men you will have realized the
wisdom of strategy.
—Miyamoto Musashi

The history of Japan is one of beauty and blood. Beware: Blood can be just as seductive as beauty, sometimes even more so!

The Japanese kanji *bu* means "sword." Hence a *"bu-shi"* is someone carrying a sword, a warrior. But "bu" can also mean "pen." This reflects that samurai were expected to be both men of action, as well as patrons of the arts. Thus the ideal: *"Bunbu itchi,"* to have "pen and sword in accord."

We find this ideal exemplified throughout Japan's violent history, not just up through their Middle Ages with warrior-author Miyamoto Musashi, but further on to World War II kamikaze who took time out of their busy schedule dying to calmly write death poems, down to modern-day mystery man Yukio

Mishima, the famed Japanese author and actor who, at the head of his own samurai secret society, committed hara-kiri ritual suicide—in 1970!

Thus the samurai spirit is without question worthy of our time and effort to study: from Musashi's masterpiece of strategy, *A Book of Five Rings,* down to the study—and mastery—of the mind-set, discipline, and focus it would take to pull off "a Mishima".

Yoritomo: The Twelve Cuts

> *To influence others! What a marvelous gift, and what assured success to him that possesses it!*
> —B. Dangennes

Around 762 C.E. a specialized cadre of knights were commissioned in Japan. Drawn from well-to-do families and known as *Kondei* ("stalwart youth"), they were the first samurai. Up till this time, the Japanese army had been made up mainly of spear-wielding foot soldiers, but these new samurai preferred the sword, symbol of both their rank and their willingness to do bodily harm at the least trespass. Their code was Bushido, "The Way *(do)* of the Warrior *(bushi)."*

When not busy protecting the realm from real and imagined threats, samurai clan leaders *(Daimyo)* entertained themselves by manufacturing reasons to go to war against rival samurai clans. Finally in 1192, Yoritomo, Daimyo of the Minamoto clan, succeeded in beating down his rivals to become Japan's first shogun (warlord).

Yoritomo was aided in his conquest by his younger brother Yoshitsune, later credited with founding the Karuma-hachi-ryu, a martial-arts school that specialized in teaching ninja tactics to Minamoto troops. (See: Laughing with the Long-nose, later.)

Legend says Yoshitsune learned his unorthodox martial arts from half-human/half-crow forest demons known as *Tengu,* a thinly disguised reference to the Shinobi ninja clans who lived in Japan's central forests. Given Yoritomo's ruthlessness, it is hardly surprising he would stoop so "low" as to ally himself with hated ninja. In order to swell his ranks, Yoritomo even knighted samurai from the "barbarian" Ainu (lit. "hairy ones"), the original Caucasian inhabitants of the Japanese islands ("Samurai Anthropologist," *Discover,* September 1989).

Despite his great accomplishments, Yoritomo has gone down in history as the Stalin of his day—a ruthless and paranoid dictator who no sooner

seized power by mercilessly crushing his present enemies than he began settling scores with all past foes—real and imagined—including his brother
Yoshitsune, whom Yoritomo wrongly accused of plotting a coup. Yoshitsune
prudently escaped to become Japan's version of Robin Hood.

And like Stalin, Yoritomo outlived his enemies. But ironically the warlord, who finally succeeded in bridling and breaking Japan, died mundanely
after a fall from his horse.

While moralists belittle Yoritomo's accomplishments by maintaining he
slaughtered his way to power, and hung on to that power by making swift
and sanguine examples of any who opposed him, the truth is Yoritomo used
diplomacy just as often as he did decapitation; his steel was wrapped in
seductive silk.

Early on, Yoritomo realized that the key to both conquest and control
over both individuals and empire lay in one's ability to exert influence, sub-
stituting one's will for that of others.

Yoritomo's thoughts and techniques for mastering the "art of influence"
were finally rendered into English, via his "interpreter" B. Dangennes, in 1916.

Yoritomo exposes twelve ways we can increase our "influence" and,
thereby, our personal power:

- *Increasing our psychic forces. Psychic forces* is a synonym for "mental ability and agility"—our powers of perception, concentration, and decision making. Yoritomo maintains that all individuals have an innate
  need for what he calls the "perpetual pursuit of the highest," a desire
  to strive to be the best we can be, to experience and express ourselves fully:

  > The struggle for life becomes more and more arduous, and
  > the power of our hidden faculties should expand in accor-
  > dance with ever-growing necessities.

Seven hundred years later, on the other side of the world, Nietzsche
called this same innate urge to influence our world the "will to power." Failing to live up to this potential, either because of our own indolence or
because of deliberate interference from our adversaries, causes that vague
feeling of dissatisfaction so many of us carry around, feelings of dissatisfaction an alert and adroit adversary can all too easily encourage into more and
even more self-destructive feelings of doubt, defeatism, and self-loathing.
(Of course, we can do the same to our adversary!)

Thus, the first step to increasing our influence—if only in order to protect ourselves—is to make full use of our mental abilities. It's a myth—and an excuse!—that we only use 10 percent of our brain. The average person only uses their brain 10 percent *efficiently.*

Increasing our psychic forces, our mental abilities, we thereby increase our influence over others.

- *By persuasion.* Exercising influence by persuasion requires our subtly bringing ourselves more into sync with another person in order to nudge them in the direction and into the deeds we desire. We do this in four ways:
  - Establishing trust.
  - Learn to listen, both to what others are saying (consciously and unconsciously) and to what they aren't saying.
  - Don't browbeat. Learn to win gracefully. Recognize when the other person is giving in.
  - At least pretend to share their sympathies.

- *By influence of the eyes.* From that stern look of reproach from parents and teachers that we're taught to cringe from as children, to those alluring, wallet-draining looks cast by fashion models, to the will-sapping gaze of Rasputin and Charlie Manson, eyes hold the power to scold, seduce, and stupefy:

> Few persons escape the influence of the human eye. If its look is imperious, it subjugates; if it is tender, it moves; if it is sad it penetrates the heart with melancholy. (Yoritomo)

Yoritomo says we can take this to the next level by developing the ability to communicate (influence) with our eyes, allowing our emotions—sincere or fake—to freely flow from our eyes. This means not only developing a forceful, dominating stare guaranteed to stop someone in their tracks, it also means mastering those sincere, compassionate, and caring looks that are the key to unlocking the heart of another. Just think what a person's eyes can tell us about them (or them about us?):

- Eyes downcast tell people we're subservient . . . and no threat.
- Eyes demurely turned aside tells a person you're modest . . . and maybe a little bit shy. (Guys take note, gals love it when you do the "shy guy" routine.)

- Eyes wide means very interested.
- A surreptitious wink instantly makes someone our accomplice.
- A smiling wink can stir thoughts of passion.

Thus, with a single practiced glance we can show approval, sow confusion, incite passion, or instill paranoia.

- *By words and speech.* Yoritomo advised us to keep it short and sweet, warning that "Too great wealth of words is hostile to conviction." And:

  The word is the most direct manifestation of thought; hence it is one of the most important agents of Influence when it clothes itself with precision and clearness, indispensable in cooperating in creating conviction in the minds of one's hearer.

Yoritomo was well ahead of his time in understanding the value of concise propaganda, inventing the idea of countering short attention span syndrome with a well-crafted sound-bite:

  Those that know how to present their thought in a few phrases, in a way that impresses itself on their listeners, may easily become leaders of the masses.

Yoritomo's method for creating simple and effective messages is (1) think deeply on what we want to say beforehand, then (2) transform your thoughts into images by (3) using incisive words that (4) draw mental pictures you can easily (5) implant into the minds of others using what Yoritomo calls "the form of lights and shades," (openness when appropriate, subterfuge when expedient, depending on the situation).

And when we're speaking, Yoritomo advises us to: speak with concision, speak with clearness, speak with moderation, speak with discretion. Warns Yoritomo:

  From indiscretion to lying the step is short . . . Speech is the distributor of the thoughts that surround us, of which the reiterated suggestions, after impregnating certain groups of cells in our brain, travel by affinity to haunt the same group of brain-cells in other auditors.

Get the other guy talking and keep him talking—answering all your questions, providing you with invaluable intelligence. The more he talks, the more you know.

This especially holds true when trying to seduce women. No matter how much you think she wants you to talk about you . . . get her to talk about herself instead. And do your best to sincerely pretend to be interested!

- *By Example.* J. Paul Getty once said: "No psychological weapon is more potent than example." In other words, you're known by the company you keep. Or as Yoritomo puts it:

> Our most frequent associations are never indifferent to our mentality, and we always submit, voluntarily or unconsciously, to the ascendancy of those that surrounds us, unless we have sufficient influence over their minds to compel them to submit themselves to us.

We influence those around us. They influence us. Sometimes those around us form a positive support network, one that strengthens us by stimulating our imagination and challenging our abilities—making us better people. Our association can also be negative, and we can find ourselves trapped in toxic relationships, surrounded by vampires who drain our life's blood while they ravage our precious resources. (See Shadow Warriors, later.)

It's been said you can't teach what you don't know, and you can't lead where you don't go . . . *Sure you can!* Political leaders no longer fight beside the troops they send to die in senseless foreign wars, and high school coaches are still called in to substitute for the sick algebra teacher. In a pinch, you "fake it till you make it" . . . or at least until you can make it out the door!

Tell the truth, would you really be surprised to find out that, in most situations, most people don't have a clue what the hell they're doing? That's why they're so relieved when some "take-charge guy" shows up who seems to know what's going on . . . someone willing to take responsibility off them (to take the weight of making decisions at the risk of later being blamed when it all goes horribly wrong!).

No surprise that a lot of women (and quite a few men) are looking for this kind of guy.

We lead by example. We teach by example. And we are influenced by example—often without being consciously aware of it.

Nothing inspires the faint of heart so much as seeing the example of someone else standing up against impossible odds, boldly defying the merciless juggernaut. Think Gary Cooper in *High Noon* (1952). And who can forget the image of that lone June 1989, prodemocracy demonstrator defiantly holding his ground in front of that advancing line of Chinese tanks in Tiananmen Square?

Politicians and cult leaders are all quite adept at manufacturing convenient enemies for their followers to take a stand against, inspiring their followers by their "heroic" rhetoric . . . inspiring those gullible followers (and constituents) to dig deeper into their pockets.

Chapter one/verse one from "The Cult Leader's Bible" reads: Relieve the sheep of any responsibility (fear of future, guilt, blame). Did you notice you can't write relieve or believe without sticking a *"lie"* smack-dab in the middle?

> *Ability and achievement are bonafides no one dares question, no matter how unconventional the man who presents them.*
>
> **—J. Paul Getty**

- *By psychic influences.* Dangennes defined "psychic influences" thus:

    It is the art of substituting for the want of resolution in others our own will, which they obey blindly, sometimes unconsciously, ever glad to feel themselves guided and directed by a moral power which they cannot elicit in themselves. (1916:82).

Yoritomo is careful to point out that this overpowering psychic influence is *not* some magical force, nor is it outright hypnosis—though, as a student of Black Science you'll quickly spot elements of hypnosis technique in it (See Lung and Prowant, 2000:89).

Yoritomo describes psychic influence as "an intensity of determination" that surges outward from us like a wave, to wash over and inundate the will of others:

    It is not necessary to have, as many pretend, recourse in magic in order to become past masters in the art of influencing our fellows; what is needed above all is to keep ourselves constantly in a condition of will-power sufficient to impose our commands on minds capable only of obedience. Intensity of determination, when it reaches a certain point, possesses a dazzling influence which few ordinary mortals can resist, for it envelops them before they are aware of it and thus before they have dreamt of endeavoring to withdraw themselves from it.

- *By decision.* Yoritomo assures us:

> You can thus instruct yourself in this art, so difficult and nevertheless so important, for the influence which he who is accustomed to wise and prompt decisions exerts over others is always considerable.

We admire people who can make decisions. And we like others to see in us someone capable of making decisions. But studies show we also like others to make decisions for us, to take responsibility away from us.

The sorry fact is that most people are not very good at making decisions. The more things change . . . the more people stay the same. Schools today teach regurgitation, not problem solving. It was much the same in Yoritomo's day:

> The majority of the irresolute love to deceive themselves by delusions which their imagination creates, and thus becomes only too often the architects of their own misfortune.

Let's review "Problem-Solving 101," a prerequisite for exercising mind-controlling influence:

- *Clearly define the problem.* Most people never get past this first step. When you fail to progress beyond this initial step, it's "just bitching."
- *Brainstorm options.* Write down every possible solution, no matter how seemingly farfetched. Don't stop until you come up with at least twelve options.
- *Prioritize options.* Cut your brainstormed options in half, keeping only those six options with the most likelihood of success . . . now, cut them in half again. Take the three options you're left with and put them in order of most likely, most do-able.
- *Implement your best option.* Just do it.
- *Adjust* to changing circumstance. If necessary, move on to your second option, and then your third, keeping those elements of options one and two that were at least viable in part.

Yoritomo adds that decisions should be made through use of:

- *Reflection and concentration*
- *Presence of mind* (awareness)
- *Will* (the determination to see a decision through)
- *Energy* (the strength to see a decision through)

- *Impartiality* (the ability to observe and decide objectively);
- *A desire for justice,* a quest for recompense, balance and completion (an idea expressed centuries after Yoritomo by the Gestalt school of psychology);
- *Forethought,* with an eye toward stopping problems before things get out of hand.

(FYI: One man's desire for justice is another man's revenge!)

Don't forget: To the indolent and the uninitiated, our foresight and forethought will make it look like we possess ESP:

> We should not confound forethought with the art of divination, although, in the eyes of the vulgar, it sometimes takes on the appearance of it. (Yoritomo)

According to E. B. Condillac (1715–1780):

> He who would influence others should above all things know how to influence himself in order to acquire the faculty of self-concentration which will allow of his reaching the highest degree of discernment. Many soothsayers have owed their influence over the multitude only to that spirit of concentrations that passed for prophecies. It is wrong and delusive to give credence to magic which is trickery, but we bear within us a power equal to that of the sorcerers whose deeds are related; this is the magic of the influence which the prudent and self-possessed man always exercises over his fellows.

Of course, you would never personally be tempted to take advantage of such a misperception on the part of others.

It could work to your advantage if your adversary believes you possess the power to read his thoughts, to anticipate his every move. One man's superstition is another man's salvation. (More on the ninja art of Kyonin-No-Jutsu to come. See also Lung and Prowant, 2001:76.)

- *By ambition.* Nowadays, ambition is a dirty word. But, back in his day, Yoritomo saw ambition as a good thing:

> It is by believing steadfastly that we shall attain the highest power, that we shall acquire the qualities that make a man

almost more than man, since they allow him to govern and subdue those by whom he is surrounded.

Likewise Joseph Von Hammer (1935) said: "It is nothing to the ambitious man what people may believe, but it is everything to know how he may turn them for the execution of his projects."

It used to be a good thing to be called "a real go-getter." But nowadays, if you're caught trying to better yourself you're all too often accused of trying to be better than the next guy (or gal), that ambition means you're somehow inherently racist, sexist, or otherwise chauvinistic.

Yoritomo goes on to give two examples of how ambition helps produce influence:

First, ambition shows courage and boldness, making us an example to others. Second, ambition overcomes poverty. Says Yoritomo:

> Poverty is only allowable if it is voluntary, that is to say, if it is the result of a decision which prefers that condition to another more brilliant but less independent. . . . Nevertheless, riches are the key of many marvels and they are above all the key of many influences.

Riches give us power that can be used to help others, as well as a means of exciting interest and influencing the multitude. After all, Yoritomo is not shy about reminding us: "The poor man exercises little influence over the multitude."

Yoritomo also warns that our ambition should be (1) *without false modesty,* (2) *without unworthy means,* (3) *without intrigue* and (4) *without illusion,* as these are all flaws in character an alert adversary can all too easily exploit.

Speaking of which, how does "a man of influence" deal with his enemies? Yoritomo advises us to take the high ground:

> He lifts his eyes too high to recognize the vulgar herd of the envious who swarm around his feet, he is content to spurn them with the tip of his shoe; unless, overmuch beset or tormented by their incessant attacks, he crushes them under foot, as we do with an importune insect, which we try at first to drive away and which we destroy, without ill feeling, simply to rid ourselves of its repeated and irritating stings.

Having invested our time and effort in mastering this Art of Influence, we shouldn't feel guilty when we find we can so easily exercise this power over others. Should the alert tiger feel guilty for snatching the distracted monkey who strays too far from the tree? Should a ditchdigger sweating all week to provide for his family feel guilty when he picks up his paycheck? Should the graduate feel guilty when he is finally handed his scroll and key? Yoritomo puts it this way:

> As for those in whose minds we substitute our own will for that which they tend to manifest, they are generally dull or frankly vicious souls, who combine with their natural defects a kind of moral weakness, which renders them accessible to outside influence.

In the East they call this karma. In the West, they simply say you get what your hand calls for—a paycheck or a pink slip.

It is not given to all to possess in themselves the aggressive spirit necessary to command the influences which must emanate from our brain in order to result in forming the convictions of others.

—Taishi Yoritomo

- *By perseverance.* "Perseverance" is synonym to "persistence," antonym to "pest." Being persistent pays off. Being a pest just pisses people off:

> For perseverance is the mother of many gifts; from her is born circumspection which clasps hands with application and patience. (Yoritomo)

When people view us as someone who perseveres until the job gets done, they see a dependable leader they'll gladly follow down any road. When we stay the course, we inspire respect and we exercise more influence than our "half-ass'n" competition. We persevere by simply going forward. Over obstacles, around obstacles, under them, using any and all means at our disposal to accomplish our goal. Step-by-step:

> Every work is made up of a chain of acts more or less infinitesimal; the perfection of each of them contributes to that of the whole. . . . Few persons are born with a silver spoon in their mouths, but everybody can aim at conquering fortune

by a series of continual and rational efforts. . . . The man who would spring up thirty cubits at a single leap would spend his life in ridiculous attempts, but if he wishes steadily to mount the steps that lead him to that height, he will attain it, sooner or later, according to the dexterity, the agility, and the perseverance which he displays. (Yoritomo)

- *By concentration.* Concentration is synonymous with *mindfulness,* antonym to "Huh?" It is the next-to-last step on Buddha's "Notable Eightfold Path" that leads us to enlightenment.

In Buddhism, mindfulness/concentration manifests in practice as mediation, and is the core of the Zen (Ch. Ch'an) branch of Buddhism that came to be favored by the samurai. The Zen emphasis on developing powers of concentration fit perfectly with the samurai way of life, where the already thin line between life and death must be trodden daily.

Even when only training in the dojo, the least lapse in a samurai's concentration could mean serious injury, let alone what could happen on the open battlefield.

Concentration, attention to detail. As on the battlefield, so in the bedroom.

If we reflect well on it, we shall see that most of our troubles can be set down to carelessness. . . . Without concentration, no success is possible. (Yoritomo)

Consequently, those who do not take this time to develop their powers of concentration, those who allow their concentration to waver, and those whose concentration we purposely and successfully break, are already lost. Quoting Yoritomo again:

[They] can only with difficulty concentrate themselves on a task that requires a little application; they are the slaves of the instability of their impressions; beginnings, however arduous, always find them full of enthusiasm, but this fervor soon grows cold, and if success does not present itself immediately they will hasten to give up their project and devote themselves to another which will soon have a like ending.

- *By confidence.* There are two types of confidence: Confidence we actually have and confidence we pretend to have. Any show of confidence, real or successfully acted can impress (influence) others.

Confidence wins people over. Our show of confidence often inspires others by convincing them they too can succeed.

We gain confidence by simply trying. Not necessarily by succeeding. To muster up the courage to initially try an unknown takes more effort than continuing on after a failure.

- *By sympathy.* Sympathy isn't a synonym for pity. Rather, it refers to "getting in sync" with others. Simpatico.

Confidence is also synonymous with "trust." When people believe we feel as they do, that we identify with them, it gives them the confidence they need to open up to us.

Having established sympathy, we can then exercise our newfound influence to gently lead them in the direction we want, whether onto the battlefield or into the bedroom.

One of the secrets of dominating power lies in exciting similarity of feelings by adopting for the time being those which are within the compass of the person whom we wish to influence.

—Taishi Yoritomo

Hidetsuna: Mind-Dancing

Kamiizumi Hidetsuna, sixteenth-century samurai founder of the *shinkage-ryu* "New Shade School" (so-called for the "shade" of confusion pulled over a foe's eyes) once saved a hostage child from a sword-wielding madman by using a single rice cake. Rather than physically trying to overpower the lunatic and risk further endangering the child, Kamiizumi opted to "mind-dance" around the enraged man.

Donning the robe of a Buddhist monk, Kamiizumi slowly approached the madman and his hostage, first offering the child a rice cake and then casually tossing one to the madman. When the madman instinctively reached to catch the rice cake, Kamiizumi grabbed hold of the madman's extended arm and easily restrained him with a jujitsu hold.

Kamiizumi's "mind-dance" employed the following insights:

First, by donning the guise of a Buddhist monk, Kamiizumi invoked the man's moral and social conditioning, the respect all Japanese are taught for a holy man. Second, it is universally known that Buddhist monks are sworn to peace, therefore the madman did not feel threatened by the harmless monk approaching.

Third, Kamiizumi recognized that the enraged man was functioning at a primal level. To try reasoning on a higher level with such a person would be useless and only confuse him all the more. Instead, Kamiizumi opted to meet the madman on the same basic level at which the lunatic was functioning, distracting the man with an even more basic urge, hunger. Finally, tossing the rice cakes reveals Kamiizumi's knowledge of instinctive body reactions.

To the average person such mind-dancing sounds exotic, yet mastery of such "psychological warfare"—on the battlefield, in the boardroom, in the bedroom—brings us one step closer to Sun Tzu's ideal of subduing an enemy without fighting.

Musashi: No-Sword, No-Mind

During his violent life, Ben No Soke, better known as Miyamoto Musashi (1594–1645) killed over a thousand men—sixty of those during personal duels, the rest while fighting in one of the six different wars. By the time of his death Musashi was universally acknowledged as a Kensai "sword saint," the greatest swordsman who ever lived in Japan. But ironically, Musashi defeated as many foes with his brain as he did with his sword.

Where steel fails, silk often succeeds.

First, Musashi mastered the traditional single samurai long sword, before then developing a style of fighting using two long swords, leading to the founding of his Nitten-ryu, "Two Swords," school. Not satisfied, Musashi mastered other samurai weapons—the bow, spear, and so on. Still not satisfied, Musashi mastered *Kakushi-jutsu,* the ninja art of fighting with small, easily concealed weapons. To win his scores of personal duels, Musashi often used unconventional weapons—his empty scabbard, a dagger, an unstrung bow, even a tree limb.

But no matter what the tool in Musashi's hand, he ultimately defeated his adversary first and foremost using Black Science.

Two years before his death (from old age!) Musashi wrote his opus *Go Rin No Sho.* Though written four hundred years ago, this "Book of Five Rings" remains one of the greatest classics on warfare ever written, respectfully spoken of in the same breath as Sun Tzu's *Ping-Fa.*

Far from being an "outdated" manual on medieval sword fighting, *A Book of Five Rings* is recognized for its application to every area of life. For example, successful Japanese businessmen consult Musashi on a daily basis.

Musashi was one of the original "think outside the box" guys. His main theme? All battles are first won in the mind. Therefore, we must concentrate (There's that word again!) on developing what Musashi calls *Senki,* our "war-spirit." Senki is our focus, that combination of concentration and determination. No matter how trivial the task at hand, we must focus on it with the same intensity as would a samurai in a life-and-death confrontation. As on the battlefield, so in the boardroom, so in the bedroom.

On the battlefield, the least lapse in concentration and we are treated to a quick death. So too in the equally ruthless boardroom, where a lapse in our attention means we're soon living in a cardboard box.

And coming up short in the concentration department in the bedroom means you'll never get a chance to lay down your long suit.

Closely examining the *Go Rin No Sho* we notice five basic themes running through Musashi's strategy:

- *Become your adversary.* Learn to think like your target.
- *Upset your enemy's balance.* The more upset the other person is the more balanced and in charge you appear.
- *One equals 10,000.* What works at the micro level can easily be adapted to the macro level, and vice versa.
- *Two swords are better than one.* Always get a second opinion. Always keep a pair of spare keys. Always wear clean underwear.
- *No sword is better than two swords.* Adaptability is the key.
- *Become your adversary.* Says Musashi, "To become the enemy means to think yourself in the enemy's position." This echoes Sun Tzu's dictum to "Know yourself and know your enemy, and in a thousand battles you'll never be defeated."

We want to discern our adversary's spirit, all the while following another Musashi admonition: "Don't let the enemy see *your* spirit."

- *Upset your enemy's balance.* Once we understand how our adversary thinks, we can take steps to unbalance him.

Confusion is our friend. First we introduce confusion, and then we offer to remove that confusion. It's called "CHAOS": Create Hurdles And (then) Offer Solutions.

Pose the problem . . . then pose as the solution.

Sexual feng shui tip #5: Delight her with a simple magic trick—a little sleight of hand—and then show her how to do the trick herself.

First comes the confusion (and amazement) part, then her delight, first at witnessing the trick and then because (per her inevitable request) you're going to show her how to do the trick. Of course, by agreeing to show her—and "only" her (because she's so special)—you not only convince her she's special, you've also created "a cult of two" (because the two of you now share a secret together), and you've succeeded in bringing her closer—into your confidence.

Says Musashi: "Victory is certain when the enemy is caught up in a rhythm which confuses his spirit." That's our job.

Musashi points out how we can unbalance an opponent during one-on-one combat by frightening him with our body, our voice, and our sword. It's not hard to see how these three can be applied to psychological combat as well: body language, ranging from the seductive to the intimidating; the right word dropped in the wrong ear at just the right time.

Musashi gives us five sure ways of unbalancing an adversary:

1. *Attack where his spirit is lax* (e.g., exploit lack of focus in your adversary).
2. *Throw him into confusion.* (Confusion is the beginning of wisdom . . . and woe.)
3. *Irritate him* (through the use of anger and frustration).
4. *Terrify him.* Fear is the first of the deadly warning FLAGS. Go out of your way to create this condition. Remember Machiavelli's advice that it is better (safer!) to be feared than loved.
5. *Take advantage of the enemy's disrupted rhythm* when he is unsettled.

- *One equals ten thousand.* For Musashi, the strategy of defeating one man in single combat is the same as defeating an army of men, and vice versa. He is not alone in this assessment:

   > Winning a battle by commanding a great army should be no different from winning a sword fight in one-to-one combat. (Yagu Munenori, 1529–1646).

This is an ancient concept: the idea that by studying some part of a thing, we can discern a larger pattern. (Hint: her lips smile, but what are her eyes really saying?)

In Japan the saying goes, "The little Do leads to the big Do." *Do* in this case means "way," the path in life we follow. In other words, the essence and meaning of the universe at large can be understood through diligent attention to a little "do", as in Ken*do* (swordsmanship), Ju*do,* and Cha*do* (tea ceremony).

Whether a swordfight or a contest of wills, battlefield or bedroom, noticing minute flaws of movement and motivation, thought and action, is the key to finding that all-important gap in our adversary's defenses—physical and psychological. The most armored of warriors can easily be brought low by the least unguarded emotion. Small success paves the way to bolder undertakings.

- *Two swords are better than one.* Philosophically, "two swords" means using all our resources, developing what Musashi called a twofold gaze of both sight and perception. According to Kensei, "Perception is strong, sight is weak." One might argue that Musashi is also telling us to arm ourselves with both steel and silk. Where steel fails, silk often succeeds. (Yeah, if we repeat it enough times you're bound to remember it!)

In other words, the eye (and our other senses) can easily deceive us. To counter this, we must develop a deeper, more intuitive perception, one that uses the "twin swords" of both heart (instinct/intuition) and mind (thought and reason).

In samurai culture this was known as *"Bunbu Itchi,"* literally "pen and sword," reminding samurai to seek a balance in their studies of both the martial arts and the liberal arts. Musashi himself took time to master calligraphy and painting.

On still another level, "two swords" means using both sides of our brains, left and right hemispheres, concrete and abstract thinking, our full faculties.

- *No sword is better than two swords.* The tale is told that when the Shihan of the first (of many) sword academics Musashi attended decided to retire, he passed his most prized katana along to his eldest student . . . but that he gave *the* empty scabbard to Musashi. Students of Zen will be quick to grasp the significance of this. This gift foreshadowed Musashi's eventual creation of his "No-Sword" school.

In *Go Rin No Sho* Kensei expresses his disdain against what he calls "narrow spirit," or closemindedness and predictability. In the same breath, Musashi also warns us against having a favored weapon or favoring one combat stance/attitude over another because it makes us predictable.

Never limit yourself. That's your adversary's job.

If you favor no specific weapon or strategy, then your adversary has no idea what you're going to bring to the party, so he has to try and prepare against all possibilities, against all possible angles of attack . . . an impossible task! Sun Tzu understood this:

> If my enemy doesn't know where I am going to attack he is forced to prepare everywhere. Forced to prepare everywhere, he is strong nowhere.

As on the battlefield, so in the bedroom: keep her guessing and sooner or later, she'll guess *you!*

Nothing better illustrates Musashi's "no-sword" thinking outside the box than the following tale:

> One day Musashi is challenged by a belligerent samurai while the two are crossing between islands by ferry.
>
> "What's your style of fighting," the samurai demands to know. "no-sword" replied Musashi.
>
> Fast forward: Despite Musashi's best efforts to ignore him, the samurai picks a fight and Musashi finally agrees to duel the challenger. But, suggests Musashi, rather than fight on the cramped ferry, they should instead fight on that sandbar the ferry is approaching.
>
> The challenger quickly agrees and leaps overboard as the ferry passes the sandbar.
>
> Landing on the sandbar, the samurai whirls, sword at the ready—only to watch the ferry continue on toward the far shore—a smiling, waving Musashi still on board!
>
> Hours later, drenched in humiliation and dripping rage, the challenger finally wades ashore where he finds Musashi patiently fishing out of a small rowboat.
>
> "You tricked me!" screams the samurai.
>
> "Your eagerness to die tricked you," shrugs Musashi.
>
> "Your no-sword cannot defeat my real sword!" declares the challenger, advancing menacingly.
>
> "It already has," Musashi says smugly.
>
> Confused by his intended victim's apparent lack of concern for his own safety, the challenger hesitates, for the first time noticing Musashi is unarmed.

"Where is your sword?" the samurai demands, on guard against more chicanery.

"The No-Swordsman keeps his sword where it will do the most good," Musashi replies cryptically.

"No more tricks! Where is your weapon?" demands the samurai, his sword raised high.

"There," sighs Musashi, pointing to the water lapping at the side of the boat.

Still suspicious, the samurai cautiously bends over the gunwale . . .

"Bah! I see nothing but my own reflection?"

"And that is where the no-swordsman keeps his weapon . . . *in the mind of his enemy!*" Musashi explains as he caves the samurai's skull in with the rowboat's heavy oak.

The tale is perhaps anecdotal, although, during what most consider to be Musashi's greatest duel, in 1612, Musashi did kill master Sasaki Kojiro using a wooden sword he'd carved from an oar.

Miyamoto Musashi taught we should make our combat attitude the same as our everyday attitude. Like samurai on the battlefield, we must always be alert and prepared to deal with danger—whether an actual physical attack or a psychological incursion into our mental space. Likewise, we should carry our calm and collected attitude from home, our everyday life, out into the stressful world at large.

In seeking to balance these two "worlds," Musashi was as astute as he was honest enough to acknowledge the fact we "carry ourselves" differently at work than at home than at church than at a nightclub.

We all wear different "faces"—*masks,* if you will—we hope will better fit specific situations. (See "All The World's A Stage," which follows.)

What Musashi called *attitude,* Black Science calls "posture" and includes how we sit, stand, fold our arms—all the subtle and subconscious twitches, tics, and "tells" of our body that all too often betray our true feelings and intent. So much about our body posture—from minor fidgeting to "flight or fight"—is beyond our control, whether because we are *unaware* of these reactions or because we are *too lazy* to make the effort needed to master them.

Other body reactions we can learn to control. For example, recall how Indian yogis can control their heart rate and how Tibetan lamas use tumo to deliberately raise their body temperature, allowing them to endure extremes of cold.

Likewise modern-day spies successfully use biofeedback and self-hypnosis to control body responses during intense interrogation—often successfully outwitting polygraph machines.

Accomplished actors, con men, and spoiled children can cry on cue. And most of us can deliberately make our lips smile, even if our unsmiling eyes give away the fact we're faking it!

Helpful mind-control hint #469: Always squint and "crinkle the crows-feet" around your eyes when sporting a "genuine" fake smile.

Fortunately, so far as strategy and seduction are concerned, natural reactions like sweating when anxious, blushing in embarrassment, and laughing nervously at funerals are beyond most people's ability to control. Thus our adversary's discomfort stands out like a neon ad for antiperspirant.

> **When you cannot be deceived by men you will realize the wisdom of strategy.**
> **—Musashi**

The *Pen* Is At Least as Mighty as the Sword

> *The weak ones do have a power over us.*
> **—The Tale of Genji**

While samurai are most identified with the sword, some were just as skilled with the pen. Musashi is the best example of this, embracing both steel and silk strategy in both his life and his writings.

Medieval Japanese women also had time to put pen to paper.

The eleventh-century *Tale of Genji,* written by Murasaki Shikibu, a woman at court, tells a tale of seduction and intrigue in the Japanese royal court. Though ostensibly a novel, it nonetheless gives insight and advice into how to act, dress, and talk so as to most easily seduce someone.

Author Robert Greene credits Murasaki with "a kind of mental transvestism—the ability to enter the spirit of the opposite sex, adapt to their way of thinking, mirror their tastes and attitudes—[which] can be a key element in seduction. It is a way of mesmerizing your victim." (Greene, 2001:50)

The story centers around the character of the rogue Genji, the young son of the Emperor's favorite concubine. A Japanese Casanova, Genji has a well-deserved reputation as the court's most amoral—albeit most successful—seducer and manipulator. Genji was probably based on real-life court intriguer Fujiwara no Korechika. (Greene, 2001:65)

Female author Sei Shunagon had a real-life encounter with Korechika (Greene, 2001:65) and the latter reportedly had incredible charm and a hypnotic effect on women, inspiring Sei Shunagon to write *The Pillow Book.*

Both these novels reveal how Japanese courtiers were skilled at *Hyori,* a catch-all meaning "double-dealing," defined as "the stratagem of obtaining truth through deception":

> Like Genji, you must attune your senses to your targets, watching them carefully, adapting to their moods. (Greene, 2001:271)

Hyori means we hide our intent using *kyoku* ("deception") techniques crafted to lure an adversary in by feigning weakness ("When strong, appear weak," wrote Sun Tzu), and by such ploys as *suigetsu* (lit. "moon on water"), getting close to an enemy (via disguise, by feigning friendship, etc.). These are the same techniques taught by the Kama Sutra for getting closer to a respective love interest.

These techniques for psychologically outmaneuvering a rival were gleaned from actual physical confrontations. War is war; it matters little whether your adversary hides his true face behind castle walls or a courtiers' fan, or whether he thrusts at you with a blade or with a witty barb.

I have heard people suggest that no reply at all is better than a bad one.
—*The Pillow Book*

Laughing with the Long-Nose

Discard even the True Law, let alone the false ones.
—Takuan (1573–1645)

Everyone knows samurai have nothing in common with ninja. Samurai were guided by Bushido, a strict code of conduct and chivalry requiring them to meet other samurai face-to-face on a brightly lit field of combat.

Ninja have only one code: "Masakatsu!" whatever works—fighting face-to-face with a foe only when left no choice.

The underhanded tactics of the ninja were so anathemic to the samurai ideal of honorable comportment and confrontation that one samurai shogun banned even the speaking of the word ninja (lit. "one who sneaks in") under penalty of death. Yet it's common knowledge that several medieval ninja clans were founded by ronin samurai. And, quiet as it's kept, even "respectable" samurai were not above using the occasional "ninja trick" or two.

When a samurai (like Yoshitsune) used ninja tactics and succeeded, he went down in history as a brilliant and unconventional martial genius. When he failed, even after resorting to ninja tactics only out of desperation, he not only literally went down but also was declared despicable for daring to trespass the Bushido Code.

Samurai euphemistically referred to their use of "ninja" ploys as "Laughing with the Long-Nose," so called because the Shinobi Ninja of medieval Japan encouraged the belief that they were descended from half-man/half-crow demon-spawn known as *Tengu* (lit. "long nose").

Musashi was not the only medieval samurai to be caught "laughing with the long-nose," augmenting his samurai skills with ninja tactics and technique. Yagu Munenori was another.

Munenori was the son of Yagu Muneyoshi (1529–1606), himself a respected samurai strategist. As a young man, Munenori studied with the Rinzai school of Zen under Master Takuan, learning the five samurai virtues: humanity, loyalty, courtesy, wisdom, and trust. However, to give himself the edge, Munenori also studied with the *Shinkage-ryu,* the "New Shade" school founded by sixteenth-century master Kamiizumi Hidetsuna (whom we've already met).

The Shinkage-ryu taught sword fighting and other tactics derived from ninjutsu.

Like Musashi, Munenori knew enough to never be satisfied with yesterday's accomplishments. Once he'd mastered the sword and numerous other martial-arts weapons, Munenori had a revelation: What if he got caught *without* a weapon? Taking the next logical step, Munenori devoted the rest of his life to developing the unarmed art of *Muto* (lit. "no sword," not to be confused with Musashi's "no-sword"). The "Mu" in Munenori's Muto comes from the Chinese *Wu,* meaning "nothing." "To" is "sword." Munenori's Muto specialized in disarming an armed opponent.

Musashi and Munenori died a year apart. But whereas Musashi and his masterpiece *Go Rin No Sho* became world renowned, Munenori's equally insightful *Heiho Kaden Sho* are little appreciated outside Japan.

Munenori's text was written in 1632, thirteen years before Musashi's *A Book of Five Rings,* and we can only speculate how much influence Munenori's strategy may have had on the unfolding of Musashi's own developing strategy.

Munenori's ideal was the samurai ideal, to become a man of *daiki taiku,* expressed by one Samurai thus:

> A man of *daiki taiku* does not at all concern himself either with things learned or with laws. In everything, there are things learned, laws, and proscriptions. Someone who has attained the ultimate state brushes them aside. He does things freely, at will. Someone who goes outside the laws and acts at will is called a man of *daiki taiku.* (Hiroaki Sato, *The Sword and the Mind*)

In Japan they call this *shibumi*—to live flawlessly. This is the concept at the core of Zen, that in order for us to truly master an art we must first learn proper form and technique . . . and then forget those techniques when we reach the point where our art and craft becomes second nature and can be done sans conscious thought. Thus, we transcend "the laws" that govern that particular art.

Within Munenori's overall strategy for getting—and keeping!—the upper hand, we find several distinct tactics, all of which were, by necessity, practical, applicable for both combat and equally deadly court intrigue:

- *Chance.* "Seizing the chance ahead of time means carefully observing your opponent's mind and making an appropriate move just before he makes up his mind."
- *Practice.* "An unpolished jewel attracts dirt and dust. A polished one doesn't become soiled even if put in the mud. Train hard and polish your mind so that it may remain."
- *Experience.* ". . . few explore and bring it to light what the mind is really like, everyone continues to be misled by the mind. . . . Those who happen to have brought its nature to light have a hard time putting what has been learned into practice. The ability to speak eloquently of the mind may not mean enlightenment on the subject. Even if you hold forth on water, your mouth does not become wet. Even if you speak eloquently of fire, your mouth doesn't become hot. You cannot know the real water and real fire without touching

them; you cannot know them by explaining them from books. Likewise, even if you speak eloquently of food, hunger will not be cured. The ability to speak is not enough for knowing the subject at hand . . . as long as they do not behave as they preach, they have yet to know the mind. Until each person explores the mind in himself and knows it fully, the matter will remain unclear."

- *Humility.* "I am not saying these things because I have mastered my own mind. I say these things even though it is difficult for me to conduct myself, move, and stay still as if my mind were correct, as if I met the dictates of a correct mind. I note this because it is a state to strive for."

NINJA: THE ONE-EYED SNAKE

A keen insight into human psychology and predictability has
always proven the ninja's greatest weapon. This remains
true today.
—Dirk Skinner, *Street Ninja*

Of all the corps and cadre down through history to successfully use mind manipulation, the most adept were the ninja of Japan.

Experts disagree as to when and where the craft of Japanese ninjutsu (art of the ninja) actually began. Ninjalike practices, including their mind-manipulation tactics and techniques, can be found within the mysterious Thuggee cult of India, the sDop sDop of Tibet, the Moshuh Nanren of China, and the Black Crows of Vietnam. Some "ninja" strategies can be traced back to the ancient Hindu writings of Indian strategist Kautilya and to the *Arthasastra,* which contains instructions on the art of espionage, mind manipulation, and seduction.

Other portions of Japanese ninja strategy can be traced back to ancient China's Warring States Period (453–221 B.C.E.), when ruthless rival princes routinely employed subterfuge, spies, and mind manipulation both on the battlefield and in the bedroom to further their ambitions. Recall that it was during this tumultuous period that the greatest of Asian strategists, Sun Tzu, wrote his *Ping-Fa (Art of War),* one of the first military books to carry a chapter devoted specifically to the use of secret agents. This is important because "turning" (recruiting) a spy to your cause in wartime often involves a mastery of the art of seduction, in many ways similar to the same tactics and techniques involved in seducing one lover away from another lover, or in convincing a member of her posse to "turn traitor" to help you get closer to her. (Hint: Convince the posse member that they're doing their friend a favor.)

Many Moshuh Nanren espionage techniques filtered into Japan between the first and fifth centuries, a period that saw a large influx of Chinese Buddhists into Japan. Undoubtedly, Sun Tzu's *Art of War* came along for the ride.

In addition to Sun Tzu, early Japanese strategists may have also studied other notable Chinese writers, for example Wu Ch'i (330–381 B.C.E.) and Tu Mu (803–852 C.E.), both of whom wrote extensively on the proper recruitment and employment of spies and double agents, especially spies gleaned from an enemy's own country.

Japanese ninja techniques came into their own in the sixth century, when Prince Shotoku, contestant for the Imperial throne, recruited a *yamabushi* (mountain warrior-monk) by the name of Otomo-No-Saijin as a spy. Where Otomo came by his extraordinary espionage skills and keen insight into human nature is not known. What is known is that Otomo was adept at stealth craft and instrumental in helping Shotoku outthink his enemies. Otomo's alias was Shinobi ("one who sneaks in"). The word "ninja" comes from the Japanese written character for Shinobi and refers generically to anyone who uses stealth, subterfuge, and mind manipulation to accomplish their goals.

Over the next few centuries, ninja techniques of espionage, subterfuge, and psychological warfare continued to be refined.

In the fourteenth century, Japan was ripped end to end by savage fighting between rival samurai clans. The barbarity of this period stimulated an increase in "ninja" activity, as "ninja" criminal bands took advantage of the chaos to rob and plunder, and every freelance "ninja" spy peddled information on opposing forces. Any act of savagery or subterfuge occurring during this time was attributed to "ninja," a catchall term not indicative of the great organized ninja clans of the fourteenth century, more than fifty Shinobi-ninja clans—including the powerful Hattori, the Momochis, and the Fijibayashis—who would collectively carve an almost autonomous state in the central provinces of Iga and Koga.

Insulated by dense forests, these Shinobi-ninja perfected their stealth and intelligence-gathering craft, their martial arts, and, most importantly, their *satsujin-jutsu* (insights into the minds of men).

In the mid-1500s, Shogun Oda Nobunago and his two generals, Leyasu Tokugawa and Hideyoshi Toyotomi, launched a campaign to wipe out defiant ninja clans in central Japan. In his zeal, Nobunago drew no distinction between defiant ninja clans and those Shinobi folk merely wanting to be left to themselves. In 1582, Nobunago was assassinated by one of his own men, a devout Buddhist, who had simply had enough of Nobunago's persecution of peaceful Buddhists. Following the death of Nobunago, his general, Hideyoshi Toyotomi, seized power.

By 1590 Toyotomi, a commoner, had succeeded where all emperors, shogun, and Daimyo before him hadn't, uniting all of Japan under his banner. Toyotomi began his rise to power as a juvenile henchman for a group of ruthless "ninja" highwaymen. From there, he manipulated his way into Nobunago's confidence: first as a valuable spy, then as an accomplished strategist, and eventually cocommander of all Nobunago's forces. (Remind you of Lu Büwei, the Chinese kingmaker?)

Not surprisingly, whispers were that "the Ninja" Toyotomi had engineered Nobunago's death. How ironic that Toyotomi, a man who owed his rise to ultimate power to ninja mind-manipulation tactics and techniques, would be the same man who would spell the beginning of the end of the great ninja clans.

As government, military, and law-enforcement became more centralized, most of the smaller, purely criminal "ninja" gangs dispersed. Others however remained defiant, forming even larger criminal leagues and helping foster the emergence of the Yakuza, the so-called Japanese Mafia.

Ironically, still other ninja became policemen and operatives for the centralized military's intelligence network. These "converted" operatives lent their ninja expertise (especially Satsujin-Jutsu techniques) to the creation of the Japanese military's feared *Kenpeitai* (Thought Control Bureau) and to the national *Tokko* (Thought Police). Established in 1911 to suppress left-wing movements in Japan, the Tokko's power continued to expand up through World War II, when it specialized in enforcing the thought-control policies of the pre–World War II militarist regime.

Back in the seventeenth century, the conservative Tokugawa regime that succeeded Toyotomi's reign made it a capital offense to even say the word "ninja" since merely acknowledging the existence of such rogues challenged the very nature of "respectable" Japanese social structure.

What frightened proper Japanese society in general, and pretentious samurai in particular, was that ninja did not stop at unconventional physical warfare. Ninja also used psychological attacks, targeting their enemy where that enemy was most vulnerable and least able to defend themselves—their secret lusts, inner fears, and superstitions. You never knew when a wily ninja mind manipulator might succeed in "overshadowing" your brother, your wife, even your priest—any one of whom could slip a dirk into your back or poison into your cup while under the control of an accomplished ninja mind wizard!

Ninjutsu training teaches students a myriad of concentration and meditation techniques designed to focus and strengthen the student's mind. Advanced ninja students are then taught techniques of mind manipulation (for example, evoking a foe's emotions, the use of subliminal suggestion, or hypnotism) designed to give ninja an edge against foes.

Attacking an enemy's mind is known as *saimen-jutsu* ("storming the mind-gate").

For a complete training course in all the nine training halls of ninjutsu, see *The Nine Halls of Death* by Dr. Haha Lung and Eric Tucker, Citadel, 2006.

Saimen-Jutsu: Storming the Mind-Gate

> *Your greatest weapon is in your enemy's mind.*
> —the Buddha

Ninja compare attacking another's mind to invading an enemy fortress, literally overwhelming their mental defenses (either through direct attack or through entering by stealth).

Recall from our discussion of Indian arts of strategy and seduction that accomplished mind masters often use the metaphor of "the City of Nine Gates" when speaking of the mental vulnerabilities of the body: the nine bodily openings (eyes, ears, nose, mouth, urethra, and anus) through which we interact with the world, receiving information, expressing ourselves, experiencing pleasure.

Thus an adversary can be overcome by breaching one of these gates, referred to collectively as "the Mind Gates." For example, false gossip and propaganda attacks his ear gate; a sexual ploy can be used to attack the (urethra) sex gate.

Ninja mind-manipulation experts employed a two-step strategy when attacking the mind-gate of an enemy—first discerning and discovering, then distorting and destroying.

> Step 1: *Discovering an adversary's mind-set* (overall attitude toward life, personal beliefs, etc.) and then *discovering the inherent*

weaknesses they carry through the use of satsujin-jutsu allowing us to prepare a mind strategy for invading a foe's mind castle.

Step 2: *Distorting our adversary's version of reality,* figuratively and literally *destroying his trust in the world* and his confidence in himself.

Ninja techniques to accomplish these two steps, collectively known as *Satsujin-Jutsu,* consist of several ploys and practices.

Having discerned an individual's overall modus operandi, having discovered his innate weaknesses, ninja *sennin* then deployed a variety of *kiai-shin* ("shout into the mind") tactics and techniques designed to distort the victim's world and eventually destroy him. (See China section, "The Twelve Animal Passions.")

In-Yo-Jutsu These tactics are designed to unbalance an opponent, to sow doubt and distrust in his mind. *In-yo* is the Japanese version of the Taoist concept of yin-yang (balance). The theory behind all in-yo tactics is to throw an opponent off balance by making him doubt himself and distrust others.

Amettori-Jutsu ("A Man of Straw") Encompasses all tactics and techniques of deception. The name comes from the ploy of dressing up a scarecrow to make an enemy think it is a real sentry or soldier.

Gojo-Goyoku ("Five-Element Theory") This strategy, derived from the Chinese *wu-hsing,* teaches that all reality (including actions and attitudes) is composed of five basic forces: earth, air, fire, water, and void. In all things and all times, one of these elements is dominant. Each element has a corresponding element in opposition to it. When gojo-goyoku is specifically applied to emotions, it is referred to as the Five Weaknesses or simply the Five Feelings. (Refer to Figure 25, page 173.)

Jomon-Jutsu Consists of the use of special words and phrases designed to affect an individual's emotional stability; the words evoke fear, lust, patriotism, and so on.

Yugen-Shin-Jutsu ("Mysterious Mind") Uses various methods of hypnotism and subliminal suggestion to influence and control the minds of others.

Ekkyo These are divination methods that allow us to determine a victim's birth order and examine his interactions with others, especially close relatives. This allows us to attack an adversary by psychologically "cutting at the edges" of his world, undermining his confidence by eroding his comfort zone. This would include studying such arts as astrology.

Junishi-Do-Jutsu Employ the ancient art of Chinese astrology to determine a person's overall temperament as well as his weakest time of the day, when he is most susceptible to physical attack and mental manipulation.

Kyonin-No-Jutsu Ninja Use of Superstition From shamans to Buddha, from ancient soothsayers to modern psychiatrists, many have tried to take apart the human mind with methods ranging from reading animal entrails and tea leaves to the use of modern electronic devices. Many undertake this search in order to better understand themselves and benefit others. Others—mind-slayers—use the insights of the ancients and the inventions of modern researchers to control—and kill—others.

A superstition should not be confused with spiritual beliefs and practices. Spiritual practice has—or should have—a basis somewhere in fact. Superstitions, on the other hand, are unfounded personal or cultural-religious beliefs that spring from either the misinterpretation of an actual occurrence or simply from wishful thinking. A simpler definition is that "superstition" is what we call the other guy's religion. (Our religion is, of course, "the Truth"!)

Superstitions abound worldwide and vary from culture to culture.

In the West, the number thirteen is unlucky, while in the East it is the number "four," because the word for "four," *"shi,"* is a homonym of the word for "death" in both Chinese and Japanese.

In the West, breaking a mirror is seven years' bad luck. In Russia it is bad luck to give a mirror as a gift, but in Japan a mirror is an honored gift, one of the three sacred imperial objects.

Recall that Sun Tzu taught that "Knowing your own mind is only half the battle." The other half is discerning the mind-set of others—their personal perceptions, motivations, flaws, fears, and prejudices that correspond to or differ from your own.

The deadly and arbitrary nature of medieval Japanese warfare ensured that the majority of samurai clung stubbornly to traditional beliefs in ancient shamanism, Shinto mythology, and the power of esoteric chants and spells *(jomon)* designed to protect them from sickness and death and to exorcise evil spirits *(kami)*. This samurai "superstitious streak" was not lost on their enemies, the ninja.

Ninja sennin understood that an adversary's superstitions provide invaluable insight into that foe's behavior.

The most important of kyonin-no-jutsu ploys used by Shinobi was their encouraging the belief they descended from the storm-god Susano via mysterious *tengu* demons, *kinjin* (goblins). Whether medieval ninja actually believed themselves to be descended from tengu, or whether they simply encouraged the myth in order to further instill fear in their foes, is a moot point. What matters is the strategy worked and medieval ninja were neither first nor the last secretive group to use such a ploy.

One ninja-trained warrior who wielded superstition like a fine sword was twelfth-century samurai hero Yoshitsune, who did nothing to stop the spread of stories that he'd been schooled by tengu demons.

Yoshitsune founded the Karuma-hachi school of martial arts responsible for teaching the guerrilla (ninjutsu) tactics that helped his Minimoto clan defeat their enemies. Through Yoshitsune's efforts, his brother Yoritomo became Japan's first shogun in 1192.

No sooner had Yoritomo ascended to power than he began killing anyone he imagined posed a threat to his absolute rule. A superstitious paranoid, Yoritomo performed daily cleansing rituals designed to prevent the angry ghosts of those that he killed from returning to haunt him.

Eventually Yoritomo turned to killing even those loyal to him, and Yoshitsune was forced to flee.

Some say Yoshitsune was eventually murdered by Yoritomo's agents, others that Yoshitsune committed hara-kiri rather than be taken captive. According to Shinobi lore, however, Yoshitsune used his ninja skills to escape to China, but not before getting revenge against his evil brother.

Shortly after Yoshitsune's reported death, small, inexplicable incidents began happening to Yoritomo: Objects belonging to his dead brother began appearing and often Yoritomo would hear Yoshitsune's voice from behind a screen, yet when the screen was jerked aside no one was there!

Yoritomo, an accomplished rider, died in 1198 after a fall from his horse. Critically injured, the shogun lingered in agony for days and died screaming to his last breath that he had been attacked by the ghost of his dead brother!

Shinobi lore tells it this way: Yoshitsune first faked his death and then began harassing his brother by making Yoritomo believe he was being haunted by the restless ghost of the brother he had unjustly killed. This kyonin-no-jutsu campaign culminated in the "ghost" of Yoshitsune (Yoshitsune himself or a confederate) suddenly "materializing" before his already frazzled brother during Yoritomo's evening ride.

Shadow Warriors

There are certain persons who when near you seem to draw something
from you, to pump you, to absorb your force and your life; a species of
vampire, without knowing it, they live at your expense.
—DePote De Sennevoy

In *The Secret Power Within: Zen Solutions to Real Problems* (1998), martial-arts great, movie star, and all-around nice guy Chuck Norris devotes an entire chapter to what he calls "the Shadow Warrior," his term for troublemakers, gossipmongers, and backbiters:

> Shadow warriors are no joke, especially when they take the form of lawyers, friends, and advisors to one or both of the parties who are having a problem. In that capacity, like the ninjas of legend, the shadow warrior is most often invisible, but the havoc he creates is very real indeed. . . . One of the problems in dealing with shadow warriors is that their presence may be unknown to you. (104)

Such shadow warriors often first appear as friendly faces offering us free advice that we later pay through the nose for, after they've sown what Chuck calls "seeds of discord," turning friendly ground into battleground.

Your particular shadow warrior could be a coworker, subtly making you look bad in the eyes of the boss, or even a loved one who "out of concern" is always telling you how your latest venture is already doomed and how you're fated to fall flat on your face "So why even bother trying?"

How can we avoid falling victim to the defeatism and/or deliberate manipulations of such shadow warriors? Chuck tells us to: (1) create good perimeter defenses, (2) prepare for an all-out battle, and (3) never overestimate the damage a shadow warrior can do.

Of course Chuck, being the nice guy he is, doesn't consider that it might sometimes work to our advantage to temporarily don the dark garb of the shadow warrior ourselves.

All's fair in love and war, remember.

Recall our warning about the T'zi-bu, Chinese vampires?

Vampires do exist. Perhaps not the bloodsucking, albeit always impeccably dressed and always witty vampires from *Buffy the Vampire Slayer,* but vampires nonetheless.

These vampires also suck at your life's blood—often your financial life's blood—or else undermine your relationships. (Sounds a lot like Chuck's "shadow warriors," huh?)

And, yes, her cock-blockin' posse do qualify as "shadow warriors"—ninja of the nookie—undermining your plans for a great night of not-sleeping!

YAKUZA: BEHIND THE BLACK CURTAIN

You stand in the way not merely of an individual, but of a mighty organization, the full extent of which you, with all your cleverness, have been unable to realize. You must stand clear . . . or be trodden underfoot.
—Professor Moriarty

Yakuza. The Japanese "Mafia." Some see them as a benevolent "Freemason"-like organization (some Yakuza groups even openly advertise themselves as such). Others see them as *shugo-rei,* "guardian angels," Robin Hoods who flout the law and help the needy. Still others know them not as saving angels but as *Oni*—demons! Or, at the very least, *kanjin* ("bad guys") with *kuro-kakure,* dark and hidden agendas.

Yakuza clans began appearing after Japan's Sengoku, "Warring States," era (1467–1572), when the Tokugawa shogun finally succeeded in uniting Japan under one iron fist, ending years of internecine warfare between rival samurai, ninja clans, religious factions, and anybody else with a sharp stick.

Some Yakuza clans were founded by samurai (now ronin) defeated and dispossessed by the Tokugawa regime. Other Yakuza clans were formed by out-of-work ninja. Still other Yakuza came from already established criminal gambling and prostitution gangs.

"Yakuza" comes from the unlucky numbers "8-9-3," the worst score possible in a popular underworld game called *hanafuda* ("flower cards").

Today it's estimated there are tens of thousands of Yakuza members in Japan, not counting those outside Japan looking out for Yakuza overseas "interests."

Yakuza groups are called *uji* (lit. "crews"). Its members, *ujiko,* are led by an *uji-no-kami,* a chief of a particular uji.* Groups of uji make up Yakuza

---

*In this case "kami" means "superior," not "deity," but still implies god-like power.

"families" and "clans." A Yakuza family is lorded over by a *Kuromaku,* a "Black Curtain." Appropriately enough, the word "Kuromaku" originated in Kabuki theater, where an unseen wire-puller controls the stage, manipulating props and players from behind a black curtain. Today "Black Curtain" likewise connotes a powerful "godfather" operating behind the scenes. (Kaplan and Dubro, 1986:78)

Today, it is said not a grain of rice falls to the floor in Japan that there are not at least two Yakuza uji there to fight over it. This is a nice way of warning us that Yakuza have their hands in every pocket, purse, and potential moneymaking venture conceivable—legal or otherwise, from *turukuos,* who run "harmless" houses of prostitution, to *sokaiya* gangsters, who specialize in shaking down Japanese corporations.

At one time or another various Yakuza clans have been caught between the sheets with any number of shadowy conspiracies, cliques, and cults: from the infamous pre–World War II *Kokuryu-kai* (Black Dragon Society), to working for the Tokko during World War II, to allying themselves with cults like Sun Moon's Unification Church (called *Genri Undo* in Japan and since linked to the Korean CIA).

Many Yakuza uji trace themselves (factually or fancifully) back to samurai, thus it's not surprising to find them embracing both the "silk" and the "steel" aspects of samurai philosophy.

To outsiders, Yakuza are simply *gutentai,* "hoodlums," but within their own brotherhood they have their own unforgiving code of honor, similar to the Bushido Code of the samurai. This Yakuza code includes:

- *Giri:* fulfilling all duty and obligations to self and clan;
- *Shojiki:* honesty, veracity, and frankness, at least among fellow Yakuza brothers; and
- *Shojin:* devotion to one's uji, diligence in carrying out instructions from one's uji-no-kami, and performing acts of restitution and purification for mistakes. The latter ranging from the ritual cutting off of a finger, to performing assassinations.*

The worst thing for a Yakuza soldier is to be declared *dasoku,* a word that literally means "a snake's legs," something totally useless. Better dead than useless.

---

*See Robert Mitchum's *Yakuza* (1975) and the 1989 movie *Black Rain* with Michael Douglas.

Despite their fearsome reputations, the Yakuza's ideal is to maintain "balance" and promote "harmony." Thus a "balance" of "silk" and "steel" methods are used to accomplish their goals—restoring balance, maintaining harmony. Bloodshed is bad for business.*

This "silk and steel" approach applies even when it comes to the Yakuza's four main areas of operation: (1) *Tobaku* (gambling), (2) *Baishum Torimochi* (pimping), (3) *Kyohaku* (extortion), and *Satsujin* (homicide).

Japanese in general, and the Yakuza in particular, view gambling and prostitution as harmless vices (if ones not to be talked about in polite company).

Depending on your particular proclivity—and pocketbook—you might bargain for the company of a *tayus,* the highest class of courtesans. Or perhaps your tastes lean more toward the company of an *okama*—young men as accomplished in the arts of . . . "distraction" as their sisters:

> Seduction is another world into which you initiate your victims. Like the UKIYO,** it depends on a strict separation from day-to-day world. When your victims are in your presence, the outside world—with its morality, its codes, its responsibilities—is banished. Anything is allowed, particularly anything normally repressed. (Greene, 2001:436)

So far as extortion is concerned, Yakuza view this as a business opportunity ("my enemy's weakness and indiscretion has added to my strength by giving me an opening through which to stab at him"). Second, extorting someone who has done something dishonorable is seen as karma, as setting an example for others to be more discreet (or, at the very least, destroy the videotape after the party!).

And murder? That's also seen as the (last resort) price of doing business, and as a way of restoring balance, of righting a wrong (an insult, most likely), and of exacting "an eye for an eye." And, as already mentioned, one of your enemies dying a most horrible death sends a point-blank message to your other enemies.

On a more cerebral "less mess to clean up" level, there are psychologi-

---

*Unless the blood is spilled in so spectacular a way as to send a message to others to modify their behavior and see things *your* way! (See *Theatre of Hell: Dr. Lung's Complete Guide to Torture,* Loompanics Unlimited, 2003.)

**Geisha.

cal ploys to be derived from these four. They call this *Kuroi Kiri,* the "Black Mist," a dark record of all the dirty tricks, corruption, and organized crime in Japan. But it's hardly unique to Japan.

The Asian "old school" of intrigue and intelligence, double-dealing and poisoned dirks in the dark, stretches back through the Middle Ages to ancient times, and includes as its alumni those adept at Chinese counterespionage, Indian intrigue, and Tibetan treachery.

THE THREE DIAMONDS' WAY

I know what you're thinking. How does all this ancient Asian warrior philosophy affect me? I don't carry a samurai sword, ninja aren't dropping out of the trees on top of me, and I don't plan on joining the Japanese mafia any time soon.

But what about that plotting piss-ant shadow warrior in the computer cubicle next to you, the one even now scheming on how to get your job for his brother-in-law? Oh well, worst-case scenario: He succeeds, and you and your whole family end up living in a cardboard box . . . at least you're still living. Maybe that's a blood-baptized "ninja" sitting in the seat next to you on the plane . . . think 9/11.

So maybe ninja are dropping out of the trees—and out of the sky—all around you . . . And maybe you do carry a sword, the sword of the mind, or even two: Musashi's twin blades of sight and insight.

And don't tell me your love life couldn't benefit from learning a trick or two from a geisha adept?

Take a good look around and you'll find plenty of uses for both "silk" and "steel" in your everyday life.

Dirk Skinner, in his *Street Ninja: Ancient Secrets for Mastering Today's Mean Streets* (Barricade Books, 1995) convincingly argues that, despite what we might think, the pressures and dangers of current times are not that far removed from similar threats faced by the beleaguered Shinobi ninja clans of medieval Japan. Consequently, says Skinner, many of the ninjas' tried-and-true tactics, both physical and psychological, will still work for us today. Says Skinner, "The old ways still work. There are no new answers, only new questions."

Still think names like "Musashi" and "Munenori" mean nothing to you? What about "Mitsubishi"? You may have a samurai to thank for that automobile you're driving.

In 1870, samurai Yataro Iwasaki founded the Mitsubishi ("Three Diamonds") corporation and, because of his nine insightful guiding principles his company has prospered down to the present day, making civilian vehicles during peacetime and fighter planes during wartime.

All agree Iwasaki possessed rare insight into human nature. A student of Sun Tzu? Musashi? All the above. But all the philosophical insight in the world means nothing, unless it can be translated into practical action. Iwasaki's method has stood the test of time and is as easily applicable to our lives today. Following are Iwasaki's nine guiding principles:

- *Do not be preoccupied with small matters but aim at the management of large enterprises.* Translation: "Think big!" . . . and then do big! Note that Iwasaki doesn't say we should ignore small matters, only that we must not be preoccupied with small matters—squandering precious resources on trivial concerns. (That's what they make "lackeys" for!)

Hence we follow the advice of every Black Science master from Sun Tzu on down: Deal with little matters before they become big matters.

- *Once you start an enterprise be sure to succeed in it.* Translation: Finish the job or the job'll finish you.
- *Do not engage in speculative enterprises.* Get the facts and then act on the facts.
- *Operate all enterprises with the national interest in mind.* Translation: See the "big picture." No enterprise operates in a vacuum.
- *Never forget the pure spirit of public service and makoto ("sincerity").* Translation: Do what you say, say what you do. Someone is always watching.
- *Be hardworking, frugal, and thoughtful to others.* Translation: Set the bar for subordinates . . . and set it *high!*
- *Utilize proper personnel.* Translation: Don't send a boy to do a man's job. Breasts can't type. And no matter how much your wife bitches, don't hire your brother-in-law.
- *Treat your employees well.* Translation: Take care of your people and they'll take care of you. And, take care of your enemies, before they take care of you!
- *Be bold in starting an enterprise but meticulous in its prosecution.* Translation: *Do it now!* And do it well.

SEDUCTION MAGICK

Do not neglect to show hospitality to strangers, for thereby some
have entertained angels unawares.
—Hebrews 13:2

The Japanese are not an overly superstitious lot, but they do know a devil when they see one. They knew the *tengu,* those half-man, half-crow demons who materialized out of thin air dressed all in black, with their pointed hats and capes made of feathers. Some argued that these were merely men—ninja, it was whispered—but men nonetheless. Thankfully most of these sons of Susano the storm god kept to their own clans in the great forest.

Occasionally an *Oni* (demon) might cross your path, fierce-faced, dressed in a tiger's pelt, who could alter their size at will, a giant one minute, a tiny mischief-maker the next.

But the worst of all were the *Marebito* ("spiritual guests"), mysterious visitors who would show up on your doorstep unexpected. In the north they call them *Namahage,* but in the south they're simply *Dons* (brutes and devils), who look like young men wearing horned demon masks and straw caps. Those that came at New Years were called *Toshidon.* It was bad luck to forbid them entrance into your home. These are spirits that must be placated with food and drink and by never daring to refuse whatever burden or obligation they ask of you. Not that one could resist, for it was widely known that these visitors possessed *kotadama,* the ability to command "the spirit of the word," the power to entrance with just a word, to freeze a victim in their tracks. Such was the power of their words.

The notion of kotadama has in the twentieth century been elevated
to a pseudo-science by some popular writers who view the entire
Japanese language as uniquely endowed with spiritual power.
—Bocking, 1997

Japanese in general and practitioners of the Shinto religion in particular understood the power of the spoken word, believing a spirit resides within each word. To speak the word, sometimes even to merely write the word, invokes the spirit within that word. Some of these spirits are good. Some not. For not all words are created equal:

Imi-kotoba ("taboo words") include words that should not be spoken during sacred ritual, nor in the vicinity of shrines, negative words such as *blood, sweat, meat, grave,* and *cry.* Should this occur, an often elaborate ritual is required to cleanse the site.

Other words were more mundane, but no less forbidden. As already mentioned, at one time using the word ninja merited the death penalty since it was considered an insult to the Japanese people in general and to the Bushido Code of the Samurai in particular that any Japanese would ever think of engaging in such underhanded acts.

Tatari, on the other hand, are curses, powerful spells that spell certain doom. Dons were thought to possess this power, having the power to curse—or bless—with a single word, and with a single whisper to literally spellbind a person to performing a specific task. (See "The Control of Candy Jones" in *Black Science,* Lung and Prowant, 2001.)

The power of words wielded by word wizards are well documented: Rasputin, Charles Manson, Rush Limbaugh. From words that incite riots ("Burn, baby, burn!") to words designed to quell riots ("Can we all just get along?"), words have the power not just to move people but to raze cities. Coming out of the mouth of an accomplished politician, the right words all too often lead us into the wrong war. Out of the mouth of an unscrupulous hypnotist and, despite what they tell us, you *can* be convinced to do acts you wouldn't normally think of doing, up to and including murder:

> Case in point: On March 29, 1951, a thirty-three-year-old man named Hardrupp shot and killed two people in Copenhagen during a botched robbery. When arrested Hardrupp's defense was that he had been repeatedly *hypnotized* into committing the robbery by a man named Nielsen. After a sensational trail, Hardrupp was found guilty and sentenced to a mental asylum (with possible release in two years). Nielsen the hypnotist was also tried and convicted . . . and received a life sentence for committing murder by hypnotism!
>
> Predictably, prosecutors had argued the commonly held belief that it's impossible to make someone do something while under hypnosis they wouldn't normally do. However, the defense's expert witnesses, including Paul Reiter, former Director of the Denmark insane asylum and later head of the psychiatric department at the Copenhagen City Hospital, testified that when Hardrupp committed the crime he was clin-

ically insane since he was in "a semi-conscious state while deprived of his free will by repeated hypnotic suggestion."

According to Dr. Reiter, *any person* is capable of committing any act while under hypnosis so long as the hypnotist presents the crime as being for a worthy purpose. (In this instance Nielsen had convinced Hardrupp that the money from the robbery would be used to combat communism!)

During *Shogatsu,* the Japanese New Year's, young men do indeed don straw capes and horned devil masks to harass the homes of honest Japanese folk, Japan's version of Halloween. Tradition demands that these *Toshidon* be invited into your home, where they will be fed fish and sake. In return, they give a blessing to the household and/or threaten unruly children. This custom is rooted in darker times past, when households were visited by true Don devils.

At the very least these "devils" were ninja armed not only with hidden dirks but also sinister agendas. No one dared refuse their "requests." If you were lucky they only wanted food or shelter. Other times, though, they would recruit your son's strong arm or your daughter's ready smile to their cause.

Of course some superstitious hosts still suspected these Dons were not true men; recognizing them for the shape-shifting devils they were, demons, who only took on the shape of men when they passed through the *kuro-torji* "dark gate," which joins our world to theirs!

There are few accounts of Dons using physical force to accomplish their aims; more often it was the power of persuasion inherent in their words alone that crumbled any hope of resistance. Sometimes these words were recognizable to their hosts, other times Dons spoke in foreign tongues, commands with the power to paralyze, or else singsong chants that seemed to lull the listener into calm acquiescence. Some of the "foreign" words employed by the Dons were *majinai,* "magic words," perhaps derived from ancient mantras, perhaps from as far away as India. Other Don "spells" and chants were passed down from ancient shamanistic times, from the Ainu, the original peoples of the Japanese archipelago.

Use of majinai is part of *Ninjo.*

In Japan, Miko (recall them from our China section?) and other women whose livelihood—and often their very lives!—depended on their ability to please, or at the very least placate their gentlemen callers, mastered the art of *Ninjo.**

"Ninjo" means "human emotion," in particular, the emotion of "empathy"—feeling sympathy for another person, offering them generosity. On a deeper, (darker) level, Ninjo also refers to "reading" what another person is thinking by how they talk, how they walk, and how they use body language. The art of Ninjo studies all human emotions, and then refines the best ploys and platitudes to (1) elicit those emotions or (2) short-circuit already existing emotions. Yes, this does sound a lot like the ninjas' Gojo-Goyoku, the "Five Weaknesses," better known at the Black Science Institute as the Five Warning F.L.A.G.S. (Fear, Lust, Anger, Greed, and Sympathy).

All human interaction is predicated on emotion. Figure out how to tap into another person's emotions and you can run the show. Remember our discussion on "Hitting Her E-Spot" in *Mind Control* (2006)?

Everybody's got their emotional "buttons." Everybody's got their price. As soon as you go thinking you're the exception, that's when you've placed yourself in the worst kind of danger.

They say you catch more flies with honey than with vinegar. But what about bullshit? Flies are attracted to bullshit, too. In the same way, the tactics and techniques that rely on emotion to seduce can easily be applied to both male and female, in the bedroom or the boardroom.

ALL THE WORLD'S A STAGE

For in and out, above, below
'Tis nothing but a Magic Shadow-show,
Play'd in a Box whose candle is the Sun,
Round which we Phantom Figures come and go.
—**Omar Khayyam,** *Rubaiyat*

The immortal Bard, through his bipolar mouthpiece Hamlet, taught us—or is that warned us?—that "All the world's a stage, all the men and women, merely actors."

The imperial Japanese court often used "small talk" about the popular Noh theater to hide what they were really saying—and plotting.

---

*Not to be confused with "Ninpo," a synonym for ninjitsu, the art of the ninja.

Noh is a stylized, ritualized form of theater, and imperial intriguers were all well acquainted with the traditional settings, roles, and plotlines for the most popular Noh plays. References from popular Noh dramas were often used to "side-talk" and scandalize a rival without doing so openly. Such references could be used to alert a person of plotting against him and his house without your being seen to openly side with his cause (just in case he lost!). Should he win, however, your secret help would undoubtedly be rewarded by him.

Of course, we also use such roundabout talk in the West. For example, you might venture, "Look at that happy couple over there, just like Romeo and Juliet!"—since everyone understands the reference to the great lovers. However, your friend snickers, "More like Delilah and Othello!" warning you that the woman in question is a schemer and not to be trusted (Delilah, betrayer of Samson, from the Bible?), and that her new boyfriend is the jealous type (Shakespeare's Othello, who went mad with jealousy and murdered his wife).

But you don't have to have a literature degree. We all use such references every day:

- You ask a coworker about the "new guy" and he tells you, "He's the kinda guy who spends all his off-hours reading Machiavelli." You've just been warned to keep an eye on your job.
- "Hey, since you're not dating Sally anymore, think I could ask her out?" Reply, "Sure, if you're the kind of guy who likes living in a soap opera." Translation: she's a drama queen.
- "What do you think about Bob?" Smirk precedes reply, "Oh, I hear he's a real outdoorsman . . . visits Brokeback Mountain every chance he gets." Hmmm.

"Noh" (meaning both "talent" and "skill") began in the fourteenth century, having developed from ancient forms of shamanistic dance and drama performed at Shinto shrines and temples. Traveling groups of secular actors soon picked up on the popularity of these plays and eventually took this Noh show on the road. Like their European counterparts, some of these bands of thespians doubled as bands of thieves. Ninja sometimes infiltrated existing bands or else sent their own troupe of players, in order to move about freely through enemy territory, or in order to weasel their way inside a town or a Shogun's castle.

Noh (also written No) predates Kabuki, which wasn't founded until the sixteenth century. Noh also differs from Kabuki in that the former is more subtle in its storytelling. Noh's approach depends more on the use of symbolism and subtle allusions.

Westerners are often disappointed with their first encounter with Noh. Noh is less about the presenting of action than of simile and metaphor.

Noh speaks more to the subconscious. This subtle use of symbols lends itself to attacking your enemy on a subconscious (subliminal) level, under his conscious awareness. This is why Noh stories are sometimes described as *Yugen* ("dark, obscure"), since, for the uninitiated, Noh's subtle moral lessons are only partially perceived on a conscious level. This is why we must cultivate our *"merkura,"* our inner eye that sees beyond outward appearance—both in order to appreciate Noh and, more important, to see through the facepaint and elaborate "play" our adversary is putting on in order to hide their true agenda (their true face!) from us.

By learning to appreciate the overall staging of the five types of Noh plays we will more readily be on our guard should an enemy try applying those same settings and situations to his "obscene" advantage. (By the way, the word "obscene" originally meant "offstage.")

Moreover, on occasion we may find it necessary ourselves to act "obscene," finding application for our appreciation of Noh, those settings, situations, and subtleties that can "obscenely" benefit us. Likewise, by mastering the six roles used in Noh theater, we can add yet another useful skill to our already formidable Black Science repertoire, a skill that allows us to instantly recognize when we are being "played" by an enemy and, most important, a skill that allows us to take on those roles necessary to help us adapt to any situation and achieve any goal.

And finally, by familiarizing ourselves with "the masks we wear" (the kind used in Noh), we will become better adept at slipping on the "face" du jour that best serves our immediate ends, whether that end be the protection and promotion of self, and/or bring the curtain crashing down onto our enemy's stunned head!

The Five Types of Plays

All of us play out "scenes" beforehand in our head, mapping out how we'd like a future encounter to go. Some of us are good at it, most not so good. We do this every time we try to pick up a honey-filled piece of eye candy in a bar, every time we rehearse for a job interview, every time we're trying to work up enough gumption to ask the boss for a raise.

Some people write entire "life scripts" in their heads, the way they think their life is supposed to play out.

Today there are Noh plays called *Gendai Mono* (lit. "present-day play") that offer various contemporary types of stories, even mixing the five traditional types of Noh plays:

- *Kami Mono* ("God" and "Spirit" plays) center around the actions of deities *(kami)* and spirits *(rei)*. Often these deities interact with demon folk, usually *Oni* or *Tengu*.

This kind of Noh scenario could be compared to the spirit and sprite shenanigans going on in Shakespeare's *A Midsummer Night's Dream,* the Bible's Book of Job, and in Greek epics where gods take an active interest in the fortunes of man.

- *Shura Mono* (lit. "fighting play"), centers on warriors and conflict.
- *Katsura Mono* (lit. "wig play") always have a female antagonist and usually concerns itself with *kokoroa* ("the human heart") or love and relationship problems.
- *Kyojo Mono* (lit. "madwoman play"). The female antagonist has been driven insane from loss, most often because of the loss of her lover or her child.
- *Kiri Mono,* also known as *Kichiku Mono* ("final" or "demon" play) has a supernatural theme: death, unsettled ghosts, earthly debts that won't allow the dead to rest in peace.

Each of these types of plays are dominated by a central character whose personality literally sets the stage for the type of play it is.

These five play types easily lent themselves to Imperial Court intriguers identifying these same "personality types" in the real world. Once this connection was realized, it was a simple matter for them to assign specific characteristics to specific personality types. Once a person's dominant type was determined, it was—is still!—a simple matter of "flipping the script," disrupting our enemy's choreography and direction.

Many of us have a tendency to become caught up in—and even subconsciously create for ourselves—situations that reflect our dominant (core) personality type.

For example, Type A personalities seek out danger, excitement, and high-risk ventures. So, logically, we'd expect these types of personalities would actually find themselves caught up in that kind of action more often than a more cautious, less adventuresome, Type B personality.

Likewise, it isn't uncommon for a man prone to anger to keep finding himself in situations where his anger has more of a likelihood to explode. This is what's called a "self-fulfilling prophecy."

I hate to be the one to have to break it to you, but fantasies don't always come true. Having unrealistic expectations that the world owes you a living makes you a prime candidate for every "Get ahead without sweat," "Too good to be true," "You're a member of the master race/God's chosen people" scam coming down the pike.

Conversely, we want to do everything in our power to encourage our adversary's fantasies. The more fantastic—illogical and unrealistic—the better!

Our enemy wants to play one role, never suspecting we have another role for him in mind.

Review the "Art of Seduction" section in *Mind Control* (Lung, 2006). You remember? Where that hot babe you just met wants you to play one role (her future baby's daddy) while you have a completely other role in mind: Johnny-come-lately . . . and often!

The Six Roles

> *To beguile the time, look like the time.*
> —Shakespeare, *Macbeth*

Within Noh drama are six traditional roles, three principal roles and three peripheral or subsidiary. The six roles are:

- *Shite,* principle actors around whom the action centers. (Players, movers, and shakers);
- *Waki,* secondary and subordinate actors. (Who just might want to be *shite?*)
- *Kyogen,* who acts as the narrator. Kyogen can also refer to those actors who perform humorous sketches in between short plays. (Distractions.)
- *Tsure,* attendant(s) who interact to support the main players. (Her posse.)

- *Kokate,* "boy," often used as a go-between, or through whose "naïve" eyes we view the unfolding drama. (Agents and snitches.)
- *Tomo,* "walk-ons," nonspeaking parts. (The "little people" who can sometimes become big problems if you piss them off.)

In the real world, "Tomo" are those worker bees in the background, we seldom notice but who—either because we've somehow slighted them or because our overly generous adversaries have "turned" them—can all too easily be used against us.

Japanese imperial court intriguers knew these stage roles could easily be applied to life outside the theater. They became adept at first recognizing the role a (targeted) person had chosen for themselves, and then "recasting" that person into the roles that better suited the intriguer's script. (See Figures 27a & 27b, pages 238–39.)

In real life we all have our different roles to play, and not just the six allotted us by Noh. Roles vary from time to time, place to place but, consistently, there are three ways we come by these roles:

- We take on roles *consciously,* adopting and adapting those roles that best fit our goal(s).
- We also take on roles *unconsciously by ourselves,* because it's our nature, and we're inexorably drawn to certain roles, even though we are *unaware* of our unconscious reasons for choosing such roles.
- We assume roles *unconsciously, but from others,* when a role is "thrust" upon us by others. In turn, the person foisting this role upon us might be doing so deliberately, or else may be unconscious of their actions themselves.

For example, a father dies and a young, inexperienced son is forced to assume the role and responsibilities of the "man of the house." Or in relationships, where you (unconsciously) turn your new bride into your surrogate mother, and then you're flabbergasted when she takes to the role like flour to a rolling-pin and starts treating you like her domineering mother treated her father!

NAME	PERSONALITY FOCUS	POSITIVE TRAITS	NEGATIVE TRAITS	APPROACH /ATTACK
KAMI	AUTHORI-TARIAN	Fatherly, benevolent, enterprising.	Dictatorial, overly ambitious will hitch his/her wagon to any horse to get ahead. LUST.	*Feed his ambitions; cater to his "God complex." Push him to become even more dicta-torial. Encourage him to overextend himself. Lure and corrupt him with promises of power. He can't be trusted, will ally with anyone who promises power.*
SHURA MONO	COMBATIVE	A defender, benevolent, enterprising.	Aggressor, fundamentalist. ANGER.	*Maneuver him into situations where his combative nature will reveal itself. Justify his need to do violence.*
KATSURA MONO	RELATIONSHIP-ORIENTED	Believes in love, a giver.	Jealously, possessiveness. GREED.	*Suspicious by nature, stir up his jealousy, feed his latent para-noia. Undermine his relationships. Othello.*
KYOJO MONO	EMOTIONAL	Compassionate, empathetic.	Unpredictable, unstable. SYMPATHY.	*Responds on an emotional level, acts first without thinking. Trap him in situations where he acts without thinking. Sympathy ploys.*
KIRI/ KICHIKU	BELIEVER	Faithful, helpful	Supersititious. FEAR.	*Unseen forces move him. Prone to blind faith. Show him a miracle, let him talk to his dear departed mother and he'll follow you anywhere. Steal his lucky rabbit's foot, jinx his ball team. He is haunted by guilt. Prime candidate for blackmail.*

Figure 27a.

WAKI

Undermine his authority. Demote him. Secretly stifle his advance at every turn. Neuter his support network.

KYOGEN

Play the understudy. Take over his position and role the moment he stumbles (over the block you've placed in his path). Feed him false information designed to make him play the fool.

SHITE

TOMO

Make friends with the "walk-ons" in his life, the "little people" he interacts with everyday but hardly notices. Pump them for information, inflame any petty grievances they have against him for real or imagined slights. Where such actual slights do not already exist, invent some.

TSURE

Undermine his support network, her "posse." Use "Cutting at the edges" and "Six Degrees of Separation" ploys to get at him (*Mind Manipulation*, 2002) Weaken him by taking away and otherwise hindering his "attendants."

KOKATE

Play the "innocent" role in order to get close to him. Become his confidant, his "gopher," his "boy." Infiltrate his camp (either personally or through agents). Read Sun Tzu's chapter on "Secret Agents." Pretend weakness until strong enough to challenge him.

Figure 27b.

The Masks We Wear

*In every social encounter a person brings a "face" or "mask"—
which constitutes the value he claims for himself.*
—Stanford Lyman and Marvin Scott, *A Sociology Of the Absurd* (1989)

The key to successfully pulling off a flawless performance hinges on (1) *acting like the character* you're portraying, and (2) *looking like that character* as well. This requires the correct dress and deportment and, most importantly, wearing the right false face. (See "The Art of Disguise" in *Nine Halls of Death,* Lung and Tucker, Citadel, 2007.)

Noh actors accomplish this through the use of masks—friendly and fearsome. In fact there are 125 varieties of Noh masks: males, females, elderly characters, gods, goddesses, devils, and goblins; masks made of wood, coated with plaster, and then lacquered and gilded. Even the color of the masks holds significance for a knowledgeable audience. White means a corrupt ruler. Red, a righteous man. Black is always reserved for violent and brutal villains.

Japanese audiences are familiar with these masks and understand the underlying attitude, emotions, and motivations inherent in each traditional mask.

Far from being a universal negative, wearing the appropriate mask at the appropriate time seems to be the Krazy-Glue holding civilization together.

Masks allow us to establish identity in an increasingly politically correct "don't ask, don't tell" world where you're free to pretend to be anything and anybody you want so long as you don't blow the cover of anybody else busy being anything and anybody else they want to be!

Unfortunately, once we take on a specific role, whether suited to that role or not, we can all too easily become caught up in the identity/role. Having put considerable emotional investment into the role, we then become trapped, finding ourselves spending more time maintaining that role than in enjoying the fruits of being that role. This is what Lyman and Scott call "characterological survival," or keeping up your front (Lyman and Scott, 1989:83).

For example, a young—perhaps inexperienced—girl decides she's going to play the role of "sexy vamp" complete with false facepaint and a slinky dress cut all the way up to "thar"! What are the chances of more than one barfly calling her bluff, challenging her to put up or shut up?

In other words, there's a danger we'll get caught up in our playacting and start believing our own line of bull. Again, Lyman and Scott:

For the rebel, art does not imitate life. It becomes life. The rebel's very existence is theater. And when the rebel begins to regard clothes as costumes, facilities of all kinds as props, and streets as stages, he is capable of wreaking havoc in the social world—as his dramaturgical innovations break down the line between theater and taken-for-granted reality. But in the process of destroying the world, he has made himself. (Ibid, 196)

An even worse scenario: We get caught up in someone else's playacting, a charismatic con man, a crooked politician (yes, I realize that's redundant), or a crazed cult leader (twice redundant!).

The only thing worse than forgetting you're wearing a costume is to actually start taking the other guy's costume too seriously. Remember from *Mind Control* that any "power" that comes from outside yourself (such as the uniform you wear), power given you by another, isn't real power.

The story is oft told of accomplished cross-dressing actor/actress RuPaul once being approached by a leathered-out, heavily tattooed outlaw biker type who felt the need to question RuPaul's dressing in . . . well, dresses. The ever-composed entertainer coolly looked the biker up and down—beard, tattoos, Harley chainbelt—before sighing, "Honey, it's *all* drag."

In other words, we all dress for effect, to portray the *character role* we want the world to see. Part of that is choosing the right outfit (or ensemble, if you will) to fit the time, place, and affect we are trying to project. Whether that time and place be a drag queen ball or a barroom full of bikers, we dress for success . . . and survival!

Curiously, the word "outfit" originally comes from "outside fit"—the clothes (and masks) we wear outside, for the world. Your "drag" or "outfit," depending on your preference, can range from the coveralls you wear and the bucket you push that allows you to mop your way past the guard in the bank lobby without arousing suspicion, to the three-piece suit and false FBI badge you flash to convince that old lady into withdrawing her life savings so you can use it "to bait a trap to catch some scumbag who's stooping so low as to rip off seniors of their life savings."

We have to make ourselves aware of the various roles, masks, and "drag" both our potential lover and potential adversary might don.

Likewise, we must always take into consideration the background—the stage—against which our seduction (and strategy) drama—or tragedy!—is being played out.

Setting the Stage

Sitting in a darkened theater, we can all too easily get caught up in the action on stage or on that silver screen to the point where sometimes it's hard to tell where the play ends and the reality begins.

Life imitates art and sometimes events and encounters happen right in front of our eyes and we become caught up in them, never suspecting (until too late!) that these events are being staged for our benefit.

Larcenous con men and would-be lotharios are masters at "setting the stage," catching us up in a well-crafted "scene" where everyone involved is in on the scam, except "the mark."

Likewise, medieval ninja were masters when it came to "setting the stage," preparing areas and "actors" for future operations. For example, a group of travelers on the way to the shogun's castle are attacked by masked highwaymen but are saved at the last minute by a brave young ronin. To ensure their safe passage, the young ronin agrees to see them safely to the castle. Predictably, once the shogun hears from the travelers how this young ronin saved then, on the spot, the shogun enlists the ronin to work for him.

It doesn't take a genius to figure out that the local ninja clan has just succeeded in infiltrating one of their agents inside the shogun's castle and, more important, into his confidence.

"Setting the stage" can be as elaborate as a "fleeing" general choosing the time and place from which to turn and confront his enemy, to something as simple (but no less potentially disastrous!) as that pretty young thing accidently-on-purpose dropping her hanky for you to pick up.

The Show Must Go On

In any stage play, beyond the actors we see, there are the scores of support personnel behind that Black Curtain we don't see, but without whom the show could not go on.

When we can't cast ourselves in the main role, or even get out on stage, there are still five influential "behind the scenes" roles available to us:

- *Prop-master.* Using props (tools, disguises, and costumes) can work to our advantage, since so many people will automatically obey a uniform (police, fireman, security guard, military), and/or someone with impressive-looking credentials (badges, bills of sale, college degrees) without question.

People can be props, too. That pretty-boy actor, the one who the tabloids keep wondering why he's never married or ever even been seen with a girlfriend for that matter? His agent makes darn sure he shows up on the red carpet at every awards show with a buxom blond bombshell (prop!) dripping off his arm.

Accused of neglecting his minority constituents, the next time you see that wily lily-white politician you can bet he'll be "pumpin' the flesh" and/or receiving an honorary humanitarian award (prop!) down at that NAACP banquet/photo op.

So we use props to our advantage while at the same time sabotaging our adversary's "props." Can you say "wardrobe malfunction"?

- *The Critic.* By refusing to acknowledge an adversary's "acting" ability, we expose him for the poseur he is.

We draw attention to the flaws and faux pas in his acting technique. We openly challenge his facts and statistics; we put him on the defensive and keep him there. As long as an adversary is kept on the defensive, he can't rally his forces to go on the offensive.

There's that marvelous scene in *Good Will Hunting* (1997) where blue-collar hero Matt Damon takes the girl away from the obnoxious college boy rival when he simply humiliates the snob by pointing out the flaw in the Ivy Leaguer's pretentious recitation of facts.

- *Talent Agent.* An alternative script calls for us to use the judo principle: instead of openly opposing him, feed his fantasy, become his confidant.

He wants to play leader, give him what he wants. Feed his delusions, encourage him to overextend himself. Convince him he can handle it. Give him enough rope . . .

- *The Director.* Feed him misquote, misstep, and miscue, encourage his mistakes. Make him miss his mark and stumble over his lines. He memorizes his lines, force a last-minute rewrite on him. Break the routine to break his concentration. Keep him doubtful and in the dark: give him the "Mushroom Treatment."*
- *The Understudy.* Whatever theater you play in life, there's always some

---

*The Mushroom Treatment, "Keep 'em in the dark and feed 'em plenty of bullshit!"

eager young understudy waiting in the wings—salivating—just praying you'll stumble over your lines and literally break a leg. You always ignore this person, often passing them over for (real or imagined) praise and promotion. Be careful what enemies you leave in your wake. What's that old African saying? "He who shits on the road going, has to deal with flies on the return!"

As soon as . . . uh, I mean, if something should ever happen to the "star," some highly improbable accident—if he should succumb to suspiciously good health, whatever—you will be there to step in to his shoes, to save the day for the rest of the cast. After all, the show must go on.

Duh! Can you say "identity theft"! C.H.A.O.S., remember?

We study the various types of "plays," roles assumed and masks presumed, first in order to use them effectively and, second, to keep our adversaries from using them effectively.

He wears a mask, and his face grows to fit it.
—**George Orwell**

8

Sexual Feng Shui

To borrow another adage, "to the victor go the spoils." A sexually active man who is unwilling to hone his sexual skills and correctly adjust his attitude in preparation for the "flowery battlefield" of sexual intercourse will, sooner than later, deplete his sexual potency, dissipate his vital energy, lose his immunity and foreshorten his life. Such men become expendable to the species—and are useless to women—as drones driven from the beehive.

—Daniel Reid, *The Tao of Health, Sex, & Longevity* (1989)

Love is a battlefield.

—Pat Benatar

INTRODUCTION: "TANTRIC ACADEMY"

Time to go back to school, back to the "Tantric Academy" (part of that famed Black Science Institute!), where we'll take some time to brush up on a little chemistry, history, maybe even a little math (groans all around).

Relax. You'll like these classes:

The "chemistry" part we'll be studying is body chemistry—why she smells so good, why you probably don't . . . and why it subconsciously drives you both crazy. (Right, those pheromones again. Gold star. You have been paying attention!)

The History part has to do with learning about where and how the Chinese concept of feng shui originated, more importantly, how we can adapt it to the modern day, helping multiply our chances of scoring.

Finally, Math. (Again with the groans!) This math you'll like. It's as simple as: 1 (you) + 1 (her/him) = too much fun!

We bring these lessons together by first studying Mood (what enhances versus what reduces our chances of getting them to the dances). Then comes Method (tried-and-true techniques for touching her/his mind and body) while, hopefully, sorting out (read: avoiding!) some of the Madness that always seems associated with sex in the first place.

These three: Mood, Method, and yes, a little of the Madness always found when potential lovers come together (always nice when you can come together!), are best understood in the context of feng shui, which, again, simply means our learning how to better arrange (and rearrange) our attitudes and latitudes so as to increase our chances of connecting with, and staying connected with, the right person.

In her marvelously informative *Qigong Basics* (2004), author Ellae Elinwood gives us this working definition for feng shui:

> The art of correctly analyzing the relationship of the elements within a location, especially the relationship between wind and water and their reaction to the terrain in which they flow. Once the flowing patterns are understood, placements can be made that will alter the flow. . . . Feng Shui teaches the art of placement to enhance the smooth flow of Qi. Specific elements—water, minerals, fire, mirrors, flowers, plants, mounds of earth, fresh air, and more—are combined uniquely and wisely to create a harmonious flow of qi. Qigong provides the balance within, and feng Shui balances the environment without. (53)

Simply put, feng shui is the deliberate arrangement of diverse elements designed to enhance vitality by getting a little more *qi* (a.k.a. chi) into your life.

We usually think of feng shui in connection with the layout of our homes and gardens, juxtaposing various elements so that they complement one another, encouraging a nurturing environment through which chi flows effortlessly, revitalizing us in return.

Sexual feng shui works on this same principle: seeking out those most favorable elements—time, place, and the mix of personalities—that go into creating the perfect environment for the perfect relationship . . . or at least for the perfect lay!

You automatically (unconsciously) already use feng shui whenever you decide to add anything to your seduction environment—soothing music, soft lighting, favorable foods (see "Aphrodisiacs" below), even the fabrics and flowers you choose. When it comes to sexual feng shui: All effects affect.

When it comes to chi (qi) remember three types are discerned: *tian* (heavenly chi); *di* (earthly chi), and *ren* (human chi).

Whereas sexual feng shui seeks first and foremost to bring together human elements (ren qi), don't forget that all our human dramas and exchanges of energy (not to mention bodily fluids!) are played out against an "earthly" (di qi) backdrop, subject to "heavenly" (tian qi) influences.

For the sake of our study of sexual feng shui, think of "earthly" influences as being all the hurdles and hoops you have to jump through to get where you want to go (or, in this case, where you want to come). These include time and place constraints you have to coordinate (how and where to meet Mr. Right or Miss All-that-and-a-bag-of-chips), while also factoring in any other people getting in the way of you liberally buttering your latest love muffin.

"Heavenly" in this context refers to all the mental flotsam and jetsam you'll have to swim through to reach your goal. This includes not only figuring out his/her mind-set, but also your own mind-set. (Yeah, Sun Tzu's "Know yourself/Know your adversary" again.)

This also means dealing with—or better yet, sidestepping—any "attitude" you might encounter from her cock-blockin' friends!

As we brushed upon in our section on China, the practice of feng shui is rooted in ancient Taoist arts. And like Taoism in general, feng shui above all seeks balance and harmony through figuratively and literally aligning ourselves (personality) and our world (property) so as to achieve the greatest amount of harmony with "heaven" (the universe, the tai chi).

What we think of as the "Chinese" art of feng shui is actually found throughout Asia in one form or another. Feng shui deals with how one object affects another due to proximity; studying and situating those natural (and man-made) materials that either complement one another or else crimp one anothers' style and possibly even diminish potency. (Yeah, just like people.) This natural desire for feng shui goes back to our lifelong pursuit (whether we are aware of it or not) of our striving to (re)balance yin and yang in our lives.

The earliest written record of yin/yang appears in the ancient Chinese text *I-Ching* (c.1250 B.C.E.), in which we are told that the constant intermingling and interchange of "Heaven" (yang) and "Earth" (yin) gives form to all things. (See Illustration 26)

As above, so below: the sexual union of human beings mirrors the great cosmic oneness of the universal Tao. Sexual feng shui seeks to facilitate this natural—eventual—balance:

> In Taoist sexual yoga, the abundant and powerful yin element of women is carefully balanced with the limited and vulnerable yang energy of man. (Reid, 1989:25)

As a result, as early as 590–692 C.E. we find Taoist master Sun Ssu-mo advocating a form of such Taoist "sex yoga."

SEX AND IMMORTALITY

The Chinese regard sex to be as natural and indispensable to human health and longevity as rain falling on the fields is to plant life. The intense sense of guilt attached to sexual matters in Judeo-Christian tradition is, in Chinese eyes, one of the most unpleasant and incomprehensible aspects of Western culture.
—**Daniel Reid,** *The Tao of Health, Sex, and Longevity* **(1989)**

So you want to live forever and have fun doing it? Sexual feng shui is the answer!

The Yellow Emperor of China (c.2700 B.C.E.) lived to the ripe old age of 111. The "secret" to his long—vigorous—life was no "secret" to his fellow Taoists—he kept a harem of more than 1,200 women on whom—*with* whom—he performed secret Taoist immortality rituals:

> Taoism is the only world philosophy that stresses the importance of disciplined sexual relations as an absolute prerequisite for health and longevity. The sexual school of Taoism began to blossom during the second to fourth centuries AD . . . When practiced in private by individual adepts sexual yoga had never caused much concern to Confucian authori-

ties. . . . The sexual secrets of Taoism continued to crop up from time to time right down to the present day. (Ibid., 13)

But no matter who throws the party, there's always some wet blanket determined to keep anybody else from having any fun under the blanket. Thus, even back in ancient China, you find stuck-in-the-mud moralists (mostly dour Confucianists and prudish Buddhists) always kvetching that "Those darned horny Taoists" were always up to something:

> These Taoists wantonly practice obscene disciplines from the Yellow Book [collected by The Yellow Emperor], whereby men and women indulge in promiscuous sexual intercourse like birds and beasts in order to avert disaster and death. (Chinese Buddhist monk Tao An, 292–362)

Myopically, outsiders peeping in didn't realize that Taoist practice (only some of which was "sex yoga") had a somewhat loftier goal than continuous orgasm in mind:

> A major goal of Taoist diets is to enhance sexual potency by stimulating sexual glands and strengthening sexual organs. The purpose here is not to increase sexual pleasure—though that is a definite side effect—but rather to increase the body's store of hormones, semen and other forms of "vital essence" required for optimum vitality and immunity. Sexual essence provides our greatest internal source of CHEE [chi, qi] and sexual potency is a major indicator of good health. (Reid, 1989:54)

Called the "parallel practice" (a.k.a. "dual cultivation," because it involves two people) this is the path to health and longevity through the practice—and perfection—of Taoist sexual yoga.

This five-step method centered around (1) mutual stimulation and (2) exchange of sexual essence and energy between partners during (3) properly disciplined intercourse, resulting in (4) cultivating a strong spirit and (5) a long life in the world. (Ibid., 42)

Detractors of Taoist sexual exploration always seem to overlook that, first and foremost, Taoist disciples did not just jump into the sack on day one. Years of meditation, accompanied by laborious ritual "cleansings," were used to prepare the mind for the rigor of Taoist sex yoga. (And you thought it was all just gonna be fun and games!)

All sex ultimately takes place in the mind:

> The mind is a slippery little devil with the very short atten-
> tion span and a strong penchant for drifting aimlessly in ever-
> shifting seas of thought and fantasy. Chinese Taoists call it a
> "playful monkey" and Indian yogis compare it to a "wild
> horse" that refuses to be tethered. . . . Mind is the leader of
> energy. Where mind goes, energy follows. (Ibid., 163)

Reid adds:

> According to the Taoist view, sexual excitement begins in the
> mind, which in turn arouses sexual energy, quickens the breath
> and accelerates the heartbeat, which in turn stimulates hor-
> mone secretions, increases body heat, circulates blood, and
> other physiological manifestations of sexual arousal. Unless the
> mind is properly primed for action by initial awareness and
> spontaneous thoughts of sex, neither energy nor essence can be
> fully mustered for the act. (Ibid., 330)

Sexual feng shui tip #6: Mind controls breath. Breath controls blood.
Blood controls semen. Learn to breathe.

Taoist sex yoga, much of which, as we've already pointed out, was
derived from Indian tantric practice, was ultimately a health practice. Ancient
Eastern masters seem to have realized intuitively what modern Western phys-
iologists have only recently begun to realize:

ORGASMS ARE GOOD FOR YOU!

Sex has many physical benefits (apart from the obvious!). These include:

(1) Increasing blood flow (and not just down there!).
(2) An increase in the level of endorphins (Mama Nature's "Kiss-it-
and-make-it-feel-better" chemicals).
(3) Orgasms have been shown to relieve headaches and menstrual
cramps in women.
(4) Increasing heart rate, improving overall cardiovascular fitness.
(5) Increasing overall metabolic rate, allowing you to burn more calories.

It's a no-brainer: Less fat, equals more circulation which, in turn, equals
better overall health and better self-esteem, which means (drumroll please)

a much better sex life! Better sex life equals better overall mental and physical health. Win-win.

THE SCIENTIFIC BASIS FOR FENG SHUI

I know what you're thinking. All this feng shui crap is just a bunch of Eastern superstition, right? 'Fraid not. Western science backs it up.

For example: In order to spruce up your room, you place a bouquet of roses. Those flowers release their physical fragrance molecules. These molecules are collected by your nose (sense) which then transforms them into electrochemical signals that are sent along to the brain.

The brain then "decides" that this incoming information is pleasant and releases *response signals* in the form of *pleasure chemicals* (endorphins) that make us feel good.

Thus *matter*—the flower (and its fragrance)—has been transformed into *energy*. Likewise, this new burst of *energy* we are feeling inspires us to physical action (sexual arousal), to do physical work, thus *energy* into matter (action/work).

But the feng shui effect doesn't stop there. Don't forget we see the flowers as well. And what we "see" are physical light photons impacting our eyes where, just like our nose transforming matter into energy, so too those photons make a physical impression on our eyes, which, in turn transform the impression into energy that is sent to the brain. So too with *matter* that we taste or touch. Matter (interacting with the senses) becomes (neurophysiological) Energy becomes matter (physical activity) again. $E = MC^2$.

So feng shui isn't some kind of Chinese "spookism." The objects we interact with (through our senses) physically and mentally affect our daily attitude and long-term well-being.

So if the arrangement and placement of a vase of flowers can affect us—positively or negatively—how much more so can the sexual feng shui that's in our lives—or else missing from our lives?

MOOD

We are all on loan to one another. The universe calls back the loan when it is ready."
—Ellae Elinwood, *Qigong Basics*

What kind of things influence mood? Everything from sunspots to G-spots, from fragrant smells to phony hard sells.

It's all about mood:

- Is she "in the mood"?
- What's the "mood" of the room? Will the atmosphere in the bar work for you or against you?
- Have you done everything you can to "set the mood" (a little candlelight, soft music, plenty of lubricant, the whole nine yards)?

"Reading" her mood, setting the mood, it's all just another word for getting a little more "feng shui" into your life, learning to anticipate, read, and heed what the signs and situation are saying to you—before deliberately inserting a few of your own "signs" in order to turn the situation to your advantage.

Did you know that geomagnetic storms on the sun (solar flares) increase depression among people here on Earth? True.

A 1994 British study noticed that rates of people hospitalized for depression rose more than 36 percent immediately after geomagnetic storms. (The Week, May 9, 2008:20) The pineal gland, part of the endocrine system that regulates melatonin production and circadian rhythms, is sensitive to magnetic fields. Thus, alterations in the Earth's magnetic field, in disrupting our body's own magnetic field, and disrupting our internal clocks, makes the release of mood hormones more erratic—leading to depression.

The bad news? Not much you can do about sunspots, solar flares, and your geomagnetic whatzits being all out of whack.

The good news is while you can't do anything about sunspots, you can do something about her G-spot, as well as other interesting ports-of-call. The more you "study" her, the more she'll end up studying you.

The Senses Finally Making Sense

Tell the truth: Have you been practicing those techniques (from the China section) for increasing your control over your five (or was it six) senses? Well the truth of the matter is, in practicing Sexual Feng Shui you don't just learn to use your own senses . . . you also learn how to use your lover's senses!

Using Their Sense of Sight

> Women fall in love between the ears and men fall in love
> through their eyes. . . . Men tend to be visual creatures,
> coming alive at the mere sight of a bare breast. Women are
> more aural and tactile. They need to hear and to feel a man
> in order to get excited. (Lou Paget, *How to Give Her Absolute
> Pleasure.* Broadway Books, 2000:16)

There's a reason they call it "eye candy." We see it, we want it—we even convince ourselves we need it. (Some basic Buddhism action going on there: All suffering is caused by desire, remember?)

We are indeed a visually oriented society. (More on NLP in a minute.)

Men view taller women as more intelligent, affluent, assertive, and ambitious, while they see shorter women as more nurturing and considerate. *(Psychology Today,* September/October 2005:32)

We primp, we preen, and everything in between, human peacocks, hoping the female of the species will like what she sees. Also she'll give us that ten seconds of "first impression" in which to plead our case. Yeah, she's doing the same thing.

From the muscles you wear, to the falsies she's sporting, from your spray-on tan to her glue-on nails . . . "It's all drag," remember?

But, if you're still looking for an "edge," something—anything!—to help you get one foot in the door and one hand down her . . . well, at least you can ask your old buddy from art class, ROY G. BIV, for a little help, using a little "color coordination" to your advantage.

According to feng shui, colors carry their own chi.

Take red, for instance. Red sparks vitality and increases vigor. Despite stereotypes of the "red light district" and Sting begging Roxanne not to put on that red light, red is not a good color for seduction. True, red makes you stand out in a crowd. Red has also been proven to speed up the heart rate of those who see red (but so has green—a much more user-friendly color).

Wearing red can give you a competitive edge, according to a recent study from Durham University in England. Test subjects performed worse in red rooms than they did in blue-colored rooms. In addition, Olympians wearing red uniforms performed better than those wearing blue uniforms in combat sports. The key seems to be that wearing red doesn't necessarily make you play better, but it can make your opponent play worse. This is because we tend to associate—both consciously and subconsciously—the color red with danger and with making mistakes. ("Seeing Red" by Rachel Mahan, *Psychology Today*, September/October 2008:53)

Orange is believed to increase physical strength. (This is somewhat ironic since correctional prisoners are often dressed in bright orange jumpsuits.); yellow truly is "mellow," engendering a feeling of calm; green is associated with skill, perhaps because of its connection with diligent gardeners; blue is nurturing; indigo inspires new ideas and innovation; and violet relaxes us. Additional color influences to consider:

White, in the West, is associated with both clarity of thought and purity of purpose. However, in the East white is often worn at funerals and is associated with death in some Asian cultures. Conversely, while black is associated with all things sinister in the West (from the western outlaw sporting a black Stetson to the Boneman's flowing black robe), in feng shui black is credited with the quality to absorb/counteract negative influence, its catchphrase being "acceptance."

Turquoise helps us adapt to changing circumstance; purple inspires thoughts of nobility and invokes images of authority; earthy brown literally means you're "grounded" and dependable; whereas a more subtle tan helps (re)establish internal balance and self-control.

Sexual feng shui tip #7: Someone's "favorite color" can provide a clue to what they consciously want to attain in life or else what they subconsciously need.

Sexual feng shui tip #8: Never compliment the color of her eyes, since she might be wearing contact lenses. Instead, mention "how intelligent" her eyes make her look, how "expressive" they are.

Sexual feng shui tip #9: Keep a picture of a cute baby in your wallet. Women love guys who love kids. Another option: Buy a puppy (or at least carry around a picture of your "lost" puppy). Why? The Saudi Arabian kingdom's "religious police," the Commission for the Promotion of Virtue and the Prevention of Vice, have outlawed the sale of dogs and cats to men on the grounds that pets can be used to pick up women. *(This Week, August 15, 2008:14)*

Using Their Sense of Touch

Giving her the "Big O": Oxytocin has been called the "touch drug" and the "Love hormone." This brain chemical is released by enjoyable physical touch and is part of the human sexual response.

Direct eye-to-eye contact often both encourages and indicates release of oxytocin.

During foreplay a woman's skin sends signals to her brain, resulting in the release of oxytocin. This hormone makes her feel good and makes her nipples erect.

Oxytocin also helps create uterine contractions, which, in turn contributes to her having an orgasm.

The benefits of kissing: Some good news: the simple act of kissing uses over twenty-nine muscles, and burns up to twelve calories. When "French" kissing (you know, playing tongue-hockey, not actually kissing Pierre) you exchange 250 types of bacteria! No, that's still actually good news because it's good bacteria, the kind that helps reinforce your immune system. Calcium and phosphorus are also passed from person to person through saliva and can reduce cavities. (This applies only to mouth-to-mouth kissing, not all those areas of interest you might be kissing!)

Most important, kissing also releases dopamine, serotonin, and noradrenalin, all hormones that calm your nerves and make you feel good.

Sexual feng shui tip #10: Taoist sex yoga practitioners avoid kissing during orgasm since people expel "muddy chi breath" at this time. Instead nestle your nose under your lover's ear.

Sending (and receiving) "the massage message" Your skin is your largest "sex" organ. Massage-massage-massage!

Sexual feng-shui Tip #11: Make love to a man from the top down. Make love to a woman from the bottom up. "Bottom" in this case means feet, dummy. Women love a foot massage. Especially working women. (I know, I know, you want to rub other things. Patience pays off—big-time!)

When using Chinese massage *(tui-na,* lit. "pressing and rubbing") gently but firmly press the tip of your thumb deep into the muscle tissue, joint junctures, and nerve and acupressure meridians. Apply primarily to the spine area, the major joints, and to the central nerve plexus (where muscle groups come together).

What's that, you say? You don't know how to give a proper massage? Don't know anything about those "meridian" thingies Chinese acupuncture guys always talk about?

No problem. There are only four things you need to know when it comes to giving a really good—sexy!—massage: Clean hands, smooth hands (oils help), warm hands, and "Goose bumps."

Having made sure your hands are clean, having warmed them (by rubbing them together, remember our tumo massage method?), before smoothing your hands and preparing the skin with an appropriate oil, lightly trace your fingertips along the area you intend to massage. Look for goose bumps to appear on the skin. Guess what? Goose bumps often appear following those "meridian" lines used in both Chinese acupuncture and Japanese shiatsu acupressure. Once these goose bumps appear, trace a thin line of oil along them and use this oil-line as your guide as you proceed with your massage.

Be sure to "feng shui" your massage sessions with appropriate lighting and mood music. You can also introduce various blends of scented oils, both to ease any roughness in your hands and to incorporate mood-altering scents into your overall feng shui arrangement.

According to the highly informative 1994 *Book of Massage and Aromatherapy* by Nitya Lacroix and Sharon Seager, when choosing oils for sensual massage the most important consideration is "personal taste." The massage will not be a pleasurable experience if the person giving or receiving it finds the blend of oils disagreeable, either scent-wise or viscosity-wise. According to Lacroix and Seager, ideally both partners should allow "an intuitive choice to guide them towards a blend of oils that they find most appealing."

Some oils seem to have a universal appeal, including: jasmine, rose, rosewood, sandalwood, and ylang-ylang, all of which have a "warming and enveloping quality, freeing the mind of the mundane and opening it to the exotic and romantic." (Ibid.) Finally, Lacroix and Seager suggest literally adding spice and stimulation to your chosen blend, adding either black pepper or frankincense.

Massage in general stimulates the lymph (immune) system, which, in turn, has been linked to the endocrine system (in Western medicine) and to the chakras in the East. (Surely you haven't forgotten our old friends the chakras from the section on India so soon?)

Some specific massage-oriented oils associated with specific chakras include:

- *For the base chakra:* Frankincense, black pepper, clary sage.
- *For the belly chakra:* Chamomile, fennel, marjoram, orange, peppermint, rose, sandalwood.
- *For the solar plexus chakra:* Frankincense, fennel, juniper, lavender, peppermint, neroli, rosemary, rosewood.
- *For the heart chakra:* Benzoin, bergamot, geranium, mandarin, peppermint, rose, sandalwood, ylang-ylang.
- *For the throat chakra:* Chamomile, clary sage, sandalwood.
- *For the brow "third eye" (pituitary gland) chakra:* Benzoin, clary sage, jasmine, juniper, orange, rosemary.

- *For the crown (pineal gland) chakra:* Cedarwood, cypress, eucalyptus, frankincense, juniper, lavender, mandarin, neroli, rose, rosewood, sandalwood.

To help (re)balance upper area and lower area chakras overall try jasmine, lavender, and sandalwood.

For relaxation choose three or four oils from this list: bergamot, German chamomile, clary sage, lavender, rosewood, or sandalwood.

To raise your spirits: Benzoin, bergamot, cedarwood, clary sage, frankincense, geranium, grapefruit, jasmine, mandarin, nutmeg, orange, rose, rosewood, or ylang-ylang. A blend of three or four from this list, and the comforting quality of a massage, can give you back the zest for life. (Ibid., 62)

An aphrodisiac blend can include black pepper (Ch. *Hu jiao),* cedarwood, clary sage, fennel, frankincense, ginger, jasmine, rose, and sandalwood, all to help stimulate the base-sex chakra. FYI:

> Indeed, ancient Taoist texts claim that a major cause of impotence in men is energy blockage in sexual orgasm and glands due to cramped feet and that vigorous massage of the toes and soles prior to intercourse helps solve this problem. (Reid, 1989:245)

Using Their Sense of Smell

> The human sense of smell is often seen as insignificant, dismissed as a distant also-ran to our eyesight or sensitive hearing. But this sense is keener and more influential on our species than many people realize. ("The Hidden Power of Scent" by Josie Glausiusz, in *Scientific American Mind,* August/ September 2008:38)

Chemistry started out as "alchemy" (a little science, a whole lotta mysticism). In the end (no matter whose end you're trying to end up in!) it still comes down to knowing—and sowing—a little "chemistry." Smelling is chemistry.

And now that little biology-by-way-of-anatomy lesson we promised:

The nasal cavity has roughly twelve million odor-detecting cells. Each odor-detecting cell has one of about 350 different olfactory receptor proteins and is specialized for sensing a limited number of dormant odor molecules.

These receptor proteins work in different combinations to enable people to detect at least ten thousand distinct scents. (Ibid.)

Our brain's olfactory bulb (the part of the brain that sorts through smells) has a close connection to the oldest part of the human brain, the limbic system. Odors trigger subconscious emotional responses before arriving at the brain's outermost section, the cerebral cortex (the "reasoning" part of our brain). In most people, this is usually the most underdeveloped or at least underused part!) A great deal of processing of odor is done on a subconscious level. We subconsciously evaluate people. (Yeah, that is a form of prejudice . . . and we're stuck with it.)

Ever thought to yourself, "there's just something about that guy I don't trust"? Well, odds are, you are subconsciously picking up on some nuance of body language and/or you've subconsciously picked up on a negative odor from him.

According to Glausiusz, research suggests that even at subliminal, undetectable levels, odors can influence our social preferences:

> Smell subconsciously facilitates a variety of human social interactions. People use smell to assess a person's likability, sexual attractiveness and emotional state. They can also use scent to distinguish a stranger from a friend, a male from a female and someone who is gay from someone who is straight.

Other "(s)experts" agree:

> Human social judgments and social interactions are at least partially under the control of smells we can't perceive. (neurologist Jay Gottfried, quoted in ibid.)

Some evidence suggests that humans may detect pheromones through special nerves distinct from those that govern smell. ("Sex and the Secret Nerve" by Douglas Fields, in *Scientific American Mind,* February/March, 2007)

Each of us has our very own funk fingerprint, a unique scent unlike any other person on earth. It doesn't matter how much we try to mask it. Just ask any bloodhound.

Curiously, women are, on average, marginally more sensitive than men to trace odors and are most sensitive to odors when they are ovulating. In fact, some experts believe that a woman's heightened sense of smell while fertile may aid them in mate selection. (ibid.)

Studies have shown that a man's body odor is more important than his appearance. Between the ages of eight and sixteen girls begin to dislike the odor of male sweat. *(Psychology Today,* September/October 2005:32)

Conversely, when adult women smell androstatienone (a pheromone in men's sweat) their cortisol levels increase. Cortosol, normally connected with stress, is also associated with sexual arousal.

People whose clothes smell of pine are perceived to be more successful, intelligent, sociable, sanitary, and attractive than people whose clothes smell of lemon, onion, or smoke.

A study completed by researchers from the University of Chicago has concluded that women who are breastfeeding emit pheromones that put other women in the mood for sex.

These pheromones act as a natural aphrodisiac, putting women in the mood for sex, increasing some women's libidos by 42 percent.

Don't think of "pheromones" as something exotic or mysterious. Think of them simply as the deepest (yes, subliminal) level of "smelling."

Pheromones were first discovered by science in 1986. Of course, every erstwhile, would-be Don Juan has known about pheromones since the time Og the caveman smeared dinosaur dung on his chest in the hopes of getting noticed by that Racquel Welch look-alike from 20,000 BC.

We can introduce some feng shui "sense aphrodisiacs," sights, sounds, tastes, and tactile stimulation specifically designed to excite the other person (and ourselves!).

Ancient Asians knew this. That's why Indian ayurvedic medicine lists seven hundred useful aromatics with spiritual and health-giving properties

Ready for a little more scent science?

Semen contains powerful mood-altering chemicals, including testosterone, estrogen, prolactin, luteinizing hormone, and prostaglandin. *(American Curves,* August 2008:10)

Research has shown that the scent of licorice, cucumber, and baby powder (!) can increase vaginal blood flow by 13 percent. Likewise, scents of lavender and pumpkin pie saw an 11 percent increase in vaginal blood flow. *(American Curves,* August 2008:104)

Sexual feng shui tip #12: When it comes to using their sense of smell to your advantage: If you want to be "*scent*-ual," always act-*scent* the positive with positive scents!

Using Their Sense of Hearing. Lou Paget's insightful quote bears repeating:

> Women fall in love between the ears . . . Women are more aural and tactile. They need to hear and to feel a man in order to get excited.

Always remember: Her ears are her biggest and best erogenous zone. (Of course, that doesn't mean you should ever comment on how gi-normous your date's ears actually are!)

Sexual feng shui tip #13: Provide plenty of compliments to a woman about her body—especially when she's naked. *The Journal of Sex Research* recently published a study that suggests that women who are ashamed of their bodies have fewer sexual experiences and are less sexually assertive. (We needed an expensive study to tell us this?)

Sexual feng shui tip #14: Don't criticize your lover about what he/she is doing wrong, compliment them on what they're doing right.

Sexual feng shui tip #15: Research has shown that lying down can diminish sensitivity to smell and sound. You experience more sense during sexual positions where you are standing or sitting than while in the missionary position.

Asian Aphrodisiacs

> ***Aphrodisiacs are the paints that color the art of seduction.***
> **—Cecily Knobler**

Whether we're talking about strategy or seduction, everybody's always looking for "the edge," something that will tip the fickle scale of chance in their favor, anything that will lend them an advantage. No matter how already wily your battlefield strategy, no matter how savvy your seduction scenarios, no matter how well laid those plans of mice and men—why leave things to chance when there's a chance you lock into a sure thing?

At one time or another down through history—East and West—almost every food, herb, and magic spell has been touted and tried as an aphrodisiac. A few of these met with startling success, many with tragic—even fatal!—failure.

Perhaps it only seems to us in the West that our brothers (and sisters) in the East have successfully made the leap from hairy palms to the upper hand when it comes to finding aphrodisiacs that actually (clearing throat here) stand up to scrutiny.

When looking at—and perhaps cooking with—the following list of Asian aphrodisiacs, try to keep in mind that many of these were discovered by Indian, Taoist, and Buddhist monks and therefore the proper use of such potions and portents were often accompanied by serious religious and meditative practices.

Aphrodisiacs in general and Asian aphrodisiacs in particular can be catalogued into three basic types: those derived from animals, those gleaned from foods and those found in herbs.

Aphrodisiacs Derived from Animals. In China, aphrodisiacs weren't just for men. The most famous "Dragon Lady" in Chinese history, Empress Wu Tze-tien (624–705), who died with a smile on her face at age eighty-one, attributed her long (healthy) life to drinking an alchemist's elixir of tiger's blood and fresh semen—the latter ingredient milked daily from her retinue of four hundred stalwart and strapping young men! (Reid, 1989:280)

Other animal aphrodisiacs: include: Egg yolk, raw (Yo, Adrian!); oysters (lots of zinc, each ejaculation equals a loss of zinc. Think: "More zinc, more pink!"); shrimp (lightly cooked); deer horn (especially the Sika deer of northeastern China); red-spotted lizard; sea horses; male seals and sea lions (their dried genitalia); sashimi; tortoiseshell; silkworm chrysalis; dried human placenta.*

Aphrodisiac Foods. Asparagus; banana; bee pollen; beet; black cherries; black grapes; carrot; celery seeds; chocolate (raises serotonin levels. Dark chocolate contains chemical phenylethamine that mimics an endorphin "happy chemical" that makes us feel good)**; cucumber juice; garlic (a natural blood cleanser, as is onion—good to have both in your system, bad to smell like either!); raw ginger root; lecithin (FYI: Semen consists largely of lecithin); papaya seeds (papaya contains B-17, a.k.a. laetrile, a natural birth-control method in Polynesia. Apricot kernel-pits have the same effect); pumpkin-

---

*Which we now know to be a prime source for life-giving and life-renewing stem cells.

**See "Aphrodite Aphro-Dirty: Top 7 aphrodisiacs to raise her sex drive!" by Cecily Knobler in *American Curves* 35–39.

seeds; tomatoes*; raw spinach; sunflower seeds; seaweed (kelp); oats (tradi-tional Chinese medicine maintains that green oat bran and wild oats can both raise testosterone levels); wheat germ oil; and wine (increases testos-terone, read "aggressiveness," levels—in women).

And the present author's personal favorite: jujubes *(zizyphus jujube)* a.k.a. "Chinese dates" were placed into the vaginas of young virgins and left for a while in the belief the dates would absorb the pristine yin-chi essence of the young girl. These jujubes are then eaten.

Foods to avoid: Strong coffees and teas; refined starches and sugars; vinegar; pasteurized milk; and meat preserved in potassium nitrate, better known as saltpeter, once given to prisoners to calm them and eliminate their sexual desire.

Anything nicotine. I know, not a food, but not helping! Nicotine restricts blood vessels, restricting blood flow. Blood flow . . . kinda important to the whole get-excited-about-sex thing.

Aphrodisiac Herbs and Spices. Angelica root; foxglove; garlic; pepper (contains *myrystin,* a proven sexual stimulant); cinnamon, nutmeg, saffron; ginseng (ginseng helps the body resist mental and physical stress, improves nerve function, and improves overall immune function. There are two types of ginseng: *panax schin-seng,* the Asian variety, and *panax quinquefolium,* Western—American—ginseng); *yin-yang huo,* a.k.a. "horny goat weed" (technical name *aceranthus sagittatum,* a nondescript weed that grows in the wilds of China); licorice; raspberry seeds; and Chinese wolf-berry.

Modern Western Aphrodisiacs

> *As a physician, I am well aware that if someone believed that green M&Ms were an aphrodisiac, a handful of the candy might be enough to goose the gonads.*
> —Dr. Ronald Klatz, Grow Young with HGH (1997)

---

*Once thought poisonous, called Pomme de' Moors ("Apples of the Moors"), or "love apple," we now know tomatoes contain lycopene, which is good for the health of the prostate. Rule of thumb: What's good for the prostate is good for your sex life!

Viagra: The official party line is that Viagra is *not* an aphrodisiac and cannot cause an erection in the absence of actual sexual desire and stimulation . . .

Officially, the main ingredient in Viagra is *sildenafil citrate.* Its "extracurricular" use was discovered in the 1980s by scientists at Pfizer who were researching a treatment for high blood pressure and angina. By the way, the only thing Viagra does for you is help to get the blood flowing better.

Some conspiracy theorists maintain that Viagra is actually "stolen" from ancient—and still secret—Far Eastern herb blends. (Perhaps they're only trying to get a "rise" out of the Viagra people?)

Human Growth Hormone: The *"Perfect Aphrodisiac"?* In the West, Human Growth Hormone (HGH) continues to grow in popularity, especially when it comes to sexual benefits users have noted.

Synthetic human growth hormone is a substance naturally produced in the pituitary gland, part of the endocrine system that Asians identify with the chakras. (Remember? From our section on India. See also Figures 6 and 7.)

Normally HGH is secreted daily in bursts with the largest amount released during sleep. Decline in GH level released in the body has been linked to decline in sexual function. Conversely, high levels of GH have been linked to mood elevation and enhanced sexual performance.

What goes around comes around: Increased sexual activity has a rejuvenating effect on the pituitary and the neuroendocrine axis. This, in turn, ups desire and performance.

Scientists are now convinced that by replenishing our supply of growth hormone, we can recover our vigor, our health, youthful looks, and a more potent sexuality. (Klatz and Kahn, 1997:15)

As early as the early nineties, researchers were discovering that the benefits of HGH included marked improvement in muscle strength; exercise endurance; loss of body fat; improvements in skin; increased healing capacity; a rise in energy levels; as well as an overall improvement in emotions, attitude, and memory, and, especially, in sexual drive and performance. (See *Grow Young with HGH* by Dr. Ronald Klatz, with Carol Kahn. HarperPerennial, 1997.)

One study revealed that 75 percent of male participants reported an increase in sexual potency or frequency, while 62 percent of the men reported being able to maintain an erection for longer periods, leading researchers to conclude that, since the vast majority of their participants using growth hormone therapy had evidenced increases in both their sexual appetite and performance, growth hormone plays a pivotal role in sexual health. (Ibid., 125)

The good news for the ladies:

> Women do not have a decline in sexual function that is comparable to that of men. A healthy woman can enjoy intense orgasm into old age. . . . Lack of regular intercourse can interfere with a woman's natural enjoyment and ability to have orgasm. In the same way as a man, she has to use it or risk losing it. (Klatz and Kahn, 1997:125)

Now the even better news for everybody:

> According to all the physicians who use growth hormone in their practice, the sexual changes are striking, affecting both men and women. Both sexes report increased libido, while male patients say that they have better erections, better performance, longer duration, and decreased recovery between orgasms. (Ibid., 127)

HGH has shown benefits for patients well into their eighties, improving cardiac function and circulation to every part of the body—*every* part.

Nearly half the incidence of erectile dysfunction in men over fifty is caused by arteriosclerosis of the penile arteries. Erectile dysfunction has been shown to be a preceding sign of a heart attack or stroke. Another major cause: decreased testosterone levels. Major villains: drinking and smoking.

FYI: The market for male sexual-dysfunction drugs is already a $4 billion a year industry. (Ibid.)

Most important, so far as sexual feng shui is concerned, HGH acts on your most important sex organ:

> The most important sexual organ lies not below the waist but above the neck. How we think and feel profoundly influences sexual functioning in both men and women. . . . People on growth hormone often say that they can't tell whether their enhanced sexual performance is due to psychological or physical factors. In truth the answer is both. Mind and body are intertwined. (Ibid., 132)

Sexuality is part and parcel of our being. When we are young, it seems to rule our lives. Whether we are men or women, we are driven by the need to look good, smell good, dress well, make ourselves attractive to those we wish to attract. . . . To be sexy seems to be the very essence of youth. (Ibid., 123)

Something New for the Ladies. There's a new skin patch about to be marketed in the United States that increases a woman's sex drive. Originally designed to treat a common medical condition in women called "Hypoactive Sexual Desire Disorder," this patch works by delivering testosterone (a hormone known to stimulate sexual response in women as well as in men). The patch was designed by Procter & Gamble, who already sell a similar testosterone patch called "Intrinsa" in Europe. According to research, one in three American women have reported suffering from low sexual desire. ("P&G patch stimulates sex drive in women" by Keith T. Reid, *Cincinnati Enquirer,* September 2, 2008)

The Real "Perfect" Aphrodisiac. Taoist Master Hua Tio said, "A running stream never goes bad." In other words, exercise is the "perfect" aphrodisiac. Doesn't matter if you ask ancient Taoists, or modern-day Western doctors.

The ancient Chinese Taoists knew what they were doing, that's why all Taoist exercises are essentially "aerobic," involving carefully regulated breathing patterns. (Reid, 1989:195)

For the active Westerner, body building, particularly leg squats and leg presses, enhances sexual prowess. The blood vessels that feed the leg and thigh muscles go right to the renal artery, increase size and rigidity, and increase venous tone. (Klatz and Kahn, 1997:130)

Blood flow . . . parts of the body like the penis and clitoris use blood flow, right? Are you beginning to see—or feel—the connection?

> **The brain is an apothecary. And it is the strongest drug you can purchase.**
>
> **—Bob Delmontegue**

METHOD: TANTRIC TIGERS COMING AND GOING

Most of us are constantly seducing (or being seduced) without even knowing it!
—Cecily Knobler

Eventually, no matter how much theory you stuff into your pants, sooner or later, somebody's gonna call your bluff and ask you to lay your . . . cards on the table.

Truth be known, everybody pads their . . . résumé. The trick is learning to read the other guy's (or gal's) résumé—instantly!—in order to figure out what kind of person you're dealing with. The quicker—more accurately— you can accomplish this, the better your chances of winning all the marbles—or at least being allowed to get your marbles into the game!

The best way to accomplish this is by learning to spot which of "The Eight Fate Traits" is motivating your prey or potential playmate, which NLP approach will best capture and keep their attention, and exactly what her (or his) body language is trying to tell you.

On average, "first impression" exists within a ten-second window. Keep in mind you'll also be judged by your approach—what you're wearing, how you're groomed, the swagger or lack of in your walk, whether or not you're adult enough to pull up your pants (a holler out to baggy "saggers"—stop showing your diaper!).

The Eight Fate Traits (Tipping the Sexual Scale in Your Favor)

The Optimist says "The glass is half-full." The Pessimist says, "The glass is half-empty." The Realist says, "We need to get a new glass!"

If your old game plan isn't working, get a new game plan. But before you can get a new game plan, you have to decide what game you're playing: One-night stand or lifetime commitment?

More importantly, you have to be able to instantly figure out what game she (or he) is playing. This is accomplished by figuring out which of the "The Eight Fate Traits" dominate their outlook on life:

Pleasure-seeker versus Pain-avoider,
Necessity-motivated versus Possibility-motivated,

Serial Thinker versus Parallel Thinker,
Similarities-Seeker versus Difference-Seeker.

1. *A Pleasure-seeker* moves toward pleasure. Active. She's come to have fun. Show her how much fun coming is and how much fun she's got coming.
2. *A Pain-avoider* moves away from pain. Reactive. She's coming off a bad relationship, or else she's timid and afraid of being hurt again. Come to her rescue. Take her someplace nice.
3. *A person motivated by necessity.* Her girlfriends told her she just "had to get out of the house." She doesn't really want to be here. Sympathize with her. Offer to take her somewhere quieter, nicer— maybe back to her place, back to her comfort zone?
4. *A person motivated by possibility.* She's a dreamer. She fantasizes about finding "Mr. Right." Become her fantasy and she'll help you fulfill yours.
5. *A serial thinker.* Weak on details. Moves ahead methodically, step by step. Thinks "micro." She's just there for a good time, not thinking about tomorrow. Keep her in the here and now. She might hate herself (and you!) in the morning; just make sure she enjoys herself tonight.
6. *A parallel thinker.* Thinks in "macro." Has to see the big picture first before starting out. She's thinking long-term, commitment. If you're not thinking along those same lines, don't be a tease.
7. *Someone who seeks similarities.* Optimistic. Two-edge sword. On the one hand, she's had fun before, you come on like the kinda guy who could show her a good time again. On the other hand, she sees the similarities between you and her ex, between you and every other lame guy in the place:

> If there is one secret to success, it lies in the ability to get the other person's point of view and see things from that person's angle as well as your own. (Henry Ford)

8. *Someone who seeks differences.* Cynical (or realistic) Show her you're different. Something new and exciting. Intrigue her:

> People view the world differently, depending upon their life experiences. . . . As a result of these varied experiences, different people use different—and sometimes

> conflicting—frames of reference to analyze and
> respond to what's going on in the world. . . . If we are
> to communicate effectively, we must do justice to these
> differences because such an understanding makes us
> more flexible and, therefore, more effective. (Jeary,
> 2004:47)

It all comes down to your being able to sell yourself.

The Salesman's Rules of Thumb

- **The Reason Rule:** On average, people are more cooperative when given a reason for a request.
- **The Because Rule:** Always use the word "because" in your request. The word "because," in and of itself, even without any logic or substantive evidence, helps elicit a positive response.
- **The Scarcity Rule** teaches that people are more motivated by the thought of losing something than they are of gaining something. Thus, a "limited-time offer" works better than a "rebate."
- **The Reciprocity Rule** makes us feel we have to do someone a favor in return for a favor done for us. It's called "feeling obligated."
- **The Matching and Mirroring Rule:** Intentionally put yourself in sync with the other person by "matching" their body language and actions (tapping a pencil in rhythm with the other person's breathing, etc.) and "mirroring" their movements, imitating their body language and patterns of speech. Having successfully picked up on and then mirrored their patterns, you can now begin to subtly lead them in the direction you want. If you've ever taken Psych 101 you know this is called "Operant Conditioning."

More NLP = More TLC!

Neurolinguistic Programming, NLP for short, was originally designed as a model for psychiatric therapy. NLP is defined as the study and use of language as it impacts our brain and our behavior. According to NLP, we all primarily function in one of three types of sensory modality:

> *Visually-oriented* folks are the most common in society. Look at her breathing pattern. Is she breathing shallow, from the chest? That's a clue she's visually oriented.

Also, watch her eyes for lots of eye movement when she's "remembering." Suggestion: Keep your hands moving as you tell your story, this will help hold her visually oriented attention.

Auditory-oriented people can be spotted by their distinctive breathing pattern: deeper, from the diaphragm, more rhythmic. They often have slouching shoulders. When listening, they lean their head in, tilt their head, and turn their ears toward the speaker. Suggestion: Plenty of bells and whistles. Snap your finger to emphasize a point, change the rhythm and volume of your voice in order to keep their audio-sense occupied.

Kinesthetic-oriented folks make up the smallest portion of the population. They make lots of eye contact, trying to figure out what you are feeling. They often ask the same question over and over, only worded differently. They are often slow to make a decision. Suggestion: If they initially say "no," re-word and resubmit your request.

Even when judged solely from the perspective of effectiveness, manipulation may succeed in the short term, but will often undermine long-term relationships. (Jeary, 2004:46)

Body Language

The person with the most flexibility has the best chance of
achieving the outcome he or she desires.
—Tony Jeary, *Life Is a Series of Presentations*

We can never talk enough (or learn enough) about body language.

Nonverbal communication in general predates human language by hundreds of thousands of years and is a much better indicator of what people are thinking since they are blissfully (as in "ignorance is bliss") unaware of what their own body language is so blatantly babbling about.

Nonverbal communication falls into two types. It's basic yin-yang, push-pull: either "intimacy behaviors," meant to draw you in closer and bond with you, or else "dominance behaviors" meant to establish personal space and boundaries (designed to keep others at a distance).

Intimacy behaviors include (1) repeatedly looking in your direction and (2) making eye contact; (3) smiling; (4) turning their head and perhaps their whole body facing you; (5) leaning in and/or (6) moving closer than three feet (within "intimate" distance).

Often you'll run into a fine damsel who likes a little "verbal jousting." Wordplay and innuendo can both be great foreplay but only if his/her body language betrays interest.

In other words, it's okay if he/she is "talking smack" and acting as if he/she is trying to "blow you off" so long as their body language is saying otherwise, in which case, they're just playing hard to get.

If, on the other hand, they are displaying true dominance behavior, or what's called "perceived dominance behavior," then you are wasting your time and they are only stringing you along for their own amusement and perhaps the amusement of their posse.

Dominance behaviors include: (1) talking a lot, (2) talking loud, (3) making deliberate eye contact, and (4) deliberate touching, "invading" the other person's space.

The Alpha Male commands the most space, his arms and legs extended. He scans the room, making eye contact with all available women . . . taking up a lot of space—power is demonstrated in direct proportion to how we occupy space; and successfully interrupting others; verbally challenging others' facts and "quizzing" them.

These show *perceived* dominance, in other words, this Alpha Male *thinks* they are in charge, or else they are directly challenging you to see who is in charge.

The Female Brain is better at decoding nonverbal signs (facial expression, tone of voice, and so forth). What women don't realize is that men are not as skilled in picking up on and interpreting nonverbal cues. That's why women get frustrated when they give off what they think are obvious nonverbal cues—either to come closer or get lost! and men seem oblivious to what they are "saying." *(Bottom Line Personal,* September 1, 2006:13)

That doesn't mean she's hard to learn to "read." First: Stop staring down at her . . . *personality,* and invest a little time into the overall feng shui of the situation:

- *Meet her in a side-by-side position* (at a bar, buffet table, or salad bar); that way she'll "turn into you" in order to stand face-to-face, a sure sign she's interested.

- *Keep your right hand empty, open, and inviting to shake.*
- *Don't let anything come between you and her*—literally. Don't hold your drink, buffet plate, hat, briefcase, or anything else between you and her. When sitting, choose small round tables, rather than larger, square-edged tables. (We're trying to tear down walls here, not build more.)
- *Line up your "center lines."* Our center line (imaginary line running from your face to your groin—ironic, huh?) should be lined up with her center line as much as possible.
- *Keep "line-of-sight at all times"*—like a sniper.
- *"Mirror" her body movements,* but don't mock.

Sexual feng shui tip #16: Charisma ("charm on steroids") isn't so much "chemistry" as it is "electricity," bringing the other person's wavelength into sync with our own via "mirroring and matching."

- *Match her physical tone.* If she's animated, be animated, too. If she's sedate, assume an air of calm about yourself.
- *Be eager, not aggressive.* Wait for her to lead. Follow enthusiastically.
- *Avoid aggressive gestures and postures.* For example, hand on your cocked hip or dangling near your crotch says, "I'm a gun-slinger who keeps his hand near his six-shooter at all times." Legs wide apart—you're advertising. Leaning too far forward—"Come on, let's wrestle!"

Sure Signs You Just Hit the Jackpot

- She'll glance at you and look away but leaves her head pointed in your direction.
- She does "the head cock." Like a puppy she'll lean her head toward her shoulder, putting her neck in a vulnerable position—this means she trusts you (and has decided you're not a vampire).
- She smiles and the smile on her lips is matched by a smile (twinkle) in her eye. (See Figure 28, page 272.)

Sexual feng shui tip #17: The mouth is the more expressive part of the face, and not just for the words that come out of it, but reactions in the eyes are harder to control. So while Americans (who are big on personal expression) look to the mouth to read each other, the relatively subdued Japanese rely more on "reading" the eyes. *(Psychology Today,* November/ December 2006:16)

SURE SIGNS SHE'S INTERESTED IN YOU

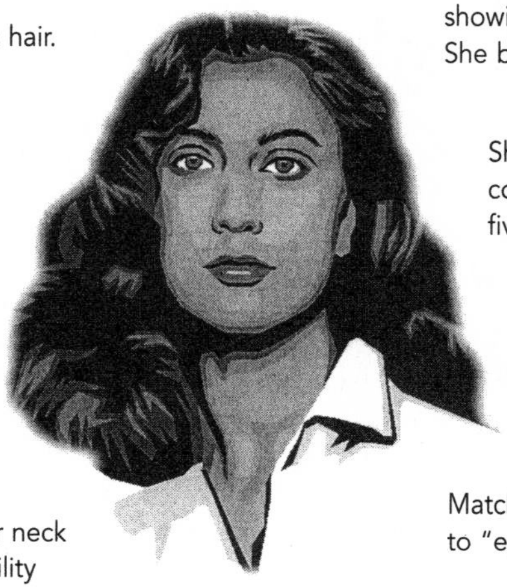

Playing with hair.

Eyebrows raised, eyes showing a lot of white. She blinks a lot.

Her smile lingers even after she looks away.

She makes eye contact for more than five to ten seconds.

Licking lips, showing teeth.

Looks at you, then looks away, but her head remains pointed in your direction.

She starts to breathe differently.

She exposes her neck (shows vulnerability and trust)

Match smiling lips to "eye-smile."

Her skin (especially face) flushes (sign of increased blood flow).

Nipples enlarge. Her breasts swell and/or she (subconsciously) thrusts her breasts more up and out.

Figure 28.

Body cues:

- *Her breathing.* She starts to breathe differently; her face becomes flushed; she starts making nonsensical noises; she grabs her hair; her breasts, nipples in particular, enlarge; her heart begins pumping harder (hint: Notice her pulse racing while holding her hand/wrist); her muscle start to contract; she extends her legs; her toes curl (sign she is beginning to experience an orgasm); and all her muscles contract.
- *Her blinking.* The average person blinks fifteen times a minute. A recent study found that women on the birth control pill blink 32 percent more than those who aren't on the pill. Women on the pill can mean a woman on the prowl! By the way, that same study found that women on the pill are more attracted to men with "rugged" features (strong wide jaws).

- *Her leaning.* She leans in closer to you. (Encourage this by dropping your voice after hooking her on an interesting story.)
- *Her looking.* She holds eye contact for more than five to ten seconds.
- *Her touching.* She touches you intentionally. If she can't keep her hands off you, chances are she wants to put more than just her hands on you!
- *She offers to buy you a drink.*

Voice and Speech cues:

- *She showers you with compliments.*

While a guest on *The Phil Donahue Show,* in front of millions of viewers, *That Girl* actress Marlo Thomas shamelessly showered Phil with compliments. Within months they were married.

- *She begins talking about her personal life,* giving you her address, telephone number, telling you where she works. We only open up to those we trust and feel comfortable with. (Unless it's only those three margaritas doing the talking!)

> Three-fourths of the people you will ever meet are thirsting for sympathy. Give it to them, and they will love you. (Dale Carnegie)

When men are in the presence of someone they deem less physically dominant, they assert themselves and their voice drops in pitch. However, when intimidated, their voice goes up. (Kate Gilbert, "Voice Messages: The Science of Your Sound" in *Psychology Today,* November/December 2006:15)

Gilbert goes on to explain how people with attractive voices have had more sexual partners and report an earlier age of first sexual encounter. They are also more likely to cheat:

> What separates the voices of Don Juans from those of average Joes? Men who score with women can more flexibly modify aspects of their voice like pitch and volume throughout a flirt session—opening up with a dynamic, loud voice and later becoming softer and more monotone to suggest tenderness. (Ibid.)

Notice in Gilbert's description that softening and lowering the voice implies more intimacy and lowering your voice tends to make people lean in closer to hear what you're saying. Once you have a person "hooked," changing your voice to a monotone can "hypnotically" relax them and can even be a precursor to full-blown hypnosis. (See *Black Science,* Paladin 2001 and *Mind Manipulation,* Citadel 2001)

Sexual feng shui tip #18: Keep the vulgarity to a minimum, unless she's already cussing like a sailor.

Men vs. Women Talk Priorities

"Having a conversation is easy. Having a conversation with a woman—not so easy." (John Eagan, *How to "Pick Up" Beautiful Women*)

Comparing a list of the nine most common topics of conversation, we find that men and women hold the first five in common, but diverge when it comes to placing priority on the remaining four:

Men and Women

1. family/home/children
2. health
3. work/job
4. professional growth (advancing careers, getting a promotion)
5. personal growth (self-actualization goals)

Men	*Women*
6. recreation	6. clothes/shopping
7. travel	7. recreation
8. women	8. travel
(especially young women)	9. men
9. sports and politics	

We judge fast talkers to be more educated, and those with varied inflection to be more interesting. Men prefer *higher* voices in women and women like *deeper* voices in men (especially when those women are ovulating or looking for a short-term relationship). FYI: A sonorous voice can help compensate for a lacking in the looks department. *(Psychology Today,* January/February. 2008:75)

Sexual feng shui tip #19: Telling a joke (1) is a great way to break the ice; (2) literally injects "happy chemicals" into the conversation by releasing endorphins in the brain; (3) makes the person associate their first impression of you with good feeling (those happy chemicals again); and (4), depending on the sophistication level of the joke—whether or not the person "gets it" and laughs—tells you a lot about both their education and sophistication level (in the case of a subtle or political joke) and/or their reaction to a more raunchy joke. Innuendo can serve this same weeding-out purpose. **Hint:** If you're trying to pick up a woman, tell a joke that makes the man in the joke look stupid by virtue of his being outsmarted by a woman and/or take her to a romantic comedy.

Master euphemism and innuendo since (1) they're a more "socially acceptable" way of putting dirty thoughts in her/his head, and (2) they mark you as someone inventive enough to actually know what "euphemism" and "innuendo" mean! Read Oscar Wilde. (Now there was a man who could tell you to "go to hell!" in such a polite and colorful a way as to make you look forward to the journey!)

In the East, innuendo and euphemism are considered high art. Asian cultures tend to have, what are to Western ears at least, wonderful euphemisms for all things sexual. See if you can figure out these examples of Chinese "dirty talk." (See Figure 29, page 276.)

Reality Rule 3.3. Whether you score depends on how you keep score.

—Boese (2006:49)

Five things to do to convince her you're sincere

1. *Let her talk.* (Take another look at "Men vs. Women Talk Priorities");
2. *Don't try to get her drunk.* Alcohol affects men and women differently: Men get a buzz on, lose their inhibitions, and want to get active. Alcohol sedates women. Hint: Less booze, more fast-tempo music (which research has shown makes women more sociable). You have better luck with energy drinks (she's "geeked" up and ready to be freaked up).
3. *Keep your hands to yourself* until you notice her orienting herself toward you (leaning closer in, aligning her shoulders square with yours, etc.);

ASIAN SEXUAL EUPHEMISMS TEST

Draw a line to the correct answer(s)

1. "Clouds and rain"

2. "Spitting the peach"

3. "Dragon-yang relations"

4. "Rubbing mirrors"

5. "Yang weapon"

6. "Jade Gate"

7. "Friendly relations"

8. "One square inch"

9. "Jade Terrance"

10. "Yin bean"

11. "Celestial Palace"

12. "Golden Gully"

13. "Mr. Kuo"

14. "Leak"

15. "Tiger Stalking"

16. "Monkey Leaping"

17. "Blowing the flute"

18. "Sipping at the vast spring"

19. "Sea of energy"

20. "Precious pearl"

21. "Pearl diver"

22. "Battle implements"

a. Woman facedown, buttocks raised

b. Face-to-face gay anal penetration with simultaneous fellatio

c. Fellatio

d. Cunnilingus

e. Sex toys, especially dildo

f. Gay intercourse

g. Lesbian clitoris-to-clitoris sex

h. Vagina

i. Sexual intercourse

j. Face-to-face intercourse (especially with navels touching)

k. Lesbian

l. Male orgasm

m. Clitoris

n. Penis

---

1 = i. 2 = f. 3 = f. 4= g. 5 = n. 6 = h. 7 = i. 8 = h. 9 = m. 10 = m. 11 = h. 12 = h.
13 = e. 14 = l. 15 = a. 16= b. 17 = c. 18 = d. 19 = j. 20 = m. 21 = k. 22 =e.

Figure 29.

4. *Don't ignore her posse.* Sometimes you have to win her friends over before you win her over. "Prime the pump" by joking with her friends about her. After a while, excuse yourself for a few minutes in order to better judge the atmosphere when you come back. They will have decided while you were gone whether you're "worthy." If yes, her friends will conspicuously leave you two alone. If her friends huddle around her, it means you got the "thumbs-down" and they've circled the wagons—move on, Hoss.

In this day and age, if she (or one of her posse) is packin' an iPhone, they can Google you instantly. Check: **Don'tdatehimgirl.com** for all those women you've ever screwed over.

Sexual feng shui tip #20: Men with female friends appear safer and more attractive to other women. For $50 an hour WingWoman.com will rent you a "female friend" who will excuse herself as soon as you hit it off with another woman. (Boese, 2006:40)

5. Don't get *caught* lying (unless it's about how *wonderful* she/he is!)

Four quick thoughts on lying

- "You only lie to two people in your life: your girlfriend and the police. Everybody else you tell the truth to." (Jack Nicholson, *Vanity Fair,* April 1994)
- "Women will lie about how many guys they've fucked in court. If she says three—that's ten! You gotta give every woman a seven-dick curve." (Chris Rock)
- Men and women lie differently when it comes to the number of sexual partners they've had. Men lie up, women lie down. (Yes, that *is* a pun!)
- Hands down, women say a "sincere" compliment is the best opening line.

  A man's fears and insecurities often concern his sense of masculinity; he usually will feel threatened by a woman who is too overly manipulative, who is too much in control. (Greene, 2001:291)

Or, in other words:

"A man of quality never feels threatened by a woman of equality." (Maureen Reagan, *The Phil Donahue Show*)

MADNESS

When the person knowingly engages in or causes contact with the
genitalia, anus, groin, breast, inner thigh or buttocks of any person
with an intent to arouse or gratify the sexual desire of any person.
—President Bill Clinton's definition of "sexual relations"*

Differences in What Men and Women Enjoy in Bed

Within every man there is the reflection of a woman, and within
every woman there is the reflection of a man.
—Hyemeyohsts Storm

According to neuropsychiatrist Louann Brizendine, in her 2006 *The
Female Brain:*

> We all start out with female brains. It's only when the devel-
> oping fetus is "marinated" in testosterone at around eight
> weeks that male and female brains diverge. . . . The female
> brain sprouts connections in areas that govern communica-
> tion and emotion, while in the male brain the cells in the
> communication centers are pruned and more cells grow in
> areas that govern sex and aggression.**

Brizendine also points out the fact that, on the one hand, on average
women think about sex once a day. Men, on the other hairy palm, think
about sex every fifty-eight seconds! (Ibid.)

When men and women do think about sex, what kind of sex do they
think about?

- Receiving oral sex: (men) 85 percent (women) 71 percent
- Giving oral sex: (men) 66 percent (women) 43 percent
- Threesomes: (men) 64 percent (women) 33 percent

---

* Given in his deposition in the Paula Jones sexual harassment case. Note that nowhere
is oral sex mentioned. Ergo, "I did not have sexual relations with that woman!" You go, Bill!

**See also "Men and Women: Maybe we ARE different . . ." by Elizabeth Weise, *USA
Today,* August 22, 2006:9D.

- Watching a mate masturbate: (men) 57 percent (women) 41 percent
- Anal sex: (men) 54 percent (women) 19 percent*

Of course, if you want something done right . . .

Masturbation: (1) puts you in touch with your own body; (2) eases tension; (3) releases mood-enhancing hormones. Masturbation is an added plus for gays and lesbians since the more they know about what feels good on them, the more likely that information is to translate to lovers of the same sex.

"Holding the Bindu." In Chinese Taoism the term *Huan-jing Bu-nau* refers to techniques designed to help a man retain and return the chi in his sperm in order to use it to nourish body and brain. This is a necessary skill for a man to cultivate because Taoists teach that yang-chi is by nature weaker and more vulnerable than yin. Yang therefore needs to be carefully nurtured, especially during sexual intercourse. (Reid, 1989:278)

Amongst Indian yogis the retention of semen is known as "holding the bindu."**

Loss of semen is prevented by applying firm pressure on the perineum between the base of the scrotum and the anus. Employ deep breathing when using this method, since deep breathing helps massage the prostate, encouraging the reabsorbing of essential (semen) elements.

Through this technique, the chi in sperm is reabsorbed within the man's body, especially in the soft tissues of the prostate gland and the spongy portion of the urethra, allowing it to enter the bloodstream and circulate throughout the body, nourishing tissues and organs, including the brain.

Some gay researchers maintain that another man's yang essence can be absorbed and exchanged during anal intercourse. (See "Gender-Benders," in chapter on China.)

FYI: According to Taoist masters, women naturally retain their sexual chi secretions during intercourse.

It seems clear that the Chinese possess some valuable secrets about health, sex and longevity from which the rest of the world stands to benefit. (Reid, 1989:284)

---

*Based on a *Marie Claire/Esquire* national survey, published in *Marie Claire,* February, 2007.
**Not to be confused with the homonym *bindu,* forehead "dot" sported by Hindu women.

Sexual feng shui tip #21: At orgasm, bellies should be tightly pressed together. Chi-nexus known as "the sea of energy" is located just below the navel.

When Longer Doesn't Necessarily Mean Better. Contrary to the myth, the best sex doesn't last all night, according to a recent survey of sex therapists. Good sex (not counting foreplay) should last more than three minutes, not more than thirteen—any more time and the experience starts to get tiresome. Previous research, involving 1,500 couples showed the average length of intercourse is actually seven minutes. *(The Week,* April 18, 2008)

Sexual feng shui tip #22: Foreplay should begin at the extremities, not at the genitals:

> In Taoist lovemaking, the emphasis lies not on romantic love but rather on correct technique; therefore it's like a football game or cricket match: wanting to win is not enough—both teams have to be "in shape," in practice, and know the rules of the game. This approach is well illustrated by the traditional Chinese literary analogy of the boudoir as a "flowery battlefield." But the Chinese image of sex as battle is not at all the same notion as the Western "battle between the sexes." The latter indicates a fundamental conflict of will and severe competition for sexual supremacy that extends beyond the boudoir, while the Chinese metaphor stresses the practical, tactical aspects of actual intercourse—what the Chinese call "bedroom strategy" . . . Unlike battles fought with swords and spears, however, it is women who hold the advantage over men in sexual engagements, and therefore men require the most "training" to prepare than women for the "battle." Most men, however, fondly regard themselves as "stronger" and therefore consider their five-minute blitzkriegs in bed to be par for the course. (Reid, 1989:266)

Sexual feng shui tip #23: Mind controls breath. Breath controls blood. Blood controls semen. Learn to breathe.

G-Spot Spotting. Using ultrasound scans, Italian physicians discovered a key difference in the anatomy of women who say they experience orgasms through sexual intercourse alone. When they scanned the urethra-vaginal space (the area in front of the vaginal canal rich in blood vessels, glands, muscle fibers, and nerves), they found that the tissue there was significantly thicker. This thickened region appears to be the oh-so-elusive G-spot.

Only about 25 percent of women appear to have thicker, more sensitive tissue there. The study would help explain the fact that most women do not reliably have orgasm through intercourse. However, experts believe it might be possible to create G-spot tissue in a woman by stimulation, or by hormone treatment. *(The Week,* March 14, 2008:22)

The G-spot is similar in size and shape to a lima bean, located directly behind the pubic bone inside the front wall of the vagina, about two inches on the front wall in from the vagina's entrance. To access it, curl your index finger into a "come here" sign, insert, and firmly and consistently massage.

A great position for accessing her G-spot is to have her lie back with her knees tucked into her chest. This shortens the vagina, making it easier for a shorter finger to do the job right. When stimulating a woman's G-spot for the first time, she may feel like she has to pee. That's because the bladder is located very close to the G-spot.

A "G-spot" for men? (See "Gender-Benders," in our China section)

Jel-Quing: Bigger and Better

A Chinese man had three daughters. He asked the youngest what kind of man she would like to marry. "I would like to marry a man with two dragons on his chest," she told her father. He then asked his middle daughter what kind of man she would like to marry. She replied, "I would like to marry a man with THREE dragons on his chest!" Finally he asked his eldest daughter what sort of man she would most like to marry. The eldest—and wisest—of his daughters thought long and hard for a minute and then told her father, "I would like to marry a man with one draggin' on the ground!"

Ever wonder what "Adam's rib" really was? The original Hebrew word that ends up translated as "rib" is "tsela." Used elsewhere in the Bible it refers to a branch, limb, or tangent extending out from the body—for example, *a penis!* Since so many of the stories in the Old Testament in general, and Genesis in particular, are derived from earlier Mesopotamian creation stories, stories used to explain natural phenomena, it doesn't take a very large leap of the imagination to see how the story of Eve explains why there is no bone in a man's penis. Figure it out: it's hard when inserted, the woman "takes away" the hardness. Simple, huh?

From Adam on down, men have obsessed about whether or not they . . . "measure up." It's not so much vanity and ego and insecurity as it is Darwin—that "survival of the fittest" thing, that innate beating out the other males in the tribe for the females, our particular DNA's struggle to survive. . . . Okay, so maybe some of it is vanity and ego and insecurity. After all, it's "Lil' Willie" we're talkin' about here! And when you're talkin' "Lil' Willie," the madness never ends!

For example, consider the many bizarre instances in history of "Koro epidemics" (a.k.a. "Shrinking Penis Panic").

In the Muslim Sudan in 2003 local papers reported that "Zionists" were using "a laser-controlled surgical robot comb" to *shrink* men's penises. (Boese, 2006:159)

In 2008 police in the Congo arrested thirteen "sorcerers" for using magic to steal men's penises. At least fourteen victims came forward to testify that the sorcerers had cast spells that caused victims' penises to either shrink dramatically or, in some cases, disappear altogether! The sorcerers then demanded a ransom for the organs' return. One witness, a twenty-nine-year old Kinshasa phone-credit salesman, assured reporters that "It's real. Just yesterday here, there was a man who was a victim. We saw. What was left was tiny." (*The Week* May 9, 2008:12)

Someone should tell those fellows in the Congo about HGH:

> It is well documented that growth hormone reverses the shrinkage of the heart, liver, spleen, and other vital organs. Now it appears that it may regrow the sexual organs as well. Starting in the fourth decade, the penis and clitoris actually start to shrink. But many patients report that with growth hormone the penis returns to its youthful dimensions. The same reversal occurs with the clitoris in women . . .
>
> Along with the increase in size comes an increase in function. It would be hard to credit the claims of sexual prowess by users of growth hormone if they weren't so consistent. (Klatz and Kahn, 1997:129–130)

In the 1940s the (in)famous Kinsey Report declared that the average penis length was 6.3 inches. However, this was based on test subjects measuring themselves . . . right. (As every woman knows, you can always trust a man to tell the truth about the size of that!)

A more up-to-date study, done in 2001, decided that the average penis size was 5.87 inches. Still another study, done the same year decided "average" was 4.7 to 5.5 inches flaccid. (Source: BJU International Journal, reported in *American Curves,* August 2008:104)

But who the heck wants to be average?

Down through the centuries men have tried everything from witchcraft to hypnosis to modern-day collagen injections and surgery to help pump up Lil' Willie.

Penis weights have always been popular. For example, men of the ZKaramojong tribe of Northeast Uganda start ritually attaching weights to their penis at puberty. They continue adding weights, eventually stretching their penises to lengths of eighteen inches. However, what they gain in length, they more than make up in lost girth "so their penises end up looking like long, thin earthworms." (Boese, 2006:28)

Speaking of penis weights: In Hong Kong there is a martial art known as *Jiu Jiu Gong,* whose practitioners often perform feats of strength, one of which is lifting heavy weights with their penis. The world record holder is a Hong Kong man who can lift a 165-pound barbell with his penis.

More modern—Western—methods of penis enlargement include:

- *Surgery,* which cuts the suspension ligaments at the top of the penis, increasing the "angle of the dangle," making your penis "look" longer when soft. Upside: What part of "looks longer" didn't you catch? Downside (literally): Your penis doesn't stand up as much.
- *Injections of adipose* (fatty tissue from another area of the man's body). Upside: Increases girth. Downside: Makes your penis look "lumpy" and malformed when adipose tissue is (often) reabsorbed.

Jel-Quing: Penis Enlargement Technique

Those who prefer a long sword may be able to justify their choice, but their reasoning is valid only for themselves. If you look from the point of view of the true way of this world, there is no reason for that. How can you say that with a small sword you will inevitably lose against someone with a big sword? When you fight in a tight place . . . preference for a long sword has bad consequences, because this preference comes from uncertainty about your own strategy. In addition, some people do not have the main force to handle a large sword.

As a proverb has it—"something large can replace something small"—so I do not unconditionally reject length, but, rather, it is the prejudice in favor of length that I repudiate. (Miyamoto Musashi, *A Book of Five Rings*)

Jel-quing consists of twenty–thirty minute sessions daily during which you first warm your penis with a warm bath or by wrapping your penis in a towel soaked in warm water. This helps increase blood flow. Do this with your penis semierect, never fully erect.

Having thoroughly warmed your penis, now apply lubricant along its length before then seizing a firm grip at the base, in order to ensure that no blood escapes from the penis. The penis is then "milked" by sliding your firm grip forward, forcing blood toward the end of the penis.

Complete one hundred to two hundred of these "milking" motions slowly. Do not ejaculate. Do not be alarmed by minor discoloration.

Bottom line: The nerves that benefit from sexual stimulation end only a couple inches into her vagina. It really is how you use it, stud.

A final Eastern thought on the subject of "It ain't how much you got, it's how you use it":

Most men are far too obsessed by the size and shape of their penis and pay far too little attention to the skills required to wield the Jade Stem properly. (Reid, 1989:315)

And a final Western thought on the subject:

This city fella happens to be standing at a urinal next to this big, country boy when the city fella "accidently" gets a gander at the country boy's Johnson. "Damn, country-cousin," exclaims the city fella. "Not that I'm 'funny' or anything (Not that there's anything wrong with it, Jerry!), but I couldn't help noticing you got quite a piece o'man-meat hanging off you! Is there some country secret for getting it to grow that big?" "Beans," the country boy replies.
"Beans? What do you mean—beans"? "Every day I soak it in beans," Country explains as a matter of fact. "Really, what kind of beans? Lima beans? Kidney beans?" The city fella needs to know. Country grins, "Naw . . . human beans!"

CONCLUSION
"Two Heads Are Better Than No Head!"

On the whole, human beings want to be good, but not too good and not quite all the time.

—George Orwell

They have a saying in the East: "Where steel fails, silk often succeeds." Thus the wise general always arms himself with both steel and silk.

Silk? That most delicate, most sensual of fabrics? True, but should we ever doubt the darker potential of silk, our Eastern brothers are quick to remind us of how the impatient and the overtly ambitious in the Chinese Imperial court often gifted their rivals with fine silken robes . . . robes crafted from silk spun by worms feeding on the deadliest of poisons. Your court rival donned the fine robe, the body heat activated the poison saturating the silk, and their illness and death quickly followed, as did your—now unopposed—rise up the courtly food chain.

And then there's that oh-so-deadly East Indian cult of the Thuggee, merciless stranglers whose stock-in-trade was murder and whose weapon of choice for dispatching the unwary—or just the unlucky—was likewise a simple silken scarf.

"Where steel fails, silk often succeeds" is the Eastern equivalent of the West's "two heads are better than one." Or, in other words, "it's always good to get a second opinion," "always good to have a back-up plan."

Stubbornly clinging to a single modus operandi can prove costly. Japanese Sword-saint Miyamoto Musashi warns us time and again not to have a preferred strategy, one an astute adversary spies out and soon learns to counter. Likewise, didn't Bruce Lee call his way of fighting the "style of no-style"?

How much harder, then, is it to pin down or pigeonhole an adversary who keeps switching tactics?

Nature punishes predictability.

Musashi eventually founded a school of sword-fighting that specialized in wielding two full-sized swords. His philosophy being that "Two swords are better than one sword" and he took plenty of heads to prove his point.

Which brings us to that old maxim about "If you can keep your head while all those about you are losing theirs . . ."

It's always good to have options. And it's reasonable to assume that two heads—put together—would give us a better chance of coming to the right decision. Unless, of course, one's "the big head" and the other's "the little head." Everyone knows, East and West, the "little head" more often than not gets the upper hand over the "big head"—who *should* know better!

And, should we allow that to happen, that "Little Head" overriding the "Big Head," well then it's just a short hop, skip, and *swish-thump!* to our losing our head altogether.

Of course, we're sure we can all agree that two heads are better than no head? And down through the centuries, how many have lost their heads to love? Literally lost their heads to love?

That's because, back in the day, "losing one's head" didn't mean throwing a hissy fit, instead, it usually meant the Red Queen throwing a hissy fit before then throwing her latest paramour to the tender mercies of the axman.

We're sure that poor sap being led to the chopping block would have appreciated the option of a "second opinion." We're sure he would agree with us that "two heads are better than one"—at least that would have given him a little head to spare. Then again, in his particular instance, his having two heads (that weaker "big head" and dominant dork of a "little head") is what sent him to see "the final barber" in the first place.

So maybe "two heads" aren't automatically "better than one," not if those two heads have decidedly different agendas—or if one of them is just an overly loud, horny little bastard!

None of this is surprising, considering that science tells us our own three pounds of gray matter is actually two brains: a seemingly rational left side, and an artsy-fartsy right side—the two sides often working at odds to one another.

If we can't keep it together inside our own head, inside our own "house," so to speak, how can we expect to keep it in our pants when we step outside the house?

So "two heads" aren't necessarily "better than one," if those two heads happen to be trying to occupy the same already crowded space.

But we agree—do we not?—it's good to have the option of opinions from two heads—steel and silk; preferring the latter, ready and able to fall back on the former if pressed.

Steel and silk—strategy and seduction. Two heads are really better than one, especially since being able to choose between the two actually gives us three choices, that third being the option of being able to use both—a little silk, a little steel, the proverbial iron fist sheathed in a velvet glove.

Which brings us back to deciphering, "If you can keep your head while all those around you are losing theirs . . ."

Perhaps, when it comes to strategy and the temptation of pulling out our missiles at the first—least—provocation, a second opinion might be what's needed to prevent premature launch, to ensure we don't go off half-cocked. Sounds like sound strategy.

Likewise, when it comes to seduction, if we can't rely on keeping our head while all those about us are losing theirs . . . perhaps we should settle for just keeping it in our pants!

Strategy is seduction. Seduction is strategy.

TABLE OF AUTHORITIES

Asanaro. *The Secret Art of Boabom: Awaken Inner Power Through Defense Meditation from Ancient Tibet.* Trans. Joice Buccarrey. Jeremy P. Tarcher/Penguin, 2006.

Bayer, Ronald. *Homosexuality and American Psychiatry: The Politics of Diagnosis.* New Jersey: Princeton University Press, 1987.

Bhagavad-Gita. (The Song of God) Misc. translations.

Bocking, Brian. *A Popular Dictionary of Shinto.* NTC Publishing Group, 1997.

Boese, Alex. *Hippo Eats Dwarf: A Field Guide to Hoaxes and Other B.S.* A Harvest Original/Harcourt, Inc., 2006.

Chung, Kuan. *A Tale of Three Kingdoms* (c. 1,400) Misc. translations.

Crowdy, Terry. *Military Misdemeanors.* Osprey Publications, 2007.

Dhammapada. (Sayings of The Buddha). Misc. translations.

Elinwood, Ellae. *Qigong Basics.* Tuttle Publishing, 2004.

Gordon, James. *The Golden Guru: The Strange Journey of Bhagwan Shree Rajneesh,* Stephen Greene, 1987.

Greene, Robert. *The Art of Seduction.* Penguin, 2001.

Gui Gu-Tze. Xiang Bian Wei Mang (Face Reading text, 250 B.C.E.) Misc. translations.

Herrigel, Eugen. *The Method of Zen.* Vintage, 1974.

Hucker, Charles. *China's Imperial Past.* Stanford University Press, 1975.

I-Ching. (Chinese Book of Changes) Misc. translations.

Jeary, Tony. *Life Is a Series of Presentations.* Simon & Schuster, 2004.

Kipling, Rudyard. *The Man Who Would Be King.* 1871.

Krishnamurti, J. *The First and Last Freedom.* 1954.

Kruglinski, Susan. "What You See Is What You Don't Get" *(Discover,* February, 2006).

Linn, Henry B. *What Your Face Reveals.* Llewellyn, 1999.

Lozoff, Bo. *We're All Doing Time,* Human Kindness, 1985.

Lung, Haha. *The Ancient Art of Strangulation.* Paladin Press, 1995.

———. *Ninja Craft.* Alpha Publications, 1997a.

———. *Assassin! Secrets of the Cult of the Assassins.* Paladin Press, 1997b.

———. *Knights of Darkness: Secrets of the World's Deadliest Night Fighters.* Paladin Press, 1998.

———. *Cao Dai Kung-Fu.* Loompanics Unlimited, 2002.

———. *Theatre of Hell: Dr. Lung's Complete Guide to Torture.* Loompanics Unlimited, 2003.

———. *Assassin!* Citadel Press, 2004a.

———. *Knights of Darkness.* Citadel Press, 2004b.

———. *Lost Fighting Arts of Vietnam.* Citadel Press, 2006.

———. *Mind Fist.* Citadel Press, 2008.

———. *The 99 Truths: Hannibal's Black Art of War.* Publication pending.

Lung, Haha, and Baughman, Robert. *Sexual Feng Shui.* Publication pending.

Lung, Haha, and Prowant, Christopher B. *Black Science: Ancient and Modern Techniques of Ninja Mind Manipulation.* Paladin Press, 2001.

———. *Mind Manipulation: Ancient and Modern Ninja Techniques.* Citadel Press, 2001.

———. *Shadowhand: History and Secrets of Ninja Taisavaki.* Paladin Press, 2002c.

———. *Ninja Shadowhand: The Art of Invisibility.* Citadel Press, 2004c.

Lung, Haha, and Tucker, Eric. *The Nine Halls of Death: Ninja Secrets of Mind Mastery.* Citadel Press, 2007.

Lyman, Stanford M., and Scott, Marvin B. *A Sociology of the Absurd.* (2nd Edition): General Hall, Inc., 1989.

Machiavelli, Nicollo. *Discourses.* 1531. Misc. translations.

Mahabharata. Misc. translations.

Musashi, Miyamoto. *Go Rin No Sho (A Book of Five Rings)* (1645). Misc. translations.

Omar, Ralf Dean. "Ninja Death Touch: The Fact and the Fiction" *Black Belt* magazine, September, 1989.

Ostrander, Sheila, and Schroeder, Lynn. *Psychic Discoveries Behind the Iron Curtain.* Prentice Hall, 1970.

Paget, Lou. *How to Give Her Absolute Pleasure.* Broadway Books, 2000.

Ramanujan, A. K. *Speaking of Siva.* Penguin, 1973.

Reid, Daniel. *The Tao of Health, Sex, and Longevity: A Modern Guide to the Ancient Way.* A Fireside Book/Simon & Schuster, 1989.

Schuchaud, Marsha Keith. *William Blake's Sexual Path to Spiritual Vision.* Inner Traditions, 2008.

Seagrave, Sterling. *The Soong Dynasty.* Harper & Row, 1985.

Shah, Ikbal Ali (editor). *The Book of Oriental Literature.* Garden City Publishing Company, 1938.

Skinner, Dirk. *Street Ninja: Ancient Secrets for Surviving Today's Mean Streets.* Barricade Books, 1995.

Sun Bin. (*The Lost Art of War,* 200 B.C.E.) Misc. translations.

Sun Tzu. *Ping-Fa* (*Art of War,* c. 500 B.C.E.). Misc. translations.

Than, Ker. "Step by Step, Your Brain Mimics His Moves" (*Psychology Today,* July/August 2005).

Upanishads. Misc. translations.

Victorian, Dr. Armen. *Mind Controllers.* Vision Books/Satin Pub. 2000.

Voltaire. *Philosophical Dictionary,* 1764. Misc. translations.

Von Clausewitz, Karl. *On War.* Misc. translations.

Wadler, Joyce. *Liaison.* Bantam Books, 1993.

Yourcenar, Marguerite. *Mishima: A Vision of the Void.* Trans. Alberto Manguel, University of Chicago Press, 1986.

Yu, Lee. *Prayer-Mat of the Flesh.* Misc. translations.

Yuan & Xiao. *Tales of Emperor Qin Shihuag.* Foreign Language Press, 1997.

Zaffuto, Dr. Anthony. *Alphagenics: How to Use Your Brainwaves to Improve Your Life.* Doubleday, 1974.

Zen and Shinto: The Story of Japanese Philosophy. Greenwood Press, 1959.